D0829123

⟳ Shortcut

# HAWAII
# BIG ISLAND

Jeanne Cooper &
Shannon Wianecki

FrommerMedia LLC

Published by
**FROMMER MEDIA LLC**

Copyright © 2016 by Frommer Media LLC, New York City, New York.
Frommer Media LLC is not associated with any product or vendor
mentioned in this book.

ISBN 978-1-62887-218-7 (paper), 978-1-62887-219-4 (e-book)

Editorial Director: Pauline Frommer
Editor: Alexis Lipsitz Flippin
Editorial Assistants: Margaret Day and Ashley Dubois
Photo Editor: Dana Davis and Meghan Lamb
Cartographer: Roberta Stockwell
Front cover photo: © Konstanttin / Shutterstock.com
Back cover photo: © KQRoy / Shutterstock.com

For information on our other products or services, see www.frommers.
com. Frommer Media LLC also publishes its books in a variety of
electronic formats.

Manufactured in China

5  4  3  2  1

## HOW TO CONTACT US

In researching this book, we discovered many wonderful places—hotels,
restaurants, shops, and more. We're sure you'll find others. Please tell us
about them, so we can share the information with your fellow travelers in
upcoming editions. If you were disappointed with a recommendation,
we'd love to know that, too. Please write to: Support@FrommerMedia.com

## FROMMER'S STAR RATINGS SYSTEM

Every hotel, restaurant and attraction listed in this guide has been ranked
for quality and value. Here's what the stars mean:

★ Recommended
★★ Highly Recommended
★★★ A must! Don't miss!

# CONTENTS

# LIST OF MAPS

# AN IMPORTANT NOTE

The world is a dynamic place. Hotels change ownership, restaurants hike their prices, museums alter their opening hours. And all of this can occur in the several months after our authors have visited, inspected, and written about these hotels, restaurants, museums and transportation services. Though we have made valiant efforts to keep all our information fresh and up-to-date, some few changes can inevitably occur in the periods before a revised edition of this guidebook is published. So please bear with us if a tiny number of the details in this book have changed. Please also note that we have no responsibility or liability for any inaccuracy or errors or omissions, or for inconvenience, loss, damage, or expenses suffered by anyone as a result of assertions in this guide.

## ABOUT THE AUTHORS

**Jeanne Cooper** fell in love with the real Hawaii on her first visit in 1998, after growing up with enchanting stories and songs of the islands from her mother, who had lived there as a girl. The former editor of the *San Francisco Chronicle* travel section, Jeanne writes frequently about Hawaii for the newspaper and its website, SFGate.com, home of her Aloha Friday column and Hawaii Insider blog, and for magazines such as *Sunset* and *Caviar Affair*. She has also contributed to guidebooks on her former hometowns of Boston, Washington, D.C., and San Francisco.

**Shannon Wianecki** grew up in Hawaii swimming in waterfalls, jumping off of sea cliffs, and breakfasting on ripe mangoes. An award-winning writer and editor, she writes feature stories for numerous travel and lifestyle magazines. Having served 8 years as food editor for *Maui No Ka 'Oi Magazine*, she knows the island's restaurant scene as well as her own kitchen. She once won the Maui Dreams Dive Company's pumpkin-carving contest.

## ACKNOWLEDGEMENTS

I would like to thank my editor, Alexis Lipsitz Flippin, and my husband, Ian Hersey, for their support, and all those in Hawaii who have shared their knowledge and aloha with me.

—Jeanne Cooper

Thanks to Gabe Marihugh for driving the Jeep through mudbogs in Lanai.

—Shannon Wianecki

# INTRODUCTION

by Jeanne Cooper

**L**arger than all the other Hawaiian Islands combined, the Big Island truly deserves its nickname. Its 4,028 square miles—a figure that's growing, thanks to an active volcano—contain 10 of the world's 13 climate zones. In less than a day, a visitor can easily traverse tropical rainforest, lava desert, verdant pastures, misty uplands, and chilly tundra, the last near the summit of Mauna Kea, almost 14,000 feet above sea level. The shoreline also boasts diversity, from golden beaches to enchanting coves with black, salt-and-pepper, even olivine sand. Above all, the island home of Kamehameha the Great and Pele, the volcano goddess, is big in *mana:* power and spirituality.

# ESSENTIALS
## Arriving

The Big Island has two major airports for interisland and trans-Pacific jet traffic: Kona and Hilo.

Most people arrive at **Kona International Airport** (**KOA;** http://hawaii.gov/koa) in Keahole, the island's westernmost point, and can be forgiven for wondering if there's really a runway among all the crinkly black lava and golden fountain grass. Leaving the

FACING PAGE: **Hawaii Volcanoes National Park.**

airport, the ritzy Kohala Coast is to the left (north) and the town of Kailua-Kona—often just called "Kona," as is the airport—is to the right (south).

U.S. carriers offering nonstop service to Kona, in alphabetical order, are **Alaska Airlines** (www.alaskaair. com; ✆ 800/252-7522), with flights from the Pacific Northwest hubs of Seattle, Portland, and Anchorage, and from San Diego, San Jose, and Oakland, California; **American Airlines** (www.aa.com; ✆ 800/433-7300) and **Delta Air Lines** (www.delta.com; ✆ 800/221-1212), both with flights from Los Angeles; **Hawaiian Airlines** (www.hawaiianairlines.com; ✆ 800/367-5320), with summer flights from Oakland and Los Angeles; **United Airlines** (www.united.com; ✆ 800/241-6522), with year-round flights from Los Angeles, San Francisco, Denver, and seasonal flights from Chicago; and **US Airways** (www.usairways.com; ✆ 800/428-4322), scheduled to merge with American, but at press time still offering nonstop flights from Phoenix.

**Air Canada** (www.aircanada.com; ✆ 888/247-2267) and **WestJet** (www.westjet.com; ✆ 888/937-8358) also offer nonstop service to Kona, with frequency changing seasonally, from Vancouver.

Only United offers nonstop service from the mainland to **Hilo International Airport** (**ITO;** http://hawaii.gov/ito), via Los Angeles.

For connecting flights or island-hopping, Hawaiian (see above) is the only carrier offering interisland jet service, available from Honolulu and Kahului, Maui, to both Kona and Hilo airports; its **Ohana by Hawaiian** subsidiary also flies from Kona and Hilo to Kahului on 48-passenger, twin-engine turboprops. **Mokulele Airlines** (www.mokuleleairlines.com; ✆ 866/260-4040) flies nine-passenger, single-engine turboprops between Kona and Kahului and Kapalua, Maui; between the Big Island upcountry town of Waimea and Kahului; and between Hilo and Kahului. *Note:* Mokulele discreetly weighs passengers and their carry-ons before boarding to determine seating; those totaling 350 pounds or more are not permitted to fly.

Coast of Kailua-Kona.

## Visitor Information

The **Big Island Visitors Bureau** (www.gohawaii.com/big-island; © **800/648-2441**) has two offices: one in the Kings' Shops in the Waikoloa Beach Resort, 250 Waikoloa Beach Dr., Suite 15 (© **808/886-1655**); the other at 250 Keawe St., No. 238, Hilo (© **808/961-5797**).

The free tourist publications **"This Week"** (www.thisweekhawaii.com/big-island) and **"101 Things to Do on Hawaii the Big Island"** (www.101thingstodo.com/big-island) offer lots of useful information amid the advertisements, as well as discount coupons for a variety of island adventures. Copies are easy to find all around the island.

**Konaweb.com** has an extensive event calendar and handy links to sites and services around the island, not just the Kona side. Those fascinated by the island's active volcanoes should check out the detailed daily reports, maps, photos, videos, and webcams on the

U.S. Geological Survey's **Hawaiian Volcano Observatory** website (http://hvo.wr.usgs.gov), which also tracks the island's frequent but usually minor earthquake activity.

## The Island in Brief
### THE KONA COAST

Kona means "leeward side" in Hawaiian—and that means hot, dry weather virtually every day of the year on the 70-mile stretch of black lava shoreline encompassing the North and South Kona districts.

**NORTH KONA** With the exception of the sumptuous but serenely low-key **Four Seasons Resort Hualalai ★★★** north of the airport, most of what everyone just calls "Kona" is an affordable vacation spot. An ample selection of midpriced condo units, timeshares, and several recently upgraded hotels lie between the bustling commercial district of **Kailua-Kona ★★★**,

The national historic park at Honaunau.

a one-time fishing village and royal compound now renowned as the start and finish of the Ironman World Championship, and Keauhou, an equally historic area about 6 miles south that boasts upscale condominiums, a shopping center, and golf-course homes.

The rightly named Alii ("Royalty") Drive begins in Kailua-Kona near King Kamehameha's royal compound at **Kamakahonu Bay,** which includes the off-limits temple complex of **Ahuena Heiau,** and continues past **Hulihee Palace ★★★**, an elegant retreat for later royals that sits across from the oldest church in the islands. Heading south, the road passes by the snorkelers' haven of **Kahaluu Beach ★★** and sacred and royal sites on the now-closed Keauhou Beach Resort, before the intersection with King Kamehameha III Road, which leads to that monarch's birthplace by Keauhou Bay. Several kayak excursions and snorkel boats leave from Keauhou, but Kailua Pier sees the most traffic—from cruise-ship tenders to fishing and dive boats, dinner cruises, and other sightseeing excursions.

Beaches between Kailua-Kona and Keauhou tend to be pocket coves, but heading north toward South Kohala (which begins near the entrance to the Waikoloa Beach Resort), beautiful, uncrowded sands lie out of sight from the highway, often reached by unpaved roads across vast lava fields. Among the steep coffee fields in North Kona's cooler upcountry, you'll find the rustic, artsy village of **Holualoa.**

**SOUTH KONA**  The rural, serrated coastline here is indented with numerous bays, from **Kealakekua,** a marine life and cultural preserve that's the island's best diving spot, down to **Honaunau,** where a national historical park recalls the days of old Hawaii. This is a great place to stay, in modest plantation-era inns or bed-and-breakfasts, if you want to get away from the crowds but still be within driving distance of beaches and the sights of Kailua. The higher, cooler elevation of the main road means you'll pass many coffee, macadamia nut, and tropical fruit farms, some with tours or roadside stands.

## THE KOHALA COAST

Also on the island's "Kona side," sunny and dry Kohala is divided in two distinctively different districts, although the resorts are more glamorous and the rural area that much less developed.

**SOUTH KOHALA** Pleasure domes rise like palaces no Hawaiian king ever imagined along the sandy beaches carved into the craggy shores here, from the more moderately priced **Waikoloa Beach Resort** at Anaehoomalu Bay to the posher **Mauna Lani** and **Mauna Kea** resorts to the north. Mauna Kea is where Laurance Rockefeller opened the area's first resort in 1965, a virtual mirage of opulence and tropical greenery rising from bleak, black lava fields, framed by the white sands of Kaunaoa Beach and views of the eponymous mountain. But you don't have to be a billionaire

| A Desert Crossing |
|---|

If you follow Highway 11 counterclockwise from Kona to Kilauea Volcano, you'll get a preview of what lies ahead in the Hawaii Volcanoes National Park: hot, scorched, quake-shaken, rippling new/dead land. This is the great Kau Desert, layer upon layer of lava flows, fine ash, and fallout. As you traverse the desert, you cross the Great Crack and the Southwest Rift Zone, a major fault zone that looks like a giant groove in the earth, before you reach Kilauea.

Keck Observatory.

to enjoy South Kohala's fabulous beaches and historic sites (such as petroglyph fields), all open to the public, with parking and other facilities (including restaurants and shopping) provided by the resorts.

Several of the region's attractions are also located off the resorts, including the white sands of **Spencer Beach ★★**; the massive **Puukohola Heiau ★★★**, a lava rock temple commissioned by King Kamehameha the Great; and the excellent restaurants and handful of stores in **Kawaihae,** the commercial harbor just after the turnoff for upcountry Waimea. *Note:* Despite its name, the golf course community of **Waikoloa Village** is not in the Waikoloa Beach Resort, but instead lies 5½ miles uphill from the coastal highway.

**WAIMEA (KAMUELA) & MAUNA KEA**   Officially part of South Kohala, the old upcountry cow town of Waimea on the northern road between the coasts is a world unto itself, with rolling green pastures, wide-open spaces dotted by *puu* (cindercone hills), and real cowpokes who work mammoth **Parker Ranch,** Hawaii's largest working ranch. Sometimes called Kamuela, after ranch founder Samuel (Kamuela) Parker, to distinguish it from Kauai's cowboy town with the same name, Waimea is split between a "dry side" (closer to the Kohala Coast) and a "wet side" (closer to the Hamakua Coast), but both sides can be cooler than sea level. It's also headquarters for the **Keck Observatory,** whose twin telescopes atop the nearly 14,000-foot **Mauna Kea** ★★★, some 35 miles away, are the largest and most powerful in the world. Waimea is home to shopping centers and affordable B&Bs, while the recently expanded **Merriman's** ★★★ remains a popular foodie outpost at Opelo Plaza.

**NORTH KOHALA** Locals may remember when sugar was king here, but for visitors, little-developed North Kohala is most famous for another king, Kamehameha the Great. His birthplace is a short walk from one of the Hawaiian Islands' largest and most important temples, **Mookini Heiau** ★, which dates to A.D. 480; you'll want a 4WD for the rugged road there. Much easier to find: the yellow-cloaked bronze statue of the warrior-king in front of the community center in **Kapaau,** a small plantation-era town. The road ends at the breathtaking **Pololu Valley Overlook** ★★★.

Once the center of the Big Island's sugarcane industry, **Hawi** remains a regional hub, with a 3-block-long strip of sun-faded, false-fronted buildings holding a few shops and restaurants of interest to visitors. Eight miles south, **Lapakahi State Historical Park** ★★ merits a stop to explore how less-exalted Hawaiians than Kamehameha lived in a simple village by the sea. Beaches are less appealing here, with the northernmost coves subject to strong winds blowing across the Alenuihaha Channel from Maui, 26 miles away and visible on clear days.

## THE HAMAKUA COAST

This emerald coast, a 52-mile stretch from Honokaa to Hilo on the island's windward northeast side, was once planted with sugarcane; it now blooms with flowers, macadamia nuts, papayas, vanilla, and mushrooms. Resort-free and virtually without beaches, the Hamakua Coast includes the districts of Hamakua and North Hilo, with two unmissable destinations. Picture-perfect **Waipio Valley ★★★** has impossibly steep sides, taro patches, a green riot of wild plants, and a winding stream leading to a broad, black-sand beach, while **Akaka Falls State Park ★★★** offers views of two lovely waterfalls amid lush foliage. Also worth checking out: **Laupahoehoe Point ★**, with its mournful memorial to young victims of a 1946 tsunami; and the quirky assortment of shops in the plantation town of **Honokaa.**

## HILO

Hawaii's largest metropolis after Honolulu is a quaint, misty, flower-filled city of Victorian houses overlooking a half-moon bay, with a restored historic downtown and a clear view of Mauna Kea, often snowcapped in winter. Hilo catches everyone's eye until it rains—and it rains a lot in Hilo, with 128 inches of rain annually. It's ideal for growing ferns, orchids, and anthuriums, but not for catching constant rays.

Yet there's a lot to see and do in Hilo and the surrounding South Hilo district, both indoors and out—including visiting the bayfront Japanese-style **Liliuokalani Gardens ★★**, the **Pacific Tsunami Museum ★**, the **Mokupapapa Discovery Center**

Hula dancer at the Merrie Monarch Hula Festival in Hilo.

★★, and **Rainbow Falls** ★—so grab your umbrella. The rain is warm (the temperature seldom dips below 70°F/21°C), and there's usually a rainbow afterward.

The town also holds Hawaii's best bargains for budget travelers, with plenty of hotel rooms—most of the year, that is. Hilo's magic moment comes in spring, the week after Easter, when hula *halau* (schools) arrive for the annual **Merrie Monarch Hula Festival** hula competition (www.merriemonarch.com). Plan ahead if you want to go: Tickets are sold out by the first week in January, and hotels within 30 miles are usually booked solid. Hilo is also the gateway to **Hawaii Volcanoes National Park** ★★★, where hula troupes perform chants and dances before the Merrie Monarch festival; the park is 30 miles away, or about an hour's drive up-slope.

## PUNA DISTRICT

**PAHOA, KAPOHO & KALAPANA**   Between Hilo and Hawaii Volcanoes National Park lies the "Wild Wild

East," an emerging visitor destination with geothermal wonders such as the ghostly hollowed trunks of **Lava Tree State Monument** ★★, the volcanically heated waters of **Ahalanui Park** ★★ and the **Kapoho warm ponds**, and the acres of lava from a 1986 flow that rolled through the Hawaiian hamlet of **Kalapana** and covered a popular black-sand beach. The rough ocean has carved a new beach at Kalapana, where the county opens a site to view lava flowing into the ocean when conditions are right. With or without active lava, Kalapana's Wednesday-night farmer's market and live music on Friday nights attract a large local crowd, and you're welcome to join. On June 27, 2014, a new lava flow from Kilauea's East Rift Zone began oozing its way toward the part-Hawaiian, part-hippie plantation town of **Pahoa,** the region's funky gateway. The flow consumed miles of forest before stopping in early 2015 within 550 yards of Hwy. 130, the only road in and out of lower Puna; the flow remained stalled at press time, although active "breakouts" were still occurring up-slope.

**HAWAII VOLCANOES NATIONAL PARK** ★★★ This is America's most exciting national park, where a live volcano called Kilauea has been continuously erupting since 1983. Depending on where the flow is, you may not be able to witness molten lava—or have to walk across miles of rough lava rock to do so—but there's always something else impressive to see. A towering plume of ash, which at night reflects the glow of the lava lake below it, has been rising from Kilauea's Halemaumau Crater since 2008, while steam vents have been belching sulphurous odors since long before Mark Twain visited in 1866. Ideally, you should plan to spend 3 days at the park exploring its many trails, watching the volcano, visiting the rainforest, and just enjoying this spectacular place. But even if you have only a day, get here—it's worth the trip. Bring your sweats or jacket (honest!); it's cool up here. *Note:* The vast park, most of which straddles the Puna and Kau districts, includes the separate, 116,000-acre Kahuku Unit, 43 miles west of the Kilauea Visitor Center in Kau. The former ranchlands and trails are open three to four weekends a month.

**VOLCANO VILLAGE**   If you're not camping or staying at historic, 33-room **Volcano House** ★★ inside the park, you'll want to overnight in this quiet hamlet, just outside the national park entrance. Several cozy inns and B&Bs, some with fireplaces, reside under tree ferns in this cool mountain hideaway. The tiny highland community (elevation 4,000 ft.), first settled by Japanese immigrants, is now inhabited by artists, soulsearchers, and others who like the crisp air of Hawaii's high country.

## KAU DISTRICT

Written variously in Hawaiian as *Ka'ū* or *Kā'ū,* and typically pronounced *"kah-oo,"* this windswept, often barren district between Puna and South Kona is one visitors are most likely to just drive through on their way to and from the national park. Nevertheless, it contains several noteworthy sites.

**KA LAE (SOUTH POINT)**   This is the Plymouth Rock of Hawaii. The first Polynesians arrived in seagoing canoes, probably from the Marquesas Islands, around A.D. 500 at this rocky promontory 500 feet above the sea. To the west is the old fishing village of Waiahukini, populated from A.D. 750 until the 1860s; ancient canoe moorings, shelter caves, and *heiau* (temples)

Ka Lae.

poke through windblown pili grass today. The east coast curves inland to reveal **Green Sand (Papak-olea) Beach ★★**, a world-famous anomaly that's best accessed on foot. Along the point, the southernmost spot in the 50 states, trees grow sideways due to the relentless gusts that also power wind turbines. It's a slow, nearly 12-mile drive from the highway to the tip of Ka Lae, so many visitors opt just to stop at the marked overlook on Highway 11, west of South Point Road.

**NAALEHU, WAIOHINU & PAHALA** Nearly every business in Naalehu and Waiohinu, the two wide spots on the main road near South Point, claims to be the southernmost this or that. But except for delicious *malasadas* (doughnuts) or another pick-me-up from the **Punaluu Bakery ★** or **Hana Hou Restaurant ★**, there's no reason to linger before heading to **Punaluu Beach ★★★**, between Naalehu and Pahala. Protected green sea turtles bask on the fine black-sand beach when they're not bobbing in the clear waters, chilly from fresh springs bubbling from the ocean floor. An ancient fish pond and temple ruins are among historic sites within the beach park, well worth a detour on the way to the volcano. Pahala is the center of the burgeoning Kau coffee-growing scene ("industry" might be overstated), so fans of caffeine should also allot at least 45 minutes for a side trip to the **Kau Coffee Mill ★**.

# GETTING AROUND

The Hawaiian directions of *makai* (toward the ocean) and *mauka* (toward the mountains) come in handy when looking for unfamiliar sites, especially since numbered address signs may be invisible or nonexistent. They're used with addresses below as needed.

**BY TAXI** Taxis are readily available at both Kona and Hilo airports, although renting a car (see below) is a more likely option. On the Kona side, call **Kona Taxicab** (www.konataxicab.com; © **808/324-4444**). In Hilo, call **Ace-1** (© **808/935-8303**). Set by the county, rates start at $3 plus $3.20 each additional mile—about $25 to $30 from the Kona airport to Kailua-Kona and $50 to $60 to the Waikoloa Beach Resort.

**BY CAR** You'll need a rental car on the Big Island; not having one will really limit you. All major car-rental agencies have airport pickups; some even offer cars at Kohala and Kona resorts. For tips on insurance and driving rules, see "Getting Around Hawaii" (p. 243).

The Big Island has more than 480 miles of paved road. The highway that circles the island is called the **Hawaii Belt Road.** From North Kona to South Kohala and Waimea, you have two driving choices: the scenic "upper" road, **Mamalahoa Highway** (Hwy. 190), or the speedier "lower" road, **Queen Kaahumanu Highway** (Hwy. 19). South of Kailua-Kona, Hawaii Belt Road continues on Mamalahoa Highway (Hwy. 11) all the way to downtown Hilo, where it becomes Highway 19 again and follows the Hamakua Coast before heading up to Waimea.

North Kohala also has upper and lower highways. In Kawaihae, you can follow **Kawaihae Road** (Hwy. 19) uphill to the left turn onto the often-misty **Kohala Mountain Road** (Hwy. 250), which eventually drops down into Hawi. The **Akoni Pule Highway** (Hwy. 270) hugs the coast from Kawaihae to pavement's end at the Pololu Valley Lookout.

*Note:* **Saddle Road** (Hwy. 200) snakes between Mauna Kea and Mauna Loa en route from Hilo to Mamalahoa Highway (Hwy. 190). Despite recent improvements to its once-rough pavement and narrow shoulders, it's still frequented by large military vehicles and plagued by bad weather; as a result, most rental-car agencies forbid you from driving on it. The 29 miles from Hilo to the Mauna Kea Access Road are easy to navigate in good conditions.

**BY BUS & SHUTTLE** **SpeediShuttle** (www.speedi shuttle.com; ✆ **808/329-5433**) and **Roberts Hawaii** (www.robertshawaii.com; ✆ **866/570-2536** or 808/ 954-8640) offer door-to-door airport transfers to hotels and other lodgings. Sample shared-ride rates from the Kona airport are $27 to $29 per person to Kailua-Kona, and $58 to $60 per person to the Mauna Lani Resort; Roberts' agents meet you outside security and provide porter service in baggage claim, but be aware there may be up to five stops before your destination.

The islandwide bus system, the **Hele-On Bus** (www.heleonbus.org; © **808/961-8744**), offers a great flat rate for riders: $2 general; $1 for students, seniors, and people with disabilities; and free for children under 5. Most routes have limited value for visitors, other than the Hilo–Hawaii Volcanoes National Park bus, or the Intra-Kona line between Kailua-Kona's big-box stores (Wal-Mart, Costco) and the Keauhou Shopping Center; the latter also makes two stops a day at the Kona airport. Longer-distance routes, such as Kona–Hilo, are generally designed for early-morning commuters.

Travelers staying in Kailua-Kona and the Keauhou Resort can hop on the open-air, 44-seat **Kona Resort Trolley,** running from 9am to 9:10pm daily along Alii Drive. It makes six stops a day at 29 locations from the Sheraton Keauhou Bay Resort and Keauhou Shopping Center to Kahaluu Beach, Kailua Pier, and the shops of downtown Kailua-Kona. The fare is $2, free for those with vouchers from their hotel (such as the Sheraton) or stores in the Kona Commons Shopping Centers, which give them to customers who spend $25 or more.

The **Waikoloa Beach Resort shuttle** runs from 10am to 10pm daily from Hilton Waikoloa Village and the Waikoloa Beach Marriott to the Kings' Shops and Queens' MarketPlace; it costs $2 adults, $1 ages 5 to 12 (younger free).

**BY BIKE**   Due to elevation changes, narrow shoulders (with the notable exception of the Queen Kaahumanu Hwy. between Kailua-Kona and Kawaihae), and high traffic speeds, point-to-point bike travel without a tour guide isn't recommended. However, several areas are ideal for recreational cycling and sightseeing. See

"Bicycling" under "Other Outdoor Activities" for rental shops and routes.

**BY MOTORCYCLE & SCOOTER** The sunny Kohala and Kona coasts are ideal for tooling around on a motorcycle, while those sticking to one resort or Kai-lua-vKona can easily get around by scooter. **Big Island Motorcycle Co.**, in Kings' Shops in the Waikoloa Beach Resort, 69-250 Waikoloa Beach Rd. (www.thrillseekershawaii.com; © **808/886-2011**), rents a variety of motorbikes to those 21 and older with a valid motor-cycle license (from $100 a day, including gear, insurance, and unlimited miles). Moped rentals, available to those 18 and up with a standard driver's license, are $20 an hour, $45 half-day, and $60 full day ($75 for 24 hr.). In Kailua-Kona, **Big Island Harley-Davidson,** 75-5633 Palani Rd. (www.bigislandharley.com; © **888/904-3155** or 808/217-8560), rents a variety of Harleys starting at $179 daily ($763 weekly), with gear and unlimited mileage, to qualified drivers, while **Big Island Mopeds** (www.konamopedrentals.com; © **808/443-6625**) will deliver mopeds to your door for $50 day ($250 weekly; note prices double during Ironman week in mid-Oct).

# [FastFACTS] THE BIG ISLAND

**ATMs/Banks** ATMs are located everywhere on the Big Island, at banks, supermarkets, Long Drugs, and at some shopping malls. The major banks on the Big Island are First Hawaiian, Bank of Hawaii, American Savings, and Central Pacific, all with branches in both Kona and Hilo.

## Business Hours

Most businesses on the island are open from 8 or 9am to 5 or 6pm.

## Dentists

In Kohala, contact **Dr. Craig C. Kimura** at Kamuela Office Center, 65-1230 Mamalahoa Hwy., Waimea (© **808/885-5947**). In Kailua-Kona, call **Dr. Christopher Bays** at **Kona Coast Dental Care,** 75-5591 Palani Rd., in the Frame 10 Center, above the bowling alley (www.kona coastdental.com; © **808/329-8067**). In Hilo, **Kuhio Dental Group,** in Prince Kuhio Plaza, 111 E. Puainako St. (© **808/959-3433**), is open daily from 8am to 5pm, with dental surgeon **Jonathan Mah** on staff.

## Doctors

For minor emergencies or drop-in appointments on weekdays, visit **Urgent Care of Kona,** 77-311

Sunset Dr., off Highway 11, Kailua-Kona (www.urgentcareof kona.com; © **808/327-4357**). In Hilo, **Urgent Care** (© **855/580-5923**) has offices open 8:30am–9pm weekdays and 9:30am–4pm weekends at 45 Mohouli St., Hilo, and 16-612 Old Volcano Rd., Keaau.

## Emergencies

For ambulance, fire, and rescue services, dial © **911.**

## Hospitals

Hospitals offering 24-hour, urgent-care facilities include the **Kona Community Hospital,** 79-1019 Haukapila St., off Highway 11, Kealakekua (www.kch.hhsc.org; © **808/322-9311**); **Hilo Medical Center,** 1190 Waianuenue Ave., Hilo (www.hilomedical center.org; © **808/932-3000**); and **North Hawaii Community Hospital,** 67-1125 Mamalahoa Hwy., Waimea

(www.nhch.com; © **808/885-4444**).

## Internet Access

Pretty much every lodging on the island has Wi-Fi; ask about the charges, which can be exorbitant in rooms but free in public spaces, ahead of time. **Starbucks** (nine locations), **McDonald's** (five locations) and numerous local coffee shops also offer free Wi-Fi.

## Pharmacies

The only 24-hour pharmacy is in Hilo, at **Longs Drugs'** 555 Kilauea Ave. location, one of 10 around the island (www.cvs.com; © **808/935-9075**). The rest open as early as 7am and close as late as 9pm Monday to Saturday; some are closed Sunday. Kona and Hilo's national chain stores such as **Kmart, Target, Wal-Mart,** and **Costco** (Kailua-Kona only) also have pharmacies, with varying hours.

**Police** Dial © **911** in case of emergency; otherwise, call the **Hawaii Police Department** at © **808/935-3311** islandwide.

**Post Office** The **U.S. Postal Service** (www.usps.com; © **800/275-8777**) has more than 2 dozen branches around the island, including in Kailua-Kona at 74-5577 Palani Rd., in Waimea at 67-1197 Mamalahoa Hwy., and in Hilo at 1299 Kekuanaoa St. All are open weekdays; some are also open Saturday morning.

**Volcanic Activity** Check the website of **Hawaii Volcanoes National Park**, www.nps.gov/havo/planyourvisit/lava2.

htm, to see if lava is flowing in or near the park. Hawaii County also has a recorded hotline for the **Kalapana viewing area** (© **808/961-8093**), which closes when lava is not flowing to the sea. For daily **air-quality reports,** based on sulfur dioxide and particulates from eruptions, visit www.hawaii so2network.com.

# EXPLORING THE BIG ISLAND

by Jeanne Cooper

**2**

# A WEEK ON THE BIG ISLAND OF HAWAII

Because of the distances involved, a week is barely enough time to see the entire Big Island; it's best to plan for 2 weeks—or even better, a return visit. Here's how to see the highlights, changing hotels as you go.

## DAY 1: Arrive & Amble Through Kailua-Kona ★★★

Since most flights arrive at lunchtime or later, check into your Kona Coast lodgings and go for a stroll through historic **Kailua-Kona,** by **Hulihee Palace** (p. 26) and **Mokuaikaua Church** (p. 27). Wear sandals so you can dip your feet in one of the pocket coves, such as Kamakahonu Bay, within sight of **Kamehameha's historic compound,** and enjoy a sunset dinner at an ocean-view restaurant. Don't unpack—you'll be on the road early the next day.

## DAY 2: A Morning Sail & Afternoon Drive ★★★

The day starts with a morning snorkel tour (plus breakfast and lunch) aboard the *Fair Wind II* (p. 99), sailing to the historic preserve of **Kealakekua Bay.** After returning to Keauhou Bay, head south to **Hawaii Volcanoes National Park** (p. 68), by way of **Puuhonua O Honaunau National Historical Park** (p. 36) and the **Kau Coffee Mill** (p. 75), for a pick-me-up. Check into **Volcano Village** lodgings (p. 161) or

**Volcano House** (p. 165) in the park, where you'll dine in full view of Kilauea's fiery evening glow.

**DAY 3:** Explore an Active Volcano ★★★

Stop at the national park's **Kilauea Visitor Center** to learn about current lava viewing (if any) and the day's free ranger-led walks. Take **Crater Rim Road** past billowing **Halemaumau Crater** (p. 70) to see **Thurston Lava Tube** (p. 71), and **Devastation Trail** (p. 71), and other sights before driving down **Chain of Craters Road,** leading to a vast petroglyph field and the 2003 lava flow that smothered the roadway. After sunset, visit the **Thomas A. Jaggar Museum** (open until 7:30pm; p. 71) and its observation deck for yet another look at Pele's power.

**DAY 4:** Tour Old Hawaii ★★★

It's just a 45-minute drive from Volcano to **Hilo** (p. 55), so after breakfast go to the **Imiloa: Astronomy Center of Hawaii** (p. 59), opening at 9am. Then explore **Banyan Drive** (p. 55), **Liliuokalani Gardens** (p. 57), and one of Hilo's small but intriguing museums, such as the free **Mokupapapa Discovery Center** (p. 60). Stroll through **Nani Mau Gardens** (p. 60) or **Hawaii Tropical Botanical Garden** (p. 49) before driving along the pastoral **Hamakua Coast** (p. 46), stopping at breathtaking **Akaka Falls** (p. 46) and the similarly stunning **Waipio Valley Lookout** (p. 54). Dine on farm-fresh cuisine in **Waimea** (p. 47) or **Kawaihae** (p. 54) before checking into your Kohala Coast hotel.

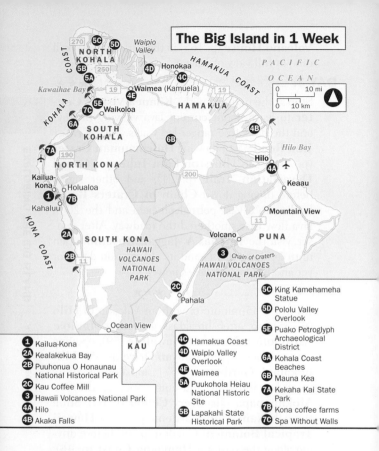

**The Big Island in 1 Week**

270 5C 5D Waipio Valley

NORTH KOHALA

250

5B

5A

Kawaihae Bay

19

Waikoloa

7C 5E

KOHALA COAST

6A

SOUTH KOHALA

NORTH KONA

7A

Kailua-Kona

Holualoa

1

Kahaluu

7B

KONA COAST

2A

SOUTH KONA

2B

11

HAWAII VOLCANOES NATIONAL PARK

190

200

Ocean View

KAU

4D Honokaa

HAMAKUA COAST

4C

Waimea (Kamuela)

4E

19

HAMAKUA

6B

4B

PACIFIC

OCEAN

0   10 mi
0   10 km

Hilo Bay

Hilo

4A

Keaau

Mountain View

Volcano

PUNA

3 Chain of Craters

HAWAII VOLCANOES NATIONAL PARK

Pahala

2C

**1** Kailua-Kona
**2A** Kealakekua Bay
**2B** Puuhonua O Honaunau National Historical Park
**2C** Kau Coffee Mill
**3** Hawaii Volcanoes National Park
**4A** Hilo
**4B** Akaka Falls

**4C** Hamakua Coast
**4D** Waipio Valley Overlook
**4E** Waimea
**5A** Puukohola Heiau National Historic Site
**5B** Lapakahi State Historical Park

**5C** King Kamehameha Statue
**5D** Pololu Valley Overlook
**5E** Puako Petroglyph Archaeological District
**6A** Kohala Coast Beaches
**6B** Mauna Kea
**7A** Kekaha Kai State Park
**7B** Kona coffee farms
**7C** Spa Without Walls

## DAY 5: Explore the Historic Kohala Coast ★★★

Start by exploring **Puukohola Heiau National Historic Site** (p. 40), the temple Kamehameha built to the war god, Ku, and sign up for a free ride on a traditional outrigger sailing canoe. Continue north on Hwy. 270 to **Lapakahi State**

Hawaii Volcanoes National Park.

**Historical Park** (p. 41) to see the outlines of a 14th-century Hawaiian village, and have lunch in Hawi or Kapaau, home of the original **King Kamehameha Statue** (p. 41) in Kapaau. The final northbound stop is the picturesque **Pololu Valley Lookout** (p. 42). Heading south in the late afternoon, stop at the **Puako Petroglyph Archaeological Preserve** (p. 39). To learn more Hawaiian lore, book one of Kohala's evening **luaus** (p. 207).

### DAY 6: Sand, Sea & Stars ★★★

You've earned a morning at the beach, and the Big Island's prettiest are on the Kohala Coast: **Anae-hoomalu Bay (A-Bay), Hapuna,** and **Kaunaoa** (see "Beaches," p. 82). Skip the scuba, though, because in the afternoon you're heading up the 13,796-foot **Mauna Kea** (p. 43), revered by astronomers. Let an expert with 4WD, cold-weather gear, and telescopes for stargazing take you there: **Mauna Kea Summit Adventures** (p. 46) or **Hawaii Forest & Trail** (p. 46).

**DAY 7:** Spa, Beach, or Coffee Time ★★★

On your last full day, visit one of North Kona's gorgeous beaches hidden behind lava fields, such as **Kekaha Kai State Park** (p. 84) or the tranquil cove at **Kaloko-Honokohau National Historical Park** (p. 27) in the morning. In the afternoon, relax with a spa treatment at the Fairmont Orchid Hawaii's **Spa Without Walls** (p. 150) or another Kohala resort spa, or tour a **Kona coffee farm** (p. 32), and pick up gourmet beans as souvenirs.

# ATTRACTIONS & POINTS OF INTEREST

While parks are open year-round, some of the other attractions below may be closed on major holidays such as Christmas, New Year's, or Thanksgiving Day. Admission is often reduced for Hawaii residents (*kama'āina*) with state ID.

### NORTH KONA

**Hulihee Palace** ★★★ HISTORIC SITE John Adams Kuakini, royal governor of the island, built this stately, two-story New England–style mansion overlooking Kailua Bay in 1838. It later became a summer home for King Kalakaua and Queen Kapiolani and, like Queen Emma's Summer Palace and Iolani Palace on Oahu, is now lovingly maintained by the Daughters of Hawaii as a showcase for royal furnishings and Native Hawaiian artifacts, from hat boxes to a 22-foot spear. You can take a self-guided tour of its six spacious rooms, but guided tours, offered throughout the day, are worth the extra $2 to learn more of the monarchs' history and cultural context; guided tours are also the only ones permitted on the oceanfront lanai. A sign directs you to remove your shoes before entering; free booties are provided upon request.

The palace lawn hosts 12 free events a year honoring a different member of Hawaiian royalty, with performances by local hula *halau* (schools) and musicians. Called **Afternoon at the Palace,** they're generally held at 4pm on the third Sunday of the month (except June and Dec, when the performances are held in conjunction with King Kamehameha Day and Christmas). Check the Daughters of Hawaii website for dates. *Note:* The www.huliheepalace.net website looks official but is unauthorized as well as outdated. 75-5718 Alii Dr., Kailua-Kona. http://daughtersofhawaii.org. ℭ **808/329-1877.** Admission $8 adults, $6 seniors, $1 children 18 and under. $2 more per adult for guided tours. Mon–Sat 9am–4pm (arrive by 3pm for guided tour).

**Kaloko-Honokohau National Historical Park** ★★ HISTORIC SITE/NATURAL ATTRACTION  With no erupting volcano, impressive tikis, or massive temples, this 1,160-acre oceanfront site just north of Honokohhau Harbor tends to get overlooked by visitors in favor of its showier siblings in the national park system. That's a shame for several reasons, among them that it's a microcosm of ancient Hawaii, from fish ponds (one with an 800-ft.-long rock wall), house platforms, petroglyphs, and trails through barren lava to marshlands with native waterfowl, reefs teeming with fish, and a tranquil beach where green sea turtles bask in the shadow of Puuoina Heiau. Plus, it's rarely crowded, and admission is free. Stop by the small visitor center to pick up a brochure and ask about ocean conditions (if you're planning to snorkel), and then backtrack to Honokohau Harbor, a half-mile south, to park closer to the beach.

Ocean side of Hwy. 19, 3 miles south of Kona airport. www.nps.gov/kaho. © **808/326-9057.** Visitor center and parking lot ½-mile north of Honokohau Harbor daily 8:30am–4pm. Kaloko Rd. gate daily 8am–5pm. No time restrictions on parking at Honokohau Harbor; from Hwy. 19, take Kealakehe Pkwy. west into harbor, then take 1st right and follow to parking lot near Kona Sailing Club, a short walk to beach.

Hulihee Palace.

**Mokuaikaua Church** ★ RELIGIOUS/HISTORIC SITE In 1820, just a few months after King Kamehameha II and Queen Regent Kaahumanu had broken the kapu system at Ahuena Heiau, the first missionaries to land in Hawaii arrived on the brig *Thaddeus* and received the royals' permission to preach. Within a few years a thatched-roof structure had risen on this site, on land donated by Gov. Kuakini, owner of Hulihee Palace, across the road. But after several fires, Rev. Asa Thurston had this massive, New England–style structure erected, using lava rocks from a nearby *heiau* (temple) held together by coral mortar, with gleaming koa for the lofty interior; the 112-foot steeple is still

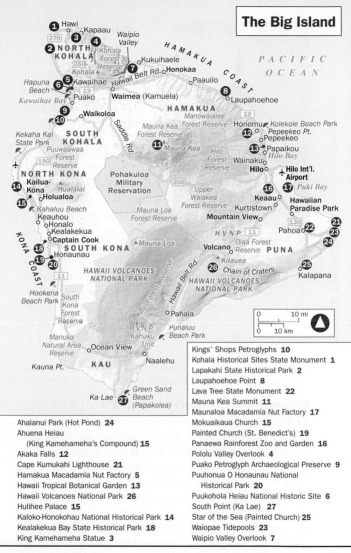

# The Big Island

**HAMAKUA COAST**

**PACIFIC OCEAN**

Hawi **1**
Kapaau **3**
Waipio Valley
**NORTH KOHALA 2**
Kohala Forest Reserve
Kohala **4**
Kukuihaele
Honokaa **7**
Kawaihae **5**
Hawaii Belt Rd.
Hapuna Beach
Kohala **6**
Paauilo
Puako **9**
Kawaihae Bay
Waimea (Kamuela)
Laupahoehoe **8**
**HAMAKUA**
Waikoloa
Manowaialee Forest Reserve
Honomu **12**
Kolekole Beach Park
Pepeekeo Pt.
Kekaha Kai State Park
Puuwaawaa Forest Reserve
**SOUTH KOHALA 10**
Mauna Kea Forest Reserve
Pepeekeo
Papaikou **13**
Hilo Bay
**190**
Mauna Kea **11**
Wainaku
Hilo Forest Reserve
Hilo
Hilo Int'l. Airport
Puki Bay **17**
**NORTH KONA**
Hualalai
Saddle Rd.
Kailua-Kona **14**
Holualoa **15**
Pohakuloa Military Reservation
Keaau **16**
Hawaiian Paradise Park
Kahaluu Beach
Keauhou
Honalo
Kealakekua
Upper Waiakea Forest Reserve
Kurtistown
Mountain View
Pahoa **22 21**
**23**
**24**
**Captain Cook**
Mauna Loa Forest Reserve
**PUNA**
**18**
**19** Honaunau
**20**
Mauna Loa
H.V.N.P. **11**
Volcano
Olaa Forest Reserve
**HAWAII VOLCANOES NATIONAL PARK**
Kilauea
Chain of Craters **26**
**25**
Kalapana
**KONA COAST**
**11**
Hookena Beach Park
South Kona Forest Reserve
Kau Forest Reserve
**HAWAII VOLCANOES NATIONAL PARK**
Hawaii Belt Rd.
Manuka Natural Area Reserve
Ocean View
H.V.N.P. Kahuku Unit
Pahala
Punaluu Beach Park
Kauna Pt.
**KAU**
Naalehu
Ka Lae
Green Sand Beach (Papakolea) **27**

0        10 mi
0        10 km

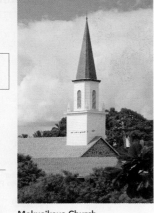
Mokuaikaua Church.

the tallest structure in Kailua-Kona. Visitors are welcome to view the sanctuary, open daily, and a rear room with a small collection of artifacts, including a model of the *Thaddeus,* a rope star chart used by Pacific Islanders, and a poignant plaque commemorating Henry Opukahaia. As a teenager, the Big Island native (known then as "Obookiah") boarded a ship to New England in 1807, converted to Christianity, and helped plan the first mission to the islands, but he died of a fever in 1818, the year before the *Thaddeus* sailed. (In 1993 his remains were reinterred at Kahikolu Congregational Church, 16 miles south of Mokuaikaua.) Mokuaikaua hosts a free history talk most Sundays at 12:15pm, following the 11am service.

75-5713 Alii Dr., Kailua-Kona, across from Hulihee Palace. www.mokuaikaua.org. © **808/329-0655.** Daily 7:30am–5:30pm.

**Ocean Rider Seahorse Farm** ★★ AQUACULTURE On the coastline just behind the Natural Energy Lab (NELHA) lies this 3-acre, conservation-oriented "aqua-farm" that breeds and displays more than half of the world's 36 species of seahorses. The farm began breeding seahorses in 1998 as a way of ending demand for wild-collected seahorses and, once successful, expanded its interests to include similarly threatened sea dragons and reef fish. Although the $40 cost of the biologist-led, 1-hour tour (the only way to see the farm) may seem excessive, proceeds benefit the farm's research and conservation. In any case, people still find their way here in droves, excited to see pregnant male seahorses and their babies, and to have one of the delicate creatures wrap its tail around their fingers.

73-4388 Ilikai Place (behind Natural Energy Lab), Kailua-Kona. From Hwy. 19 (at mile marker 94), follow OTEC Rd. past Wawala-loli Beach Park to 1st left; farm is on the right. www.seahorse.com. © **808/329-6840.** $40 adults, $30 ages 7–12, $28 ages 3–6, younger free. Tours Mon–Fri noon and 2pm; also 10am Thanks-giving week, Dec 19–Apr 30, and June 1–Labor Day. Reserva-tions recommended. Gift shop Mon–Fri 9:30am–3:30pm.

## SOUTH KONA
### Amy B. H. Greenwell Ethnobotanical Garden ★
GARDEN   You can pick up a brochure to tour this 15-acre garden yourself, home to more than 200 native plants as well as Polynesian introductions, but you'll learn so much more about Hawaiian culture and plants on a guided tour (especially since the lush vegetation can occasionally overgrow pathways and signs). Amy Greenwell, Stanford-educated granddaughter of Kona coffee pioneer Henry Nicholas Greenwell, performed botanical and archaeological surveys in the area and cre-ated this "pre-Cook" garden on her estate, which she willed to the Bishop Museum at her death in 1974. Rari-ties include six varieties of the only native Hawaiian palm tree, loulu, and a highly endangered species of hibiscus. The garden, which has an intriguing gift shop, also hosts a lively farmer's market every Sunday from 9am to 2pm.

82-6188 Mamalahoa Hwy. (Hwy. 11, *mauka* side), Captain Cook, 200 yards south of mile marker 110, across from the Manago Hotel. www.bishopmuseum.org/greenwell. © **808/323-3222.**

# CRAZY FOR KONA coffee

More than 600 farms grow coffee in the Kona Coffee Belt on the slopes of Hualalai, from Kailua-Kona and Holualoa in North Kona to Captain Cook and Honaunau in South Kona. The prettiest time to visit is between January and May, when the rainy season brings white blossoms known as "Kona snow." Harvesting is by hand—one reason Kona coffee is so costly—from late August through early winter. At least 40 farms offer regular **tours with tastings,** and many more provide samples. You can make impromptu stops along Mamalahoa Highway (Hwy. 11 and Hwy. 180), or find more obscure farms and those requiring reservations via the **Kona Coffee Farmers Association** (www.konacoffeefarmers.org). Here are some highlights, heading north to south, of coffee growers offering drop-in tours and free samples:

o **Mountain Thunder Coffee Plantation,** 73-1944 Hao St. (off Kaloko Dr.), Kailua-Kona (www.mountainthunder. com; **℃ 808/325-2136**): In the hills known as Kaloko Mauka above the airport, Trent Bateman mills award-winning coffee from his own 21-acre organic farm Mountain Thunder, as well as from other Kona growers. Mountain Thunder also grows organic coffee, pineapple, *mamaki* (used for herbal tea), cacao, sugarcane, and green tea

at another location: Kainaliu, on Highway 11, just south of mile marker 113. Both farms offer free tours on the hour from 10am to 4pm daily; farmstands open at 9am.

o **Kona Blue Sky Coffee Company,** 76-973 Hualalai Rd., Holualoa (www.konablueskycoffee. com; **℃ 877/322-1700** or 808/322-1700): The Christian Twigg-Smith family and staff grows and sells its coffee on a scenic, 400-acre estate, with free guided walking tours and tastings weekdays from 9am to 4pm.

- **Holualoa Kona Coffee Company,** 77-6261 Mamalahoa Hwy. (Hwy. 180), Holualoa (www.konalea.com; **800/334-0348** or 808/322-9937): Owned by Desmond and Lisen Twigg-Smith, this farm and mill sells its own and others' premium, organic Kona coffee. Tour the orchards (mowed and fertilized by a large flock of geese) and witness all phases of processing, weekdays from 8am to 4pm.

- **Kona Joe Coffee,** 79-7346 Mamalahoa Hwy., Kainaliu (Hwy. 11 between mile markers 113 and 114; www.konajoe.com; **808/322-2100**): The home of the world's first trellised coffee farm offers a free, self-guided tour with 8-minute video, as well as guided tours by request ($15 adults, free for kids 12 and under), daily from 8am to 5pm. Guided tours of the 20-acre estate include a mug, coffee, and chocolate, with reservations recommended for groups of six or more.

- **Greenwell Farms,** 81-6581 Mamalahoa Hwy., Kealakekua (www.greenwellfarms.com; **808/323-2295**): If any farm can claim to be the granddaddy of Kona coffee, this would be it. Englishman Henry Nicholas Greenwell began growing coffee in the region in 1850. Now operated by his great-grandson and agricultural innovator Tom Greenwell, the farm offers free tours daily from 8:30am to 4:30pm. On Thursday, join volunteers at the **Greenwell Store Museum** ★ just south of the farm in baking Portuguese sweet bread in a stone oven from 10am to 1pm; bread sales start at 12:30pm and sell out quickly.

$7 adults, $6 seniors 65 and older, free for children 12 and under. Tues–Sun 9am–4pm; guided tours at 1pm.

## Kealakekua Bay State Historical Park ★★

NATURAL ATTRACTION    The island's largest natural sheltered bay, a marine life conservation district, is not only one of the best places to snorkel on the Big Island, but it's also an area of deep cultural and historical significance. On the southern side, now called Napoopoo *(nah-poh-oh-poh-oh),* stands the large stacked-rock platform of **Hikiau Heiau,** a temple once used for human sacrifice and still considered sacred today. A rocky beach park here includes picnic tables, barbecues, and restrooms. On the north side, a steep but relatively broad 2-mile trail leads down to the historic Kaawaloa area, where *alii* (royalty) once lived; when they died, their bodies were taken to **Puhina O Lono Heiau** on the slope above them, prepared for burial, and hidden in caves on the 600-foot-cliff above the central bay. An obelisk known as the **Captain Cook Monument** stands on Kaawaloa Flat, near where the British explorer was slain in 1779, after misunderstandings between Hawaiians and Cook's crew led to armed conflict. The Hawaiians then showed respect by taking Cook's body to Puhina O Lono before returning some of the remains to his crew. Please be careful not to walk on the reef or any cultural sites; to protect the area, only hikers and clients of three guided kayak tour companies have access to Kaawaloa Flat (see "Kayaking" on p. 104).

From Hwy. 11 in Captain Cook heading south, take right fork onto Napoopoo Rd. (Hwy. 160). Kaawaloa trailhead is about 500 ft. on right. By car, continue on Napoopoo Rd. 4¼-mile to left on Puuhonua Rd., go ⅕-mile to right on Manini Beach Rd. www.hawaiistateparks.org. Daily during daylight hours.

**Kona Coffee Living History Farm ★** FARM/
HISTORIC SITE   With money earned from working
the sugar plantations, a number of Japanese immigrants bought land and became coffee-growing pio-
neers. Learn about their daily lives during the 1920s to
1940s and how their flavorful, hand-picked beans are
still produced today on the 5½-acre **Uchida Coffee
Farm,** where costumed interpreters demonstrate tasks
and "talk story" with visitors. After you explore the vintage farmhouse, stroll the orchards of coffee and macadamia nut trees, meet the chickens and donkey, and
pick up a bag of 100% Kona coffee.
*Makai* side of Hwy. 11 at mile marker 110, Captain Cook. www.
konahistorical.org. © **808/323-3222.** $15 adults, $13 seniors, $5
children 5–12, free for children under 5. Mon–Fri 10am–2pm.

**The Painted Church (St. Benedict's) ★★** RELI-
GIOUS SITE   Beginning in 1899, Father John Ber-
chman Velghe (a member of the same order as Father
Damien of Molokai) painted biblical scenes and
images of saints inside quaint St. Benedict's Catholic
Church, built in 1842 and restored in 2002. As with
stained-glass windows of yore, his pictures, created
with simple house paint, were a way of sharing stories
with illiterate parishioners. It's a wonderfully trippy
experience to look up at arching palm fronds and shiny
stars on the ceiling. Health issues forced the priest to
return to Belgium in 1904 before finishing all the pictures. The ocean-view church, which also boasts an
ornate belfry, is typically open during daylight hours,
but keep in mind it's an active parish, with Mass celebrated most days.
84-5140 Painted Church Rd., Captain Cook. www.thepainted
church.org. © **808/328-2227.** From Kailua-Kona, take Hwy. 11
south 20 miles to a right on Rte. 160. Go 1 mile to the 1st

The Painted Church.

turnoff on the right, opposite from a King Kamehameha sign. Follow the narrow, winding road about ¼-mile to church sign and turn right. Free admission.

**Puuhonua O Honaunau National Historical Park** ★★★ HISTORIC SITE With its fierce, haunting idols *(ki'i)*, this sacred site on the black-lava Kona Coast certainly looks forbidding. To ancient Hawaiians, it served as a 16th-century place of refuge *(pu'uhonua)*, providing sanctuary for defeated warriors and *kapu* (taboo) violators. A great rock wall—1,000 feet long, 10 feet high, and 17 feet thick—defines the refuge where Hawaiians found safety. On the wall's north end is **Hale O Keawe Heiau,** which holds the bones of 23 Hawaiian chiefs. Other archaeological finds include a royal compound, burial sites, old trails,

## SWEET ON chocolate

Tucked between coffee orchards in the uplands of Keauhou, the **Original Hawaiian Chocolate Factory** (www.ohcf.us; ✆ **888/447-2626,** 808/322-2626) began growing cacao in 1993. It was the first in the islands to produce 100% Hawaiian chocolate. The 1-hour walking tour ($15 adults, free kids 11 and under) includes the orchard, small factory, and chocolate sampling, plus the option to buy the expensive but delectable chocolate bars and plumeria-shape pieces. Tours take place at 9am Wednesday and 9 and 11am Friday by reservation only; book well in advance. The factory store is open Tuesday through Friday 10am to 3pm.

and a portion of an ancient village. On a self-guided tour of the 420-acre site—much of which has been restored to its pre-contact state—you can see and

learn about reconstructed thatched huts, canoes, and idols, and feel the *mana* (power) of old Hawaii, but do try to include one of the free daily ranger talks, held at 10:30am and 2:30pm in a covered amphitheater. A free, 2-day cultural festival, usually held the last weekend in June, allows you to join in games, learn crafts, sample Hawaiian food, see traditional hula, and experience life in pre-contact

**Some of the idols at Puuhonua O Honaunau National Historical Park.**

Hawaii. ***Note:*** There are no concessions in the park, other than bottled water at the bookstore, but there are picnic tables on the sandy stretch of the park's south side.

Hwy. 160, Honaunau. From Kailua-Kona, take Hwy. 11 south 20 miles to a right on Hwy. 160. Head 3½ miles and turn left at park sign. www.nps.gov/puho. ✆ **808/328-2288.** Admission $5 per vehicle; $3 per person on foot, bicycle, or motorcycle; good for 7 days. Visitor center daily 8:30am–4:30pm; park daily 7am–sunset.

## SOUTH KOHALA

### Hamakua Macadamia Nut Factory ★ FACTORY
TOUR    The self-guided tour of shelling, roasting, and other processing that results in flavored macadamia nuts and confections is not that compelling if production has stopped for the day, so go before 3pm or plan to watch a video to get caught up. But who are we kidding—it's really all about the free tastings here, generous samples of big, fresh nuts in island flavors such as chili "peppah," Spam, and Kona coffee glazed. (Just the plain salted ones are fine by me, thank you.) The affable staff can pack your purchases in flat-rate priority-mail boxes (you just pay postage). Outside the hilltop factory warehouse are picnic tables with an ocean view.

61-3251 Maluokalani St., Kawaihae. www.hawnnut.com. ✆ **888/ 643-6688** or 808/882-1690. Free admission. Daily 9:30am– 5:30pm. From Kawaihae Harbor, take Hwy. 270 north ¾-mile, turn right on Maluokalani St., and drive ⅓-mile uphill; factory is on right.

### Kohala Petrogylph Fields ★★ ROCK CARV-
INGS    The Hawaiian petroglyphs are a great enigma of the Pacific—no one knows who made them or why. They appear at 135 different sites on six inhabited islands, but most are found on the Big Island, including images of dancers and paddlers, fishermen and

chiefs, and tools of daily life such as fish hooks and canoes. The most common representations are family groups, while some petroglyphs depict post–European contact objects such as ships, anchors, horses, and guns. Simple circles with dots were used to mark the *puka,* or holes, where parents would place their child's umbilical cord (*piko*).

The largest concentration of these stone symbols in the Pacific lies in the 233-acre **Puako Petroglyph Archaeological Preserve** next to the Fairmont Orchid Hawaii on the Mauna Lani Resort. Some 3,000 designs have been identified. The 1.5-mile **Malama Trail** through a kiawe field to the large, reddish lava field starts north of the hotel, *makai* side. Take Highway 19 to the resort turnoff and drive toward the coast on North Kaniku Drive, which ends at the Holoholokai Beach parking lot; the trailhead on your right is marked by a sign and interpretive kiosk. Go in the early morning or late afternoon, when it's cooler; bring water, wear shoes with sturdy soles (to avoid kiawe thorns), and stay on the trail.

Local expert Kaleiula Kaneau leads a free 1-hour tour of the petroglyphs near the **Kings' Shops** in the Waikoloa Beach Resort Thursdays at 9:30am; meet lakeside by Island Fish & Chips. You can also follow the signs to the trail through the petroglyph field on your own, but be aware that the trail is exposed, uneven, and rough; wear closed-toe shoes, a hat, and sunscreen.

*Note:* The petroglyphs are thousands of years old and easily destroyed. Do not walk on them or take rubbings (the Puako preserve has a replica petroglyph you may use instead). The best way to capture a petroglyph is with a photo in the late afternoon, when the shadows are long.

### Puukohola Heiau National Historic Site ★★★

HISTORIC SITE   This seacoast temple, called "the hill of the whale," is the single most imposing and dramatic structure of the early Hawaiians, built by Kamehameha I from 1790 to 1791. The *heiau* stands 224 feet long by 100 feet wide, with three narrow terraces on the seaside and an amphitheater to view canoes. Kamehameha built this temple to the war god, Ku, after a prophet told him he would conquer and unite the islands if he did so. He also slayed his cousin on the site, and 4 years later fulfilled his kingly goal. The site includes an interactive visitor center; a smaller *heiau*-turned-fort; the homestead of John Young (a trusted advisor of Kamehameha); and, offshore, the submerged ruins of what is believed to be **Hale O Kapuni,** a shrine dedicated to the shark gods or guardian spirits, called *'aumakua.* (You can't see the temple, but shark fins are often spotted slicing through the waters.) Paved trails lead around the complex, with restricted access to the heiau. In mid-August, Puukohola Heiau hosts a 2-day Hawaiian cultural festival, with games and crafts in which visitors are welcome to participate. *Makai* side Hwy. 270, near Kawaihae Harbor. www.nps.gov/puhe. ℭ **808/882-7218.** Daily 8:15am–4:45pm. Free admission.

### NORTH KOHALA

It takes some effort to reach the **Kohala Historical Sites State Monument ★**, but for those with 4WD vehicles or the ability to hike 3 miles round-trip, visiting the windswept, culturally important site on the on the island's northern tip is worth it. The 1,500-year-old **Mookini Heiau,** once used by kings to pray and offer human sacrifices, is among Hawaii's oldest, largest (the size of a football field), and most significant shrines (off coastal dirt road, 1½ miles southwest of

Upolu Airport; www.hawaiistateparks.org; free admission; Thurs–Tues 9am–8pm).

**King Kamehameha Statue** ★★ MONUMENT
Here stands King Kamehameha the Great, right arm outstretched, left arm holding a spear, as if guarding the seniors who have turned a century-old, New England–style courthouse into an airy civic center. There's one just like it in Honolulu, across the street from Iolani Palace, and another in the U.S. Capitol, but this is the original: an 8-foot, 6-inch bronze by Thomas R. Gould, a Boston sculptor. Cast in Europe in 1880, it was lost at sea on its way to Hawaii. After a sea captain recovered the statue, it was placed here, near Kamehameha's Kohala birthplace, in 1912. Kamehameha is believed to have been born in 1758 under Halley's Comet and became ruler of Hawaii in 1810. He died in Kailua-Kona in 1819, but his burial site remains a mystery.
In front of North Kohala Civic Center, *mauka* side of Hwy. 270, Kapaau, just north of Kapaau Rd.

**Lapakahi State Historical Park** ★★ HISTORIC
SITE  This 14th-century fishing village, on a hot, dry, dusty stretch of coast, offers a glimpse into the lifestyle of the ancients. Lapakahi is the best-preserved fishing village in Hawaii. Take the self-guided, 1-mile loop trail past stone platforms, fish shrines, rock shelters, salt pans, and restored *hale* (houses) to a coral-sand beach and the deep-blue sea of Koaie Cove, a marine life conservation district. Wear good walking shoes and a hat, go early in the morning or late in the afternoon to beat the heat, and bring your own water. Facilities include porta-potties and picnic tables.
*Makai* side of Hwy. 270, Mahukona, 12.4 miles north of Kawaihae. www.hawaiistateparks.org. © **808/327-4958.** Free admission. Daily 8am–4pm.

**Pololu Valley Lookout** ★★★ NATURAL ATTRAC-
TION  At this end-of-the-road scenic lookout, you
can gaze at the vertical dark-green cliffs of the
Hamakua Coast and two islets offshore or peer back
into the often-misty uplands. The view may look familiar once you get here—it often appears on travel post-
ers. Linger if you can; adventurous travelers can take a
switchback trail (a good 45-min. hike) to a secluded
black-sand beach at the mouth of a wild valley once
planted in taro; bring water and bug spray, and avoid
the surf, subject to strong currents.

At the end of Hwy. 270, 5½ miles east of Kapaau.

**Pua Mau Place** ★ GARDEN  Perched on the sun-
kissed western slope of Kohala Mountain and dotted
with deep, craggy ravines is one of Hawaii's most unusual
botanical gardens, Pua Mau Place, a 45-acre oasis with
views of both the ocean and the majestic mountains. It's
dedicated to plants that are "ever-blooming," an expan-

sive collection of continuously flowering tropical
flowers, trees, and shrubs
that can handle the arid
heat (in other words, don't
expect orchids). The gar-
dens also have peacocks
and wild turkeys, which
children are invited to
feed, and a unique hibis-
cus maze planted with
some 200 varieties. Take
the self-guided tour along
mulched pathways, where
plants are clearly marked.

Pua Mau Place.

10 Ala Kahua Dr., Kawaihae. www.puamau.com. © **808/882-0888.** Admission $15 adults, $13 seniors, $5 students, free for children 9 and under. Daily 9am–4pm. From Hwy. 270, turn *mauka* at mile marker 6 onto Ala Kahua Dr. (in Kohala Estates), head ½-mile uphill to the gate at lava rock wall.

## WAIMEA & MAUNA KEA

**Mauna Kea** ★★★ The 13,796-foot summit of Mauna Kea, the world's tallest mountain if measured from its base on the ocean floor, is one of the best places on earth for astronomical observations, thanks to its location in the tropics, pollution-free skies, and pitch-black nights. It's home to the world's largest telescopes—and more are under construction, to the dismay of some environmentalists and Native Hawaiians who still worship here—but the stargazing is fantastic even with the naked eye. *Note:* Some spell it Maunakea, a contraction of *Mauna a Wakea*, or "the mountain of Wakea" (the sky father), in lieu of Mauna Kea, or "white mountain."

**SAFETY TIPS** Check the weather and Mauna Kea road conditions before you head out (© **808/935-6268**). Dress warmly; it's chilly and windy by day, and after dark temperatures drop into the 30s (around 0°C). Don't go within 24 hours of scuba diving, to avoid the bends, and bring a flashlight with red filter for night visits. Pregnant women, children under 16, and those with heart or lung conditions should skip this trip. *Note:* Since many rental-car agencies still ban driving on Saddle Road, the only access to Summit Road (which requires a four-wheel-drive vehicle), those who can afford a private tour will find it's the safest and easiest bet (see "Seeing Stars While Others Drive," below).

**VISITOR CENTER** Named for the Big Island astronaut aboard the *Challenger,* the **Ellison Onizuka visitor center** (www.ifa.hawaii.edu/info/vis; © **808/ 961-2180**), is 6¼ miles up Summit Road and at 9,200 feet of elevation. It's open daily from 9am to 10pm (with 24-hr. restrooms), offering displays, interactive exhibits, and a bookstore with food, drink, gloves, and other gear for sale. Stay here at least 30 minutes to acclimate before ascending to the summit. From 6 to 10pm nightly, a guide leads a free **stargazing** program that starts with a screening of "First Light," a documentary about the cultural and astronomical significance of Mauna Kea.

**AT THE SUMMIT** It's another steep 6 miles, most of them unpaved, to the summit from the visitor center, which offers **free summit caravan tours** at 1pm on weekends. Drivers must have a 4WD vehicle with

Mauna Kea.

plenty of fuel and low gears (or risk a $1,000 towing fee); all participants must be 16 or older and in good health (and not pregnant), due to the altitude. For hikers in good shape with appropriate gear, it's a grueling round-trip of 8 to 10 hours; check with rangers for current conditions.

Up here, 11 nations have set up 13 peerless infrared telescopes to look into deep space, making this the world's largest astronomical observatory. The **W. M. Keck Observatory** has a visitor gallery (open weekdays 10am to 4pm) with informational panels, restrooms, and a viewing area of the eight-story-high telescope and dome. For cultural reasons, visitors are discouraged from hiking the narrow footpath across the road to the actual, unmarked summit, where ancient astronomers and priests came to study the skies, and where cultural practitioners still worship today. No matter: From the summit parking lot you have an unparalleled view of other peaks, such as Mauna Loa and Haleakala, and the bright Pacific.

Another sacred site is **Lake Waiau,** which at 13,020 feet above sea level is one of the highest in the world; although it shrinks in time of drought, it has never dried up. It's named for one of the sisters of Poliahu, the snow goddess said to make her home atop Mauna Kea. To see it, you must take a brief hike: On the final approach to the summit, on the blacktop road, go about 600 feet to the major switchback and make a hard right turn. Park on the shoulder of the road and look for the obvious .5-mile trail, following the base of the large cinder cone on your left to the small, greenish lake. *Note:* Please respect cultural traditions by not drinking or entering the water, and leave all rocks undisturbed.

## seeing stars **WHILE OTHERS DRIVE**

Two excellent companies offer Mauna Kea tour packages that provide cold-weather gear, dinner, hot drinks, guided stargazing, and, best of all, someone else to worry about maneuvering the narrow, unpaved road to the summit. All tours are offered weather permitting, but most nights are clear—that's why the observatories are here, after all—with pickups from several locations. Read the fine print on health and age restrictions before booking, and don't forget to tip your guide ($5–$10 per person).

o **Hawaii Forest & Trail** (www.hawaii-forest.com; © **800/464-1993** or 808/ 331-8505), the island's premier environmentally and culturally oriented outfitter, operates a daily **Mauna Kea Summit & Stars Adventure,** including a late-afternoon picnic dinner, sunset at the summit, and stargazing at the visitor center, for $199. The company uses two customized off-road buses, with a maximum of 14 passengers each, for the 7- to 8-hour tour. A new daytime option from Hilo, **Maunakea Voyage** ($169), swaps dinner and stargazing for lunch and a private tour of the Imiloa Astronomy Center, with a peek inside a summit observatory; it's limited to 12 passengers. Like all of Hawaii Forest & Trail's

## THE HAMAKUA COAST

Don't forget the bug spray when exploring this warm, moist region, beloved by mosquitoes, and be prepared for passing showers. You're in rainbow territory here. *Note:* Some sights below are in the North Hilo district, which shares the rural character of the Hamakua District, its northern neighbor.

tours, these are exceptional, with well-informed guides.

o **Monty "Pat" Wright** was the first to run a Mauna Kea stargazing tour when he launched **Mauna Kea Summit Adventures** (www.maunakea.com; © **888/322-2366** or 808/322-2366) in 1983.

Guests now ride in a large-windowed, 4WD van instead of a Land Cruiser and don parkas instead of old sweaters; otherwise it's much the same, with dinner at the visitor center before a spectacular sunset. The 7½- to 8-hour tour costs $204 (check for discounts online).

**Akaka Falls State Park ★★★** NATURAL ATTRACTION See one of Hawaii's most scenic waterfalls via a relatively easy .4-mile paved loop through a rainforest, past bamboo and flowering ginger, and down to an observation point. You'll have a perfect view of 442-foot Akaka Falls, plunging down a horseshoe-shape green cliff, and nearby Kahuna Falls, a mere 100-footer. Keep your eyes peeled for rainbows; your ears are likely to

Lake Waiau, inside the cinder cone just below the summit of Mauna Kea.

pick up the two-note chirp of coqui frogs (see below). Facilities include restrooms and drinking water.

End of Akaka Falls Rd. (Hwy. 220), Honomu. www.hawaiistate parks.org. From Hilo, drive north 8 miles on Hwy. 19 to left at Akaka Falls Rd. Follow 3½ miles to parking lot. $5 per car, $1 per person on foot or bicycle.

**Botanical World Adventures** ★ WATERFALL/ GARDEN   Just north of Hilo is one of Hawaii's largest botanical gardens, with some 5,000 species. Although it no longer offers a vista of spectacular, triple-stacked Umauma Falls (p. 51), it still lays claim to a huge children's maze (second in size only to Dole Plantation's on Oahu), a tropical fruit arboretum, ethnobotanical and wellness gardens, and flower-lined walks through its World Botanical Gardens. Waterfall lovers will be heartened to note that the owners have also created a road and trail leading to viewing areas above and below the previously hidden 100-foot Kamaee Falls ($6 if you only want to go there), as well as a trail leading past a series of shorter, bubbling cascades in Hanapueo Stream. If that's just too peaceful for you, opt for one of the Segway tours, ranging from 30 minutes to 3 hours ($57–$187) or a zipline tour

($167), which should be reserved in advance; tour rates include garden admission.

31-240 Old Mamalahoa Hwy., Hakalau. www.worldbotanical gardens.com. © **888/947-4753** or 808/963-5427. Admission $15 adults, $7 teens 13–17, $3 children 5–12, free for children 4 and under. Guided 2-hr. garden/waterfall tours $57 adults, $33 children 5–12, free for children 4 and under; 24-hr. advance reservation required. Daily 9am–5:30pm. From Hilo, take Hwy. 19 north past mile marker 16, turn left on Leopolino Rd., then right on Old Mamalahoa Hwy.; entrance is ¹⁄₁₀-mile on right.

**Hawaii Tropical Botanical Garden ★★** GARDEN More than 2,000 species of tropical plants thrive in this little-known Eden by the sea. The 40-acre valley garden, nestled between the crashing surf and a thundering waterfall, includes torch gingers (which tower on 12-ft. stalks), a banyan canyon, an orchid garden, a banana grove, a bromeliad hill, an anthurium corner, and a golden bamboo grove, which rattles like a jungle

Akaka Falls.

drum in the trade winds. Some endangered Hawaiian specimens, such as the rare *Gardenia remyi,* flourish in this habitat. The self-guided tour takes about 90 minutes, but you're welcome to linger. Pick up a loaner umbrella in the visitor center, where you register, so that passing showers don't curtail your visit. **Note:** You enter the garden via a 500-foot-long boardwalk that descends along a verdant ravine. Free golf-cart assistance is provided for wheelchair users to reach the wheelchair-accessible path below; for those without wheelchairs but with limited physical ability, the cost to ride the cart there and back is $5.

27-717 Old Mamalahoa Hwy. (4-Mile Scenic Route), Papaikou. www.htbg.com. © **808/964-5233.** Admission $15 adults, $5 children 6–16, free for children 5 and under. Daily 9am–5pm (admissions end promptly at 4pm). From Hilo, take Hwy. 19 north 7 miles to right turn on Scenic Route; visitor center is 2 miles on the left.

**Laupahoehoe Point ★** HISTORIC SITE/NATURAL ATTRACTION   This idyllic place holds a grim reminder of nature's fury. On April 1, 1946, a tsunami swept across the schoolhouse that once stood on this lava-leaf (that's what *laupahoehoe* means) peninsula and claimed the lives of 24 students, teachers, and residents. Their names are engraved on a stone memorial in this pretty little beach park, while a separate display holds newspaper stories on the tragedy. The land here ends in black sea stacks that resemble tombstones; when high surf crashes on them, it's positively spooky (and dangerous if you stand too close). The unprotected shoreline is not a place to swim, but the views are spectacular. Facilities include restrooms, picnic tables, and drinking water.

Laupahoehoe. From Hilo, take Hwy. 19 north 25 miles to Laupahoehoe Point exit, *makai* side; the exit is 31 miles south of Waimea).

## Co-key, Co-key: What Is That Noise?

That loud, chirping noise you hear after dark, especially on the eastern side of the Big Island, is the cry of the male coqui frog looking for a mate. A native of Puerto Rico, where the frogs are kept in check by snakes, the coqui frog came to Hawaii in some plant material, found no natural enemies, and spread quickly across the Big Island, concentrated on the Hilo side. (A few have made it to Oahu, Maui, and Kauai, where they've been swiftly captured by state agriculture teams devoted to eradicating the invasive species.) A few frogs will sound like singing birds; a chorus of thousands can be deafening; on the Big Island, they can reach densities of up to 10,000 an acre. In some places, like Akaka Falls, there are so many frogs that they are now chirping during daylight hours. Coqui frogs don't like the cool weather of Waimea and Volcano as much, but anywhere else that's lush and rural is likely to have large populations. Pack earplugs if you're a light sleeper.

**Umauma Falls ★★** WATERFALL/GARDEN   Formerly accessed through the World Botanical Gardens (see below), the triple-tiered, cascading pools of Umauma Falls are now the exclusive province of visitors to the neighboring Umauma Experience, which offers an array of ziplining, hiking, swimming, and kayaking excursions on its lush 90 acres. The less adventurous can also just pay $10 to drive the paved road to the waterfall lookout, and then take a self-guided garden hike with several more overlooks; it's worth it. Pick up a map at the visitor center, which also sells

# A TASTE OF the hamakua coast

When the Hamakua Sugar Company—the Big Island's last sugar plantation—closed in 1996, it left a huge void in the local economy, transforming already shrinking villages into near ghost towns. But some residents turned to specialty crops that are now sought after by chefs throughout the islands. Hidden in the tall eucalyptus trees outside the old plantation community of Paauilo, the **Hawaiian Vanilla Company** ★★ (www.hawaiian vanilla.com; © **808/776-1771**) is the first U.S. company to grow vanilla. It hosts one of the truly sensuous experiences on the Big

Island—the **Hawaiian Vanilla Luncheon**—plus shorter tastings and a weekly afternoon tea. Before you even enter the huge Vanilla Gallery, you will be embraced by the heavenly scent of vanilla. The four-course luncheon ($39 for age 12 and up; $19 for kids 4–11) takes place weekdays from 12:30 to 2:30pm; the 45-minute **Farm Tour** ($25 for age 4 and up; free for kids 3 and under), including dessert and tastings, weekdays at 10:30am, and the **Upcountry Tea** ($29), featuring vanilla-flavored savories and desserts, occurs at 11am on Saturday. Reservations required.

snacks and drinks. You can enjoy your repast at the river walk's observation area, under guava trees (feel free to sample their fruit when ripe), or on the visitor center's back lanai, which overlooks the river and the last line on the zip course (see "Ziplining" on p. 135). If you book a tour package that includes a swim in a waterfall pool, you'll also get to see one of the only petroglyphs on the island's east side.

31-313 Old Mamalahoa Hwy., Hakalau. www.umaumaexperience. com. © **808/930-9477.** Admission $10 adults, free for children 11 and under; includes waterfall viewing, garden, and river walk. Daily 8am–5pm. Various times: Zipline tours $189–$239; hike/swim/picnic $125; kayak/swim/picnic $49. From Hilo, take Hwy. 19 north past mile marker 16, turn left on Leopolino Rd., then right on Old Mamalahoa Hwy., and follow ½-mile to entrance.

**Waipio Valley** ★★★ NATURAL ATTRACTION/ HISTORIC SITE   This breathtakingly beautiful valley has long been a source of fascination, inspiring song and story. From the black-sand bay at its mouth, Waipio ("curving water") sweeps 6 miles between sheer, cathedral-like walls some 2,000 feet high. Hawaii's tallest waterfall, Hiilawe, tumbles 1,300 feet from its rear cliffs. Called "the valley of kings" for the royal burial caves dotting forbiddingly steep walls, this was Kamehameha's boyhood residence; up to 10,000 Hawaiians are thought to have lived here before Westerners arrived. Chinese immigrants later joined them

Waipio Valley.

and a modest town arose, but it was destroyed in 1946 by the same tsunami that devastated Hilo and Laupahoehoe, though luckily without fatalities. The town was never rebuilt; only about 50 people live here today, most with no electricity or phones, although others come down on weekends to tend taro patches, camp, and fish.

To get to Waipio Valley, take Highway 19 from Waimea or Hilo to Highway 240 in Honokaa, and follow the highway almost 10 miles to Kukuihaele Road and the **Waipio Valley Lookout ★★★**, a grassy park and picnic area on the edge of Waipio Valley's sheer cliffs, with splendid views of the wild oasis below.

To explore the valley itself, it's best to go with a guided tour, for reasons of safety and access. The steep road has a grade of nearly 40% in places, and is narrow and potholed; by law you must use a 4WD vehicle, and even then rental-car agencies ban their vehicles from it, to avoid very expensive tow jobs. Hiking down the 900-foot-road is hard on the knees going down and on your lungs coming up, and requires dodging cars in both directions. Most of the valley floor is privately owned, with trespassing actively discouraged. Note that unmarked burial sites lie just behind the black-sand beach, which is not good for swimming or snorkeling and has no facilities.

Instead, book a ride on the **Waipio Valley Shuttle ★★** (www.waipiovalleyshuttle.com; © **808/775-7121**) for a 90- to 120-minute guided tour that begins with an exciting (and bumpy) drive down in an open-door van. Once on the valley floor, you'll be rewarded with breathtaking views of Hiilawe, plus a narrated tour of the taro patches (*lo'i*) and ruins from the 1946 tsunami. The tour is offered Monday through Saturday at 9 and 11am, and 1 and 3pm; tickets are $55 for adults and $28 for kids 10 and under (minimum two adult fares); reservations are recommended. Check-in is less than a mile from the lookout at **Waipio Valley Artworks** (www.waipiovalleyartworks.com; © **808/ 775-0958**), on Kukuihaele Road. Waipio Valley Artworks is also the pickup point for Naalapa Stables' **Waipio Valley Horseback Adventure ★★** (www. naalapastables.com; © **808/755-0419**), a 2½-hour guided ride ($94) for ages 8 and older; see "Horseback Riding" (p. 132) for details.

All ages may take the mule-drawn surrey ride offered by **Waipio Valley Wagon Tours ★** (www. waipiovalleywagontours.com; © **808/775-9518**), a narrated, 90-minute excursion that starts with a van ride down to the valley stables. Tours are offered Monday through Saturday at 10:30am, 12:30, and 2:30pm; cost is $60 adults, $55 seniors 65 and older, and $30 children 3 to 12. Reservations are a must; weight distribution is a factor on the rides. Check-in is at **Neptune's Gardens Gallery** on Kukuihaele Road (www. neptunesgarden.net; © **808/775-1343**).

## HILO

Download the informative self-guided walking tour of Hilo, which focuses on 21 historic sites dating from the 1870s to the present, from the website of the **Downtown Hilo Improvement Association** (www. downtownhilo.com; © **808/935-8850**), which also has sightseeing guides for the greater area. Or pick up a copy in person at its office, 329 Kamehameha Ave., in the Mooheau Bus Depot.

**Hilo Bay ★★★** NATURAL ATTRACTION    Old banyan trees shade **Banyan Drive ★**, the lane that curves along the waterfront from Kamehameha Avenue (Hwy. 19) to the Hilo Bay hotels. Most of the

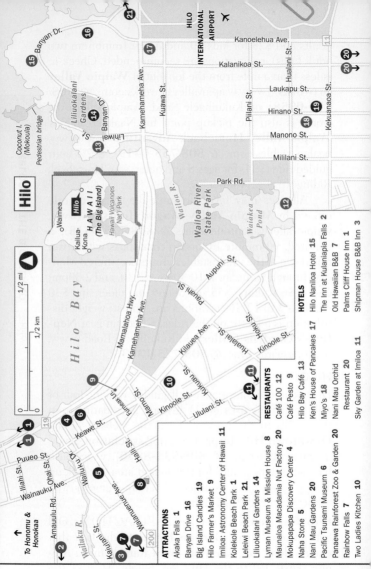

**Hilo**

Coconut I.
(Mokuola)

Pedestrian bridge

HILO INTERNATIONAL AIRPORT

Kanoelehua Ave.

Kalanikoa St.

Laukapu St.

Hinano St.

Manono St.

Mililani St.

Park Rd.

Wailoa River State Park

Waiakea Pond

Hilo Bay

*Waimea*

*Kailua-Kona*

HAWAII
(The Big Island)

*Hilo*

Hawaii Volcanoes Nat'l Park

1/2 mi

1/2 km

To Honomu & Honokaa

Puueo St.

Wainaku Ohai Ave.

Amauulu Rd.

Wailuku R.

Keawe St.

Banyan Dr.

Liliuokalani Gardens

Banyan Dr.

Lihiwai St.

Kamehameha Ave.

Kuawa St.

Piilani St.

Hualani St.

Kekuanaoa St.

Mamalahoa Hwy.

Aupuni St.

Kamehameha Ave.

Kilauea Ave.

Kinoole St.

Ululani St.

Kinoole St.

**ATTRACTIONS**

Akaka Falls **1**
Banyan Drive **16**
Big Island Candies **19**
Hilo Farmer's Market **9**
Imiloa: Astronomy Center of Hawaii **11**
Kolekole Beach Park **1**
Leleiwi Beach Park **21**
Liliuokalani Gardens **14**
Lyman Museum & Mission House **8**
Maunaloa Macadamia Nut Factory **20**
Mokupapapa Discovery Center **4**
Naha Stone **5**
Nani Mau Gardens **20**
Pacific Tsunami Museum **6**
Panaewa Rainforest Zoo & Garden **20**
Rainbow Falls **7**
Two Ladies Kitchen **10**

**RESTAURANTS**

Café 100 **12**
Café Pesto **9**
Hilo Bay Café **13**
Ken's House of Pancakes **17**
Miyo's **18**
Nani Mau Gardens **20**
Nani Mau Orchid Restaurant **20**
Sky Garden at Imiloa **11**

**HOTELS**

Hilo Naniloa Hotel **15**
The Inn at Kulaniapia Falls **2**
Old Hawaiian B&B **7**
Palms Cliff House Inn **1**
Shipman House B&B Inn **3**

trees were planted in the mid-1930s by visitors like Cecil B. DeMille (here in 1933 filming "Four Frightened People"), Babe Ruth (his tree is in front of the Hilo Hawaiian Hotel), King George V, Amelia Earhart, and other celebs, whose fleeting fame didn't last as long as the trees themselves.

It's worth a stop along Banyan Drive—especially if the coast is clear and the summit of Mauna Kea is free of clouds—to make the short walk across the concrete-arch bridge in front of the Hilo Naniloa Hotel to **Coconut Island (Moku Ola)** ★, if only to gain a panoramic sense of Hilo Bay and its surroundings.

Continuing on Banyan Drive, just south of Coconut Island, are **Liliuokalani Gardens** ★★, the largest formal Japanese garden this side of Tokyo. This 30-acre park, named for Hawaii's last monarch, Queen Liliuokalani, and dedicated in 1917 to the islands' first Japanese immigrants, is as pretty as a postcard (if occasionally a little unkempt), with stone lanterns, koi ponds, pagodas, rock gardens, bonsai, and a moongate bridge. Admission is free; it's open 24 hours.

**Lyman Museum & Mission House** ★★ MUSEUM/ HISTORIC SITE  Yankee missionaries Rev. David and Sarah Lyman had been married for just 24 days before they set sail for Hawaii in 1832, arriving 6 months later in a beautiful but utterly foreign land. Seven years later, they built this two-story home for their growing family (eventually seven children) in a blend of Hawaiian and New England design, with plastered walls, koa floors, and lanais on both floors. Long a museum of 19th-century missionary life, the **Mission House** was completely restored in 2010, and Rev. Lyman's office in an 1845 annex was opened to the public for the first time. The annex now hosts exhibits on the Hilo Boarding School for young men, which the Lymans founded near their home, and 19th-century trade. You can only visit the house as part of a guided tour, offered twice daily except Sunday.

The larger, modern **Lyman Museum** next door gives a broader perspective of Hawaiian history and culture. Walk through a lava tube and make your way through multiple climate zones in the **Earth Heritage Gallery**'s "Habitats of Hawaii" exhibit, with recorded bird sounds and full-scale replicas of sea life; mineral and shell enthusiasts can pore over an extensive collection. The **Island Heritage Gallery** examines the life of early Hawaiians, with artifacts such as stone poi pounders, wooden bowls, and *kapa,* the delicate bark cloth. Upstairs, two galleries focus on the five major immigrant groups from the era of sugar plantations.

276 Haili St. (at Kapiolani St.). www.lymanmuseum.org. ℂ **808/ 935-5021.** Admission $10 adults, $8 seniors 60 and over, $5 college students, $3 children 6–17; $21 per family. Mon–Sat 10am– 4:30pm; guided house tours at 11am and 2pm (call to reserve).

**Mauna Loa Macadamia Nut Factory ★** FAC-TORY TOUR    It's a 3-mile drive through macadamia nut orchards before you reach the visitor center of this factory, where you can learn how Hawaii's favorite nut is grown and processed. (It's best to visit Mon–Sat, when the actual husking, drying, roasting, and candy-making takes place; otherwise you can watch short videos at each station.) The gift shop offers free samples and predictable souvenirs, although a few items, such as Mauna Loa chocolate-dipped macadamia nut shortbread, appear to be exclusive.

16-701 Macadamia Nut Rd., Keaau (5 miles from Hilo, 20 miles from Hawaii Volcanoes National Park). www.maunaloa.com/ visitor-center. ℂ **888/628-6256** or 808/966-8618. Free admission; self-guided factory tours. Daily 8:30am–5pm (factory

# IMILOA: EXPLORING THE unknown

The star attraction, literally and figuratively, of Hilo is **Imiloa: Astronomy Center of Hawaii ★★★**. The 300 exhibits in the 12,000-square-foot gallery make the connection between the Hawaiian culture and its explorers, who "discovered" the Hawaiian Islands, and the astronomers who explore the heavens from the observatories atop Mauna Kea. 'Imiloa means "explorer" or "seeker of profound truth," the perfect name for this architecturally stunning center, overlooking Hilo Bay on the University of Hawaii at Hilo Science and Technology Park campus, 600

Imiloa Place (www.imiloahawaii.org; ℂ **808/969-9700**). Plan to spend at least a couple of hours here, to allow time to browse the excellent, family-friendly interactive exhibits on astronomy and Hawaiian culture, and to take in a planetarium show, which boast a state-of-the-art digital projection system. You'll also want to stroll through the native plant garden, and grab a power breakfast or lunch in the **Sky Garden Restaurant** (ℂ **808/969-9753**), open 7am to 4pm Tuesday through Sunday; the restaurant is also open for dinner Thursday through Sunday from 5 to 8:30pm. The center itself is open Tuesday through Sunday from 9am to 5pm; admission is $18 for adults, $16 for seniors, and $10 for children 4 to 12 (younger free), including one planetarium show; additional shows are $5 for adults and $3 for children.

closed Sun and holidays). Heading south from Hilo on Hwy. 11, turn left on Macadamia Nut Rd. and head 3 miles to factory; it's 20 miles north of Volcano.

**Mokupapapa Discovery Center** ★★ MUSEUM
You may never get to the vast coral-reef system that is
the Northwest Hawaiian Islands—the protected chain
of islets and atolls spanning 1,200 nautical miles is
remote (stretching from Nihoa, 155 miles northwest
of Kauai, to Kure Atoll, 56 miles west of Midway), and
visitation is severely limited. But enough people have
been intrigued by the wonders of the Papahanau-
mokuakea Marine National Monument that in spring
2014 its educational center moved into much larger
quarters in a handsomely renovated, century-old
building on the Hilo waterfront. The new center has
20,000 square feet to reveal the beauties and myster-
ies of the region's ecosystem and its relationship with
Hawaiian culture—a prime reason why the region was
named a World Heritage Site in 2010. Exhibits include
a 3,500-gallon saltwater aquarium with brilliant coral
and reef fish; the sounds of Hawaiian chants and sea-
birds; interactive displays on each of the islets; a life-
size Hawaiian monk seal exhibit; and a giant mural by
Hilo artist Layne Luna, who also created the life-size
models of giant fish, sharks, and the manta ray. Both
the content and the cost of admission—free—are
great for families.

76 Kamehameha Ave. (at Waianuenue Ave.). www.papahanaumo
kuakea.gov/education/center.html. ✆ **808/935-8358.** Free
admission. Tues–Sat 9am–4pm.

**Nani Mau Gardens** ★ GARDEN    In 1972 Makato
Nitahara turned a 20-acre papaya patch just outside Hilo
into a tropical garden. Today Nani Mau (Forever Beautiful) holds more than 2,000 varieties of plants, from fragile hibiscus, whose blooms last only a day, to durable red
anthuriums imported from South America. It also has
rare palms, a fruit orchard, Japanese gardens (with a bell

Nani Mau Gardens.

tower built without nails), an orchid walkway, and a ginger garden. The gardens went through a rough patch a few years ago, even closing the doors before Los Angeles tour operator Helen Koo purchased the site in 2012. With the help of four full-time gardeners working around the clock, she reopened the gardens in 2013, along with a **garden restaurant** that offers a surprisingly delicious buffet lunch ($17, including garden admission) daily 10:30am to 2pm.

421 Makalika St. www.nanimaugardens.com. ✆ **808/959-3500.** Admission $10 adults, $7 seniors, $5 children 4–10; with lunch, $17 adults, $15 seniors, $14 children 4–10. Daily 10am–3pm. From Hilo Airport, take Hwy. 11 south 2 miles to second left turn at Makalika St., and continue ¾-mile.

**Pacific Tsunami Museum** ★ MUSEUM  Poignant exhibits on Japan's 2011 tsunami (which caused significant property damage on the Big Island) and the 2004 Indian Ocean tragedy have broadened the international perspective in this compact museum in a former bank, where displays explain the science of the deadly phenomenon. Still, the stories and artifacts related to Hilo's two most recent catastrophic tsunamis are impressive, including a parking meter nearly bent in two by the force of the 1960 killer waves, and accounts from survivors of the 1946 tsunami that washed away the school at Laupahoehoe. Many of the

61

volunteers have hair-raising stories of their own to share—but you'll feel better after reading about the warning systems now in place.

130 Kamehameha Ave. (at the corner of Kalakaua Ave.). www. tsunami.org. © **808/935-0926.** Admission $8 adults, $7 seniors, $4 children 6–17, free for children 5 and under. Tues– Sat 10am–4pm.

**Panaewa Rainforest Zoo & Gardens** ★ ZOO/ GARDEN   This 12-acre zoo, in the heart of the Panaewa Forest Reserve south of Hilo, is the only outdoor rainforest zoo in the U.S. Some 80 species of animals from rainforests around the globe call Panaewa home, as do a couple of "Kona nightingales," the wild donkeys that have been virtually eliminated from Kona (although highway signs still warn of them)—the donkeys had escaped decades ago from coffee farms; most were relocated to California in 2011 during a prolonged drought. Panaewa's animals enjoy fairly natural, sometimes overgrown settings. Look for cute pygmy goats, capuchin monkeys, and giant anteaters, among other critters. This free attraction includes a covered playground.

800 Stainback Hwy., Keaau (off Hwy. 11, 5 miles south of its intersection with Hwy. 19 in downtown Hilo). www.hilozoo.com. © **808/959-7224.** Free admission. Daily 9am–4pm. Petting zoo Sat 1:30–2:30pm.

**Rainbow Falls (Waianuenue)** ★ WATERFALL Go in the morning, around 9 or 10am, just as the sun comes over the mango trees, to see Rainbow Falls, or Waianuenue, at its best. Part of **Wailuku River State Park,** the 80-foot falls (which can be slender in times of drought) spill into a big round natural pool surrounded by wild ginger. If you're lucky, you'll catch the rainbow created in the falls' mist. According to legend, Hina, the mother of demigod Maui, once lived in the cave behind the falls. Swimming in the pool is not allowed, but you can follow a trail left through the trees to the top of the falls (watch your step).

Wailuku River State Park, off Rainbow Dr., just past the intersection of Waianuenue Ave. (Hwy. 200) and Puuhina St. www.hawaiistateparks.org. Free admission.

## PUNA

Most visitors understandably want to head straight to **Hawaii Volcanoes National Park ★★★** (p. 68) when exploring this region, where Pele still consumes the land and creates still more. But the celebrated national park is far from the only place where you can experience Puna's geothermal wonders, or see the destruction the volcano has wrought. At press time, residents in Pahoa were still warily monitoring a slow-moving lava flow that began June 27, 2014, and halted just 550 yards before reaching Hwy. 130, the sole paved access to the rest of the island. (Officials were busy preparing unpaved roads as resident-only alternates.)

For now, the easiest way to explore the **Pahoa-Kapoho-Kalapana** triangle is still by taking Highway 130 west from Pahoa about 9 miles to Kalapana. Along the way, you'll pass **steam vents** on the *makai* side of the two-lane highway in the Keauohana Forest Reserve, near mile marker 15. (Though some have been used as natural saunas, do not enter the caves on your own.) **Star of the Sea Painted Church ★** will also be on your left, shortly before Highway 130 meets Highway 137. The wooden church was moved here in advance of the 1990 lava flow that destroyed area homes, buried the black-sand beach at Kaimu, and severed the highway link to Chain of Craters Road in the national park. Now whenever glowing lava is visible on the distant *pali* (cliffs), or steam clouds are billowing from lava pouring into the sea, Hawaii County stages an evening **lava viewing area** at the end of Highway 130 (call © **808/961-8093** to check if it's open). The church is open daily 9am to 4pm; visitor donations help pay for upkeep.

In Kalapana, you'll want to see the **new black-sand beach,** reached by walking carefully along a short red-cinder trail, past fascinating fissures and dramatically craggy rocks. A crafts stand near the start often has sprouting coconuts for you to wedge into the ground, available for a few dollars' donation; no digging is required—like the ohia lehua that have started to reappear here, coconut palms are used to tough conditions. So are the people of Puna, who gather in great numbers at the open-air **Uncle Robert's Awa Club** for the Wednesday night market and Hawaiian music on Fridays. During the day, it's open for snacks and drinks, sold "by donation" for permit purposes (be aware they'll let you know *exactly* how much to donate).

From Kalapana/Kaimu, you'll pick up Highway 137 (the Kapoho-Kalapana Rd.), and follow it east to Kapoho along 15 miles of nearly pristine coastline, past parks, forests, rugged beaches, and tide pools, some geothermally heated. The highway is nicknamed the **Red Road,** for the terra-cotta-hued cinders once used to pave it, although it's now mostly covered by black asphalt.

The adventurous (or exhibitionists) may want to make the tricky hike down to unmarked **Kehena**

**Black Sand Beach,** off Highway 137 about 3½ miles east of Kalapana. Here the law against public nudity is widely ignored, although the view of the ocean is usually more entrancing. (Clothed or not, avoid going into the water—currents are dangerous.) It's easier to take a brief detour to see the waves pounding the base of ironwood-shaded cliffs in the **MacKenzie State Recreation Area,** 9 miles northeast of Kalapana; the park was closed in 2015 for cleanup from 2014's devastating Hurricane Iselle, but expected to reopen by 2016. Another 3 miles east leads to the scenic "hot pond" at **Ahalanui Park ★★** (see below); both have picnic and restroom facilities.

From Ahalanui, Highway 137 veers inland; drive 1¾ miles to a right turn on Kapoho Kai Road and follow it for a mile to the small parking area for the **Waiopae Tidepools ★,** a state marine-life conservation district (http://dlnr.hawaii.gov/dar). Snorkelers will go crazy here, but with proper footwear, you can walk along the edges of numerous tide pools, many very shallow and teeming with coral and juvenile fish, while the breakers crash in the distance. (**Note:** The private road and parking lot are maintained by the community, with a volunteer usually on hand to collect a $3 fee.)

Back on Highway 137, head 1 mile north to Kapoho Beach Road. On your left is the **Green Lake Fruit Stand,** named for the unusual, freshwater **Green Lake,** inside nearby **Kapoho Crater ★**. The lake is actually a crater within the 360-foot-tall Kapoho Crater, formed 200 to 400 years ago. If she's not at the stand, call caretaker Smiley Burrows (© 808/965-5500) to arrange a scenic hike or drive up the crater for $5. (You can also swim in the lake, one of only two on the island, but no one knows its depths, and algae sometimes obscure the water.)

Just east of the Green Lake Fruit Stand, Highway 137 intersects Highway 132 (Kapoho Rd.). A right turn onto an unpaved portion leads to Hawaii's easternmost point and the **Cape Kumukahi Lighthouse ★**, which miraculously survived the 1960 lava flow that destroyed the original village of Kapoho. Who cares if its modern steel frame isn't all that quaint? The fact that it's standing at all is impressive—the molten lava parted in two and flowed around it—while its bright-white trusses make a great contrast in photos against the black lava, dotted with a few green trees and framed by a cerulean sea.

A left turn onto Highway 132 takes you back 9 miles to the funky, somewhat ramshackle village of Pahoa, passing eerie **Lava Tree State Monument ★★** (see below) and the towering monkeypod and invasive albizia trees of **Nanawale Forest Reserve** as you go. *Note:* If you're heading to Hilo, take the Highway 130 bypass road all the back to Highway 11, about 14 miles from Pahoa; if you're heading toward Volcano, you'll pick up another bypass in Keaau, about a mile before Highway 130 intersects Highway 11.

**Ahalanui Park (Hot Pond) ★★** PARK Warmed by one of the area's many volcanically heated springs, this balmy, shallow pool lined with lava rocks and shady trees is protected from the surging ocean by a concrete wall, although very high surf can crash over it and cool the pond. It's not a snorkeling site per se, but silver fish use inlets to dart around the pool's usually clear waters, while a few eels hide in the rocks (if you don't bother them, they won't bother you). Shaded by tall palms, it's a pretty setting even if you don't plan to

# VOG & OTHER volcanic VOCABULARY

Hawaii's volcanoes have their own unique vocabulary. The lava that resembles ropy swirls of brownie batter is called **pāhoehoe** (pa-hoy-hoy); it results from a fast-moving flow that ripples as it moves. The chunky, craggy lava that looks like someone put asphalt in a blender is called **'a'ā** (ah-ah); it's caused by lava that moves slowly, breaking apart as it cools, and then overruns itself. Newer words include **vog,** which is smog made of volcanic gases and smoke, and **laze,** which results when sulfuric acid hits the water and vaporizes, and mixes with chlorine to become, as any chemistry student knows, hydrochloric acid. Both vog and laze sting your eyes and can cause respiratory illness; don't expose yourself to either for too long. Since Halemaumau began spewing its dramatic plume of smoke in 2008, vog has been more frequent, particularly on the Kona and Kohala coasts, thanks to wind patterns; the June 27, 2014, lava flow has increased vog in Pahoa and lower Puna. The state **Department of Health** (www.hiso2index.info) lists current air-quality advisories for the Big Island, based on sulfur dioxide levels.

go into the water (which you shouldn't if you have any open cuts, due to possible bacteria, although the county does perform regular tests). Facilities include a lifeguard station, picnic tables, shower, and porta-potties—wear your bathing suit under your clothes so you don't have to change in one.

*Makai* side of Hwy. 137, between mile markers 10 and 11, Pahoa (9 miles southeast of town). Free admission. Daily 7am–7pm (closed until 1pm 2nd Wed each month for maintenance).

**Lava Tree State Monument** ★★ NATURAL ATTRACTION In 1790, a fast-moving lava flow raced through a grove of ohia lehua trees here, cooling quickly and creating lava rock molds of their trunks. Today the ghostly sentinels punctuate a well-shaded, paved .7-mile loop trail through the rich foliage of the 17-acre park. Facilities include restrooms and a few spots for picnicking (or ducking out of the rain during one of the area's frequent showers). Some areas with deep fissures are fenced off, but keep to the trail regardless for safe footing.

*Makai* side of Hwy. 132 (Pahoa–Pohoiki Rd.), 2¾ miles southeast of Pahoa. www.hawaiistateparks.org. Free admission. Daily during daylight hours.

## HAWAII VOLCANOES NATIONAL PARK ★★★

Before tourism became Hawaii's middle name, the islands' singular attraction for visitors wasn't the beach, but the volcano. From the world over, curious spectators gathered on the rim of Kilauea's Halemaumau crater to see one of the greatest wonders of the globe. A century after it was named a national park in 1916, **Hawaii Volcanoes National Park** (www.nps.gov/havo; © **808/985-6000**) remains Hawaii's premier natural attraction, home to an active volcano and one of only two World Heritage Sites in the islands.

There's never a guarantee you'll see flowing lava from the ground—helicopter flights are another matter—but it's undeniably spectacular even without liquid rocks (check the website for updates before you go). Sadly, after driving to the park, about 100 miles from Kailua-Kona and 29 miles from Hilo, many visitors pause only briefly by the highlights along **Crater Rim Drive** ★★★ before heading back to their hotels.

Hawaii Volcanoes National Park.

To allow the majesty and *mana* (spiritual energy) of this special place to sink in, you should really take at least 3 days—and certainly 1 night—to explore the park, including its miles of trails.

Fortunately, the admission fee ($10 per vehicle, $5 per bicyclist or hiker) is good for 7 days. Be prepared for rain and bring a jacket, especially in winter, when it can be downright chilly at night, in the 40s or 50s (single digits to midteens Celsius). *Note:* For details on hiking and camping in the park, see "Hiking" (p. 125) and "Camping" (p. 166).

### Crater Rim Drive Tour

Stop by the **Kilauea Visitor Center** (daily 9am–5pm) to get the latest updates on lava flows and the day's free ranger-led tours and watch an informative 25-minute film, shown on the hour from 9am to 4pm. Just beyond the center lies vast **Kilauea Caldera ★★★**, a circular depression nearly 2 miles by 3 miles and 540 feet deep. It's easy to imagine Mark Twain

## Please Brake for Nene

Nene, the endangered native Hawaiian goose and state bird, are making a comeback in Hawaii Volcanoes National Park and other high-altitude areas in the islands, where they feast on the cranberry-like 'ōhelo berries that grow at upper elevations.

Unfortunately, Hawaii's uplands are often misty, and the birds' feathers blend easily with the pavement, making it hard for inattentive drivers to see them. Drive carefully, and to discourage them from approaching cars, don't feed them.

marveling over the sights here in 1866, when a wide, molten lava lake bubbled within view in the caldera's **Halemaumau Crater ★★★**, itself 3,000 feet across and 300 feet deep.

Though different today, the caldera's panorama is still compelling. Since 2008, a towering plume of ash, visible from miles away, has billowed from Halemaumau, the legendary home of Pele. The sulfurous smoke has forced the ongoing closure of nearly half of Crater Rim Drive, now just a 6-mile crescent. The fumes normally drift northwest, where they often create vog (see "Vog & Other Volcanic Vocabulary" on p. 67), to the dismay of Kona residents. (Scientists monitor the park's air quality closely, just in case the plume changes direction, with rangers ready to evacuate the park quickly if needed.) In the evening the pillar of smoke turns a rosy red, reflecting the lava lake that rises and falls deep below. You can also admire Halemaumau's fiery glow over a drink or dinner in **Volcano House ★★** (p. 165), the only inn in the park.

Less than a mile from the visitor center, several **steam vents ★★★** line the rim of the caldera, puffing out moist warm air. Across the road, a boardwalk leads through the stinky, smoking **sulphur banks ★★★**, called Haakulamanu in Hawaiian, and home to hardy ohia lehua trees and unfazed native birds. (As with all trails here, stay on the path to avoid possible serious injury, or worse.)

Shortly before Crater Rim Drive closes to traffic (due to the current eruption), the **observation deck ★★★** at **Thomas A. Jaggar Museum ★★** offers a prime spot for viewing the crater and its plume, especially at night. By day you can also see the vast, barren Kau Desert and the massive sloping flank of Mauna Loa. The museum itself is open daily 10am to 7:30pm (gift shop until 8pm), and admission is free; watch videos from the days when the volcano was really spewing, learn about the cultural significance of Pele, and track earthquakes (a precursor of eruptions) on a seismograph.

Heading southeast from the visitor center, Crater Rim Drive passes by the smaller but still impressive **Kilauea Iki Crater ★★**, which in 1959 was a roiling lava lake spewing lava 1,900 feet into the air. From here, you can walk or drive to **Thurston Lava Tube ★★★**, a 500-year-old lava cave in a pit of giant tree ferns. Known in Hawaiian as Nahuku, it's partly illuminated, but take a flashlight and wear sturdy shoes so you can explore the unlit area for another half-mile or so.

Continuing on Crater Rim Drive leads to the **Puu Puai Overlook ★** of Kilauea Iki, where you find the upper trailhead of the aptly named half-mile **Devastation Trail ★★**, an easy walk through a cinder field that ends where Crater Rim Drive meets **Chain of Craters Road ★★★**.

Pedestrians and cyclists only can continue on Crater Rim Drive for the next .8 mile of road, closed to

Chain of Craters Road.

vehicular traffic since the 2008 eruption began. The little-traveled pavement leads to **Keanakakoi Crater** ★★, scene of several eruptions in the 19th and 20th centuries and yet another dazzling perspective on the Kilauea Caldera. Turn your gaze north for an impressive view of Mauna Loa and Mauna Kea, the world's two highest mountains, when measured from the sea floor.

### Chain of Craters Road ★★★

It's natural to drive slowly down the 19-mile **Chain of Craters Road,** which descends 3,700 feet to the sea and ends in a thick black mass of rock from a 2003 lava flow. You feel like you're driving on the moon, if the lunar horizon were a brilliant blue sea. Pack food and water for the journey, since there are officially no concessions after you pass the Volcano House; the nearest fuel lies outside the park, in Volcano Village.

Two miles down, before the road really starts twisting, the one-lane, 8½-mile **Hilina Pali Road** ★★

veers off to the west, crossing windy scrublands and old lava flows. The payoff is at the end, where you stand nearly 2,300 feet above the coast along the rugged 12-mile *pali* (cliff). Some of the most challenging trails in the park, across the Kau Desert and down to the coast, start here.

Back on Chain of Craters Road, 9¾ miles below the Crater Rim Drive junction, the picnic shelter at **Kealakomo ★** provides another sweeping coastal vista. At mile marker 16.5, you'll see the pullout parking lot for **Puu Loa ★★★**, an enormous field of some 23,000 petroglyphs—the largest in the islands. A three-quarter-mile, gently rolling lava trail leads to a boardwalk where you can view the stone carvings, 85% of which are holes known as cupules; Hawaiians often placed their infants' umbilical cords in them.

At the end of Chain of Craters Road, a lookout area allows a glimpse of 90-foot **Holei Sea Arch ★★**, one of several striking formations carved in the cliffs by the ocean's fury. Stop by the ranger station before treading carefully across the 21st-century lava, "some of the youngest land on Earth," as the park calls it. In the distance you may spot fumes from the Puu Oo vent, steam clouds in the ocean, or a red glow at night. Bear in mind it's a slow drive back up at night.

## KAU

At the end of 11 miles of bad road that peters out at Kaulana Bay, in the lee of a jagged, black-lava point, is *Ka Lae* ("The Point")—the tail end of the United States. From the tip, the nearest continental landfall is Antarctica, 7,500 miles away. It's a rugged 2-mile hike down a cliff from South Point to the anomaly known as **Green Sand (Papakolea) Beach ★★**, described on p. 94. Beware the big waves that lash the shore there.

# THE BRUTE FORCE OF THE
volcano

Volcanologists refer to Hawaii's volcanic eruptions as "quiet" eruptions because gases escape slowly instead of building up and exploding violently all at once. The Big Island's eruptions produce slow-moving, oozing lava that generally provide excellent, safe viewing when they're not in remote areas.

Even so, **Kilauea** has still caused its share of destruction. Since the current eruption began on January 3, 1983, lava has covered more than 50 square miles of lowland and rainforest, ruining 215 homes and businesses, wiping out the pretty, black-sand beach of Kaimu, and burying other landmarks. Kilauea has also added more than 500 acres of new land on its southeastern shore. (Such land occasionally collapses under its own weight into the ocean, which is why Hawaii Volcanoes National Park discourages hiking there.) The most prominent vent of the eruption has been Puu Oo, a 760-foot-high cinder-and-spatter cone 10 miles east of Kilauea's summit, in an off-limits natural reserve. Scientists are also keeping an eye on the active volcanoes of **Mauna Loa,** which has been swelling since its last eruption in 1984, and **Hualalai,** which hovers above Kailua-Kona and last erupted in 1801.

**Kahuku Unit, Hawaii Volcanoes National Park ★★** NATURAL ATTRACTION    Few visitors (or even residents) are familiar with this 116,000-acre portion of the national park, some 24 miles from the Kilauea Visitor Center and accessible only since 2009. But if your timing is right—it's only open weekends, and closed the first Saturday of each month as well as holidays—you can hike, bike, or drive to see a forested pit crater, cinder cone, and tree molds from an 1866 lava flow, plus ranch-era relics. Rangers frequently lead free hikes. **Note:** There are restrooms but no water; bring your own food and drinks.

*Mauka* side of Hwy. 11, btw mile markers 70 and 71, Pahala. www.nps.gov/havo/planyourvisit/kahuku-hikes.htm. © **808/985-6000.** Free admission. Sat–Sun 9am–3pm; closed 1st Sat of each month.

**Kau Coffee Mill** ★ FACTORY TOUR   In the former sugarcane fields on the slopes of Mauna Loa, a number of small farmers are growing coffee beans whose quality equals—some say surpasses—Kona's. More and more tasting competitions seem to agree; in any case, this farm and mill in tiny Pahala provides an excellent excuse to break up the long drive to the main entrance of Hawaii Volcanoes National Park, 23 miles northeast. Free 45-minute guided tours are offered three times daily; enjoy tastings of coffee and macadamia nuts throughout the day in the pleasant visitor center. In early May, the 10-day **Kau Coffee Festival** (www.kaucoffeefestival.com) includes hikes, music, hula, and farm tours.

96-2694 Wood Valley Rd., Pahala. www.kaucoffeemill.com. © **808/928-0550.** Free admission. Daily 8:30am–4:30pm. Guided tours 10am, noon, and 2pm, weather permitting. From Kailua-Kona, take Hwy. 11 71 miles to a left on Kamani St., take 3rd right at Pikake St., which becomes Wood Valley Rd., and follow uphill 2½ miles to farm on left.

**Kula Kai Caverns** ★★ NATURAL ATTRACTION Before you trudge up to Pele's volcanic eruption, take a look at its underground handiwork. Ric Elhard and Rose Herrera have explored and mapped out the labyrinth of lava tubes and caves, carved out over the past 1,000 years or so, that crisscross their property near South Point. Their "expeditions" range from the

Lighted Trail tour, an easy, half-hour walk suitable for families, to longer (up to 2 hr.), more adventurous caving trips, where you crawl through tunnels and wind through labyrinthine passages (some restricted to kids 8 and older). Wear sturdy shoes.

92-8864 Lauhala Dr., Ocean View (46 miles south of Kailua-Kona). www.kulakaicaverns.com. © **808/929-9725.** Lighted Trail tour $20 adults, $15 children 6–12, free for children 5 and under; longer tours $60–$95 adults ($60–$65 children 8–12). By reservation only; gate security code provided at booking.

## Organized Tours

Farms, gardens, and historic houses that may be open only to guided tours are listed under "Attractions & Points of Interest," above. For boat, kayak, bicycle, and similar tours, see listings under "Outdoor Activities."

### HELICOPTER TOURS ★

Don't believe the brochures with pictures of fountains of lava and "liquid hot magma," as Dr. Evil would say. Although there are no guarantees you'll see *any* red-hot lava (and for safety reasons, you're not going to fly all that close to it), a helicopter ride offers a unique perspective on the island's thousands of acres of hardened black lava, Kilauea's enormous fuming caldera, and the remote, still-erupting Puu Oo vent—the likeliest place to spot flowing lava. And if you're pressed for time, a helicopter ride beats driving to the volcano and back from Kohala and Kona resorts.

**Blue Hawaiian Helicopters ★★** (www.blue hawaiian.com; © **800/786-2583** or 808/886-1768), a professionally run, locally based company with comfortable, top-of-the-line copters, and pilots who are extremely knowledgeable about everything from volcanology to Hawaii lore, flies three different tours out of

# PLANTING A koa legacy tree

One of the most inspiring and memorable experiences I've ever had in Hawaii has been with **Hawaiian Legacy Tours ★★★** (www.hawaiianlegacytours.com; ✆ **877/707-8733**), which allows visitors to help restore the native koa forest high above the Hamakua Coast. More koa means more native birds and less runoff, which can harm the reefs far below. Over its lifetime, the tree can also offset the carbon impact of a week's vacation on this beautiful island. The freshly baked scones that await in the welcome center are pretty awesome, too.

After you check in at the welcome center, a handsomely restored ranch house in the tiny village of Umikoa (at 3,200 ft. elevation), guides in ATVs, or a Pinzgauer six-wheeler for larger groups, drive you even higher up the misty slopes of Mauna Kea, to the former personal forest of King Kamehameha the Great. Later cleared for ranchland, these fields at 5,000 feet bear only a few remaining old-growth trees, from which Hawaiian Legacy Hardwoods (the tours' parent company) extracts seeds to propagate seedlings in its nurseries. Amid the new groves growing on the mountainside, where the *mana* (spiritual power) and beauty of your surroundings are spine-tingling, you'll be shown how to plant a seedling. You can dedicate it to a loved one on a special commemorative certificate, and you'll also receive its GPS coordinates, allowing you to monitor its growth via Google Earth.

The 2-hour **Planters Tour,** including one tree for planting, costs $110 for adults, $55 for kids 5 to 18, while the 3½-hour **Grand Tour,** which spends more time in the nurseries and on the Umikoa Trail, costs $180 for adults, $90 for kids 5 to 18. (Children's rates exclude a tree for planting, but additional trees may be purchased for $60 each.) Private tours and shuttles (from the Kona and Hilo airports, Four Seasons Resort Hualalai, and Hilo cruise terminal) are available for additional fees. **Note:** If you can't take a tour, you can pay to have a koa ($60) or an even rarer sandalwood tree ($100) planted for you; see www. legacytrees.org for details.

Waikoloa, at Highway 19 and Waikoloa Road. The 2-hour **Big Island Spectacular ★★** stars the volcano, tropical valleys, the Hamakua Coast waterfalls, and the Kohala Mountains, and costs $450 to $563 ($396–$495 online with a 5-day advance booking). If time is money for you, and you've got all that money, it's an impressive trip, particularly if you ride in the roomier and quieter Eco-Star (the higher price in ranges quoted here). If you just want to admire waterfalls, green mountains, and the deep valleys, including Waipio, of North Kohala and the Hamakua Coast, the 50-minute **Kohala Coast Adventure ★** is a less exorbitant but reliably picturesque outing, costing $242 to $294 ($213–$259 online).

If you've "done" the volcano and have an adventurous spirit, consider Blue Hawaiian's 2-hour **Big Island–Maui tour ★★**, which includes the Kohala Mountains/Hamakua waterfalls leg and also crosses the Alenuihaha Channel to Maui, where you view Haleakala Crater (a long-dormant volcano) and dozens of waterfalls in the verdant Hana rainforest. It costs $500 to $563 ($440–$495 online, with advance booking). Blue Hawaiian also operates out of the Hilo airport (© **808/961-5600**), flying the 50-minute **Circle of Fire Plus Waterfalls ★★** tour, which is significantly cheaper—$223 to $274 ($196–$241 online)—because it's closer to the volcano and waterfalls. On the other hand, if you're willing to drive to Hilo, you really should continue on to the national park. *Tip:* Ask about a AAA discount when booking flights.

The similarly professional **Sunshine Helicopters ★★** (www.sunshinehelicopters.com; © **866/501-7738** or 808/270-3999) offers a **Volcano Deluxe**

**Tour ★**, a 105-minute ride out of the Hapuna heliport, near the Mauna Kea Resort, which includes Kohala Mountains/Hamakua waterfalls. It's even pricier: $560 for open seating, $635 reserved seating next to the pilot on the six-passenger Whisper Star choppers ($510–$585 online). Less of a splurge—and less dependent on the ooh factor of oozing lava—is Sunshine's 30- to 40-minute **Kohala/Hamakua Coast Tour ★★**, which hovers waterfall-lined sea cliffs and the Pololu, Waimanu, and Waipio valleys, for $199 ($169 online).

*Note:* On all rides, your weight may determine where you sit in the helicopter. You should wear dark shades to prevent glare, and dress in light layers; both cool rain and strong sun can occur.

## VAN & BUS TOURS

Many of the outdoor-oriented, but not especially physically taxing, excursions of **Hawaii Forest & Trail ★★★** (www.hawaii-forest.com; © **800/464-1993** or 808/331-8505) include a significant time in comfy vans heading to and from remote areas, with guides providing narration along the way. Thus, they're a good way to see large chunks of the island without being behind the wheel yourself; the eco-friendly company also has exclusive access to many sites, including the waterfalls on its **Kohala Waterfalls Adventure**. Most tours depart daily from Kona ($129–$249 adults, $139–$179 children 12 and under). The three daily tours launched from Hilo in 2015—exploring volcano country, Mauna Kea, or Hilo's heritage and "tropical wonders" ($69–$169 adults, $59–$139 children)—are perfect for cruise passengers and anyone else on the Hilo side.

Discover Hawaii ★★ (www.discoverhawaii tours.com; © 808/690-9050) offers the 9-hour **Volcano Eco-Adventure Tour,** covering all the major attractions of Hawaii Volcanoes National Park and scenic sites in Hilo. Led by expert guides, the small-group tours in large-windowed mini-coaches depart at 10:30am Monday to Thursday and Saturday. The cost is $135 for adults, $80 for children 2 and older, excluding lunch.

Kailua-Kona visitors can also book all-day volcano trips and "circle" tours, which include the black-sand **Punaluu Beach ★★★** (p. 94), the national park, Hilo, and Waimea. I recommend the environmentally conscious, community-oriented **KapohoKine Adventures ★★** (www.kapohokine.com; © 808/964-1000), which offers tours from Kona and Hilo ($119–$229 adults, $99–$179 children 12 and under).

# ACTIVE
# BIG ISLAND

by Jeanne Cooper

**3**

T oo young geologically to have many great beaches, the Big Island instead has more colorful ones: brand-new black-sand beaches, salt-and-pepper beaches, and even a green-sand beach. If you know where to look, you'll also find some gorgeous pockets of golden sand off the main roads here and there, plus a few longer stretches, often hidden from view by either acres of lava or high-end resorts. Thankfully, by law all beaches are public, so even the toniest hotel must provide access (including free parking) to its sandy shores. **Note:** Never leave valuables in your trunk, particularly in remote areas, and always respect the privacy of residents with homes on the beach. For details on shoreline access around the island, see the maps and descriptions at www.hawaiicounty.gov/pl-shore line-access-big-island. For more information on state beach parks, visit www.hawaiistateparks.org.

You'll find relevant sites on the "Big Island" map on p. 29.

## North Kona
### KAHALUU BEACH ★★

The most popular beach on the Kona Coast has reef-protected lagoons and county park facilities that

attract more than 400,000 people a year, making it less attractive than in years past. Coconut trees line a narrow salt-and-pepper-sand shore that gently slopes to turquoise pools, home to schools of brilliantly colored tropical. In summer, it's an ideal spot for children and beginning snorkelers; the water is so shallow you can just stand up if you feel uncomfortable—but please, not on the living coral, which can take years to recover. In winter, there's a rip current when the high surf rolls in; look for any lifeguard warnings. Kahaluu isn't the biggest beach on the island, but it's one of the best equipped, with off-road parking, beach-gear rentals, a covered pavilion, restrooms, barbecue pits, and a food concession. It gets crowded, so come early to stake out a spot. If you have to park on Alii Drive, be sure to poke your head into tiny, blue-roofed **St. Peter's by the Sea,** a Catholic chapel next to an old lava rock *heiau* where surfers once prayed for waves.

## KEKAHA KAI STATE PARK ★★

Formerly known as Kona Coast State Park, this beach park is known for its brilliant white sand offsetting even more brilliant turquoise water. With several sandy bays and coves well-hidden from the highway, the park has two official entrances. About 4½ miles north of the airport off Highway 19 (across from West Hawaii Veterans Cemetery) is the turnoff for Maniniowali Beach, better known as **Kua Bay.** A thankfully paved road crosses acres of craggy lava, leading to the parking lot and a short, paved walkway to an even shorter, sandy scramble down a few rocks to the beach. It has restrooms and showers, but absolutely no shade or drinking water. Locals flock here to sunbathe, swim, bodyboard, and bodysurf, especially on weekends, so go during the week, and in mornings, when it's cooler. If you have a 4WD vehicle, you can take the marked turnoff 212 miles north of the

Kekaha Kai State Park.

airport off Highway 19 and drive 1½ bumpy miles over a rough lava road to the parking area for sandy **Mahai-ula Beach,** reached by another short trail. Sloping more steeply than Kua Bay, this sandy beach has stronger currents than Kua Bay, although if you're fit you can still swim or snorkel in calm conditions. You can also just laze under the shade—you're likely to see a snoozing green sea turtle or two. The park is open 9am to 7pm daily.

## KIHOLO STATE PARK RESERVE ★★★

To give yourself a preview of why to come here, pull over at the marked Scenic Overlook on Highway 19 north of Kekaha Kai State Park, between mile markers 82 and 83. You'll see a shimmering pale blue lagoon, created by the remains of an ancient fish pond, and the bright cerulean **Kiholo Bay,** jewels in a crown of black lava. Now take the unmarked lava-gravel road (much smoother than Kekaha Kai's road to Mahaiula Beach) just south of the overlook and drive carefully to the end, taking the right fork for one of two parking areas, both a short walk from the shore (and both with portable toilets). The "beach" here is black sand, lava pebbles, and coral, but it's fine for sunbathing or spotting dolphins and seasonal humpback whales. Keep your sturdy-soled shoes on, though, because you'll want to keep walking north to **Keanalele** (also called "Queen's Bath"), a collapsed lava tube found amid kiawe trees with steps leading into its fresh water, great for a cooling dip.

Continue on past several mansions to the turquoise waters of the former fishpond, cut off by a lava flow, and the darker bay, clouded by freshwater springs. Green sea turtles love this area—as do scampering wild goats. The park opens at 7am daily year-round, with the access gate off the highway locked promptly at 7pm April to Labor Day (early Sept), and then at 6pm through March 31. Portable toilets are the only facilities.

## KOHANAIKI BEACH ★★

Hidden behind the Kohanaiki golf course development, 2 miles north of the main entrance to Kaloko-Honokohau National Historical Park off Highway 19, the 1½ miles of shoreline here include anchialine ponds, white-sand beaches, and a reef- and rock-lined bay that's home to a popular surf break called Pine Trees. Paddlers, snorkelers, and fishermen also flock to the rugged coastline, which officially became a county park in 2013. The new status means improved access and parking, restrooms, showers, water fountain, campsites, and a *halau* (covered pavilion) for cultural practices; there's also a well-marked petroglyph. Since you can't turn left from northbound Hwy. 19, directions are easiest from the airport: Head 2.2 miles south on Hwy. 19 to the Kohanaiki entrance on the right (past mile marker 95); turn right at the first fork and follow nearly 1 mile to the first parking lot for beach access; facilities and more parking are farther south along the one-lane paved road, but you can also explore the shore to the left. It's open daily from 5:30am to 9pm (no camping Tues–Wed).

## LAALOA BEACH (WHITE SANDS/MAGIC SANDS BEACH) ★★

Don't blink as you cruise Alii Drive, or you'll miss Laaloa, often called White Sands, Magic Sands, or

Kohanaiki Beach.

Disappearing Beach. That's because the sand at this small pocket beach, about 4½ miles south of Kailua-Kona's historic center, does occasionally vanish, especially at high tide or during storms. On calm summer days, you can swim here, next to bodyboarders and bodysurfers taking advantage of the gentle shorebreak; you can also snorkel in a little rocky cove just to the south. In winter, though, a dangerous rip develops and waves swell, attracting expert surfers and spectators; stay out of the water then, but enjoy the gawking. The palm-tree-lined county beach park includes restrooms, showers, lifeguard station, and a small parking lot.

## OLD KONA AIRPORT PARK ★

Yes, this used to be the airport for the Kona side of the island—hence the copious parking on the former runway, at the end of Kuakini Highway, about a half-mile north of Palani Road in Kailua-Kona. Now it's a park jointly managed by the county and state, which in 1992 designated its waters a marine life conservation district. It's easy to get distracted by all the other free amenities: two Olympic-size pools in the **Kona Community**

**Aquatic Center** (℡ **808/327-3500**), a gym, tennis courts, ball fields. Yet there's a mile of sandy beach here, fronting tidepools perfect for families with small children, and Pawai Bay, whose reefs draw turtles and rays, and thus snorkelers and divers. The beach area also has covered picnic tables and grills, restrooms, and showers.

## South Kona

### HOOKENA BEACH PARK ★

A community group known as **Friends of Hookena** (www.hookena.org) has taken responsibility for upkeep and concessions at this secluded, taupe-colored sandy beach (technically a county park) since 2007. You can rent kayaks and snorkel gear to explore Kauhako Bay's populous reefs (avoid during high surf), or beach and camping gear to enjoy the view—sometimes including wild spinner dolphins—from the shore. Reservations for gear and campgrounds can be made online; the welcome concession stand at this remote spot even accepts credit cards. Facilities include showers, restrooms, water fountains, picnic tables, pavilions, and parking. From Kailua-Kona, take Highway 11 22 miles south to the Hookena Beach Road exit just past Hookena Elementary School, between mile markers 101 and 102. Follow it downhill 2 miles to the end, and turn left on the one-lane road to the parking area.

## The Kohala Coast

### ANAEHOOMALU BAY ★★★

The Big Island makes up for its dearth of beaches with a few spectacular ones, like Anaehoomalu, or A-Bay, as many call it. This popular gold-sand beach, fringed by a grove of palms and backed by royal fishponds still full of mullet, is one of Hawaii's most beautiful. It fronts the Waikoloa Beach Marriott Resort & Spa and is enjoyed by guests and locals alike (it's busier in summer, but doesn't ever get truly crowded). The beach slopes gently from shallow to deep water; swimming, snorkeling, diving, kayaking, and windsurfing are all excellent here. At the northern edge of the bay, snorkelers and divers can watch endangered green sea turtles line up and wait their turn to have small fish clean them. Equipment rental and snorkeling, scuba, and windsurfing instruction are available at the north end of the beach. Facilities include restrooms, showers, picnic tables, and plenty of parking; look for access signs off Waikoloa Beach Road. No lifeguards.

### HAPUNA BEACH ★★★

Just off Queen Kaahumanu Highway, below the Hapuna Beach Prince Hotel, lies this crescent of gold sand—a half-mile long and up to 200 feet wide. In summer, when the beach is widest, the ocean calmest, and the crowds biggest, this is a terrific place for swimming, bodysurfing, and snorkeling. But beware of Hapuna in winter, when its thundering waves and strong rip currents should only be plied by local experts. Facilities at Hapuna Beach, part of the **Hapuna Beach State Recreation Area**, include A-frame cabins (for camping by permit), picnic tables, restrooms, showers, water fountains, lifeguard station, and parking. You can also pick up the coastal **Ala Kahakai National Historic Trail** (p. 125) here to Spencer or Hololohokai beach parks to the north and south, respectively.

### KAUNAOA BEACH (MAUNA KEA BEACH) ★★★

Nearly everyone refers to this gold-sand beach at the foot of Mauna Kea Beach Hotel by its hotel nickname, but its real name is Hawaiian for "native dodder," a lacy, yellow-orange vine that once thrived on the shore. A coconut grove sweeps around this golden crescent, where the water is calm and protected by two black-lava points. The sandy bottom slopes gently into the bay, which often fills with tropical fish, sea turtles, and manta rays, especially at night, when lights shine down from a viewing promontory. Swimming is excellent year-round, except in rare winter storms. Snorkelers prefer the rocky points, where fish thrive in the surge. Facilities include restrooms, showers, and public-access parking (go early). No lifeguards.

## SPENCER PARK (OHAIULA BEACH) ★★

Virtually in the shadow of the massive Puukohola Heiau (p. 40) to the north, this is a great place to stop heading to or from the scenic and historic sites in North Kohala. The gently sloping, white-yellow sand beach is actually called Ohaiula, though most just call it "Spencer," since it's part of **Samuel M. Spencer County Park**. Protected by both a long reef and Kawaihae Harbor, the beach has relatively safe swimming year-round. Parking is plentiful, but it may fill up on weekends and holidays. From the intersection of highways 19 and 270, take Highway 270 a half-mile north to a left turn at the sign for the park and Puukohola Heiau, and follow to either of two parking areas at the end of the road. Facilities include picnic tables, restrooms, showers, grassy lawns, and shade trees; lifeguards are on duty weekends and holidays. Campsites at either end of the beach often serve the area's homeless population. (It's safe during daylight hours, but I'd avoid walking through the tents section.)

Spencer Beach.

## WAIALEA BAY (BEACH 69) ★★

Once a hidden oasis, this light-golden sandy beach in Puako, between the Waikoloa Beach and Mauna Lani resorts, earned its nickname from the number on a former telephone pole off Old Puako Road, which signaled one of the public-access points. Still tucked behind private homes, it's now a proper beach park, with a paved parking lot and trail to the beach, restrooms, and water fountains—but no lifeguards. The bay is generally calm in summer, good for swimming and snorkeling; waves can get big in winter, when surfers and bodyboarders tend to show up. From Kailua-Kona, take Highway 19 north to a left on Puako Road, then a right on Old Puako Road; the access road to the parking area is on your left, near telephone pole No. 71 (the nickname has not caught up with the times).

## Hilo

### LELEIWI BEACH PARK ★★

This string of palm-fringed, black-lava tide pools fed by freshwater springs and rippled by gentle waves is a photographer's delight—and the perfect place to take a plunge. In winter, big waves can splash these ponds, but the shallow pools are generally free of currents and ideal for families with children, especially in the protected inlets at the center of the park. Leleiwi often attracts endangered sea turtles, making this one of Hawaii's most popular snorkeling spots. Open 7am to 7pm, the beach park is 4 miles east of town on Kalanianaole Avenue. Facilities include a lifeguard station (staffed weekends, holidays, and summer), picnic tables, pavilions, and parking. A second section of the park, known **as Richardson's Ocean Park,** includes showers, restrooms, daily lifeguards, and the marine life exhibits of Richardson Ocean Center. *Tip:* If the area is crowded, check out the tide pools and/or small sandy coves in the five other beach parks along Kalanianaole Avenue between Banyan Drive and Leleiwi, especially the protected white sand lagoon of **Carlsmith Beach Park ★,** just a 2 minutes' drive west. It has lifeguard service in summer and on weekends and holidays, as does the rocky but kid-friendly **Onekahaha Beach Park ★,** at the end of Onekahakaha Road off Kalanianaole Avenue, just under a mile west from Carlsmith.

## KOLEKOLE BEACH PARK ★

Not a place to enter the rough water, this streamside park is nonetheless an unusually picturesque spot for a picnic. The lush greenery around you contrasts with the black rock beach, aquamarine sea, and white sea foam where waves meet Kolekole Stream, several miles below **Akaka Falls ★★★** (p. 47) in Honomu. You may see local kids jumping from a rope swing into the stream, which also has a small waterfall. Facilities

Leleiwi Beach.

include picnic pavilions, grills, restrooms, and parking. It's open 6am to 11pm. From Hilo, take Highway 19 north 11 miles to a left turn on Old Mamalahoa Highway, and take the first (sharp) right, which descends a quarter-mile down to the park. No lifeguard.

## Puna District

Most of the shoreline in this volcanically active area is craggy, with rough waters and dangerous currents, although the oceanfront thermal pond at **Ahalanui ★★** (p. 66) and the **Waiopae Tidepools ★** (p. 65) are certainly worth seeking out. The still-forming black-sand beach near **Kalapana,** born in the 1990 lava flow that buried Kaimu Beach, is best viewed from the cliff above it; rogue waves may suddenly break much higher down on the beach. *Note:* Although nudism is common at secluded, unmarked **Kehena Beach** (p. 64), it is illegal.

# Kau District

## GREEN SAND BEACH (PAPAKOLEA BEACH) ★★

Hawaii's famous green-sand beach is located at the base of Puu o Mahana, an old cinder cone spilling into the sea. It's difficult to reach; the open bay is often rough; there are no facilities, fresh water, or shade; and howling winds scour the point. Nevertheless, each year the unusual olive-brown sands—made of crushed olivine, a semiprecious green mineral found in eruptive rocks and meteorites—attract thousands of oglers. From Hwy. 11, between mile markers 69 and 70, take South Point Road about 8 miles south to a left fork for the Green Sand Beach parking lot; be aware much of it is one lane. Driving from there to the top of the cinder cone is no longer permitted by the Department of Hawaiian Homelands, although enterprising locals now offer a round-trip shuttle for $10 to $20 (cash only); you can also do the windy, challenging hike along the remaining 2½ miles across unshaded dirt roads and lava rock (wear closed-toe shoes, sunglasses, and a hat, and bring lots of water). In either case, you'll still need to clamber carefully down the steep eroded cinder cone to the sand. If the surf's up, check out the beach from the cliff's edge; if the water's calm, you can go closer, but keep an eye on the ocean at all times (there are strong rip currents here).

## PUNALUU BEACH ★★★

Green sea turtles love to bask on this remote, black-sand beach, beautifully framed by palm trees and easily photographed from the bluff above. The deep-blue waters can be choppy; swim only in very calm conditions, as there's no lifeguard present. You're welcome

Green Sand Beach.

to admire the turtles, but at a respectful distance; the law against touching or harassing them is enforced here (if not by authorities, then by locals who also like to congregate in the park). Park facilities include camping, restrooms, showers, picnic tables, pavilions, water fountains, a concession stand, and parking. There are two access roads from Highway 11, at 7¾ and 8 miles northeast of Naalehu. The first, Ninole Loop Road, leads past the somewhat overgrown-looking Sea Mountain golf course to a turnoff for a paved parking lot by the bluff. The second access from Highway 11, Punaluu Road, has a turnoff for a smaller, unpaved parking area.

# WATERSPORTS
## Boat, Raft & Submarine Tours

The relatively calm waters of the Kona and Kohala coasts are home to inquisitive reef fish, frolicking spinner dolphins, tranquil green sea turtles, spiraling

95

manta rays, and spouting whales and their calves in season (Dec–Mar). A wide variety of vessels offer sightseeing and snorkel/dive tours (gear provided). Cocktail and dinner cruises take advantage of the region's predictably eye-popping sunsets. On the wild Puna side of the island, boat rides may pass lava flowing into the sea or coastal waterfalls. For fishing charters, see p. 112.

## KONA COAST

**Atlantis Submarines ★**   If you have what it takes (namely, no claustrophobia), head 100 feet below the sea in a 65-foot **submarine,** with a large porthole for every passenger. During the 45 minutes underwater, the sub glides slowly through an 18,000-year-old, 25-acre coral reef in **Kailua Bay,** teeming with fish (including, unfortunately, invasive species such as goatfish and taape) and two shipwrecks encrusted in coral. You'll take a 5-minute boat shuttle from Kailua Pier, across from the ticket office, to the air-conditioned submarine.

75-5669 Alii Dr. (across the street from Kailua Pier), Kailua-Kona. ℗ **800/548-6262.** www.atlantisadventures.com/kona. Trips leave four times a day 10am–2:30pm (check-in 30 min. earlier). $115 age 13 and older, $48 under 13 (must be at least 3 ft. tall): $10 off online bookings.

**Body Glove Cruises ★★**   Body Glove's *Kanoa II,* a 65-foot, solar-powered catamaran carrying up to 100 passengers, runs an environmentally friendly, 4½-hour **snorkel/dive** morning cruise, along with shorter lunch and dinner excursions for those who just want to enjoy the views, as well as seasonal whale-watching trips; all depart from Kailua Pier. In the morning, you'll be greeted with fresh Kona coffee, fruit, and breakfast pastries before heading north to **Pawai Bay,** a marine preserve where you can snorkel, scuba dive, swim, or just hang out on the deck. Before chowing down on the deli lunch buffet, take the plunge off the boat's 20-foot water slide or 15-foot-high diving board. The only thing you need to bring is a towel; all gear is provided, along with "reef safe" sunscreen. And if you don't see dolphins, you can do a repeat cruise for free (the same is true if you don't see whales on a whale-watching excursion). Dinner and lunch cruises feature a historian who points out significant sites on the 12 miles from Kailua Pier to **Kealakekua Bay,** where passengers feast on a buffet spread and enjoy live Hawaiian music by notable entertainer LT Smooth. All cruises are free for children 5 and under, and the boat is wheelchair accessible, including restrooms.

Kailua Pier, Kailua-Kona. www.bodyglovehawaii.com. © **800/ 551-8911** or 808/326-7122. Snorkel cruises (Tues–Sat 8am, Sun 10am) $128 adults, $88 children 6–17; see website for additional scuba charges. Dinner cruise (Tues and Thurs–Sat 4pm) $118 adults, $88 children 6–17, free for children 5 and under. Lunch cruise (Wed 1pm) $98 adults, $78 children 6–17. Whale-watching cruises (Dec–Apr only; Tues and Thurs–Sun 1pm, Mon 2pm) $98 adults, $78 children 6–17.

**Captain Dan McSweeney's Whale Watch Learning Adventures** ★★★ Hawaii's most impressive visitors—45-foot humpback whales—return to the islands' warm waters, including those on the Big Island's **Kona side,** each winter. Capt. Dan McSweeney, who founded the Wild Whale Research Foundation in 1979, has no problem finding them. During the 3-hour **whale-watching tours,** typically offered January through March, he drops a hydrophone (an underwater microphone) into the water so you can listen to their songs, and sometimes uses an underwater video camera to show you what's going on.

Cruises are aboard the *Lady Ann,* which has restrooms and a choice of sunny or shaded decks; cold drinks and snacks are provided. Trips depart from Honokohau Harbor, where parking is free and typically easy. Honokohau Harbor, 74-380 Kealakehe Pkwy. (off Hwy. 19), Kailua-Kona. www.ilovewhales.com. © **888/942-5376** or 808/322-0028. Departures 7 and 11am Mon–Tues and Thurs–Fri Jan–March. $110 adults, $99 children 11 and under who also weigh under 90 lb.

**Captain Zodiac** ★   It's a wild, 14-mile ride to **Kealakekua Bay** aboard one of Captain Zodiac's 16-passenger, 24-foot **rigid-hull inflatable rafts,** or Zodiacs. There you'll spend about an hour snorkeling in the bay, perhaps with spinner dolphins, and enjoy snacks and beverages at the site. The small size of the craft mean no restrooms, but it also means you can explore sea

Snorkeling the Big Island seas.

caves on this craggy coast. Four-hour **snorkel trips** take place twice daily, with morning and afternoon departures; the 5-hour midday tour ingeniously arrives at Kealakekua when most other boats have left, with extra time for a second snorkel site, seasonal **whale-watching,** or other experiences at the captain's discretion, plus a deli lunch. Be prepared to get wet (that includes your camera). *Warning:* Pregnant women and those with bad backs should avoid this often-bumpy ride.

In Gentry's Kona Marina, Honokohau Harbor, 74-425 Kealakehe Pkwy. (off Hwy. 19), Kailua-Kona. www.captainzodiac.com. ℂ **808/329-3199.** 4-hr. snorkel cruise (Wed–Thurs and Sat–Sun 8am and 12:30pm) $110 adults, $84 children 4–12; 5-hr. snorkel cruise (Mon–Tues and Fri 9:45am) $125 adults, $94 children 4–12. Whale-watching cruises (Jan–Apr only; Tues and Thurs 9am) $84 adults, $59 children 4–12. Online booking discounts ($15 adults, $5–$10 children) available.

## Fair Wind Snorkeling & Diving Adventures ★★★

I love Fair Wind, for several reasons, starting with its home in Keauhou Bay, 8 miles south of Kailua Pier and so that much closer to **Kealakekua Bay,** where its two very different but impressively equipped boats head for **snorkel/dive tours:**

**FAIR WIND II** When traveling with kids, I book a cruise on the *Fair Wind II,* a 60-foot catamaran that includes two 15-foot water slides, a high-dive jump, playpens, and child-friendly flotation devices with viewfinders, so even toddlers can peek at Kealakekua's glorious sea life. Year-round, the *Fair Wind II* offers a 4½-hour morning snorkel cruise that includes breakfast and barbecue lunch; most of the year it also sails a 3½-hour afternoon snorkel cruise that provides snacks, which in summer becomes a deluxe 4½-hour excursion with barbecue dinner. Swimmers age 8 and up can also try **SNUBA**—kind of a beginner's version of scuba—for an optional $69, with an in-water guide.

**HULA KAI** When traveling with teens or adults, I prefer the *Hula Kai*, the Fair Wind's 55-foot foil-assist catamaran, open only to ages 7 and up. The boat provides a plusher experience (such as comfy seating with headrests) and, on its 5-hour morning snorkel cruise, a faster, smoother ride to two uncrowded Kona Coast snorkeling sites (usually neither is Kealakekua Bay), based on conditions. Guests have the option to try **stand-up paddleboarding, SNUBA** (see above), or the propulsive **"Sea Rocket"** ($25 per half-hour) to cover even more ground underwater. The *Hula Kai* also offers a fascinating night snorkel/dive with **manta rays,** a 1½-hour tour that doesn't have to voyage far from **Keauhou Bay** to find them. At night these gentle giants (no stingers!) are lured closer to the ocean's surface by the plankton that also rise there. Like other tour companies, Fair Wind uses dive lights to attract even more plankton; on the off chance you don't get to see a manta ray, you're welcome back another evening or an afternoon snorkel tour. It's fairly balmy at night, but you'll be tempted to stay in the water with the magnificent rays as long as you can, so wetsuits, warm soup, and hot drinks are provided to ward off chills. One-tank scuba dives are also available on all *Hula Kai* excursions ($31 without gear; $45 with); the manta night trip also charges $45 per "ride-along" (no snorkeling) passenger.

*Note:* Many of Fair Wind cruises sell out several days in advance, or as much as 2 to 3 weeks in peak season, so book ahead.

Keauhou Bay Pier, 78-7130 Kaleiopapa St., Kailua-Kona. www. fair-wind.com. ✆ **800/677-9461** or 808/322-2788. *Fair Wind II* morning snorkel cruise (daily 9am) $129 adults, $79 children

4–12, $29 children 3 and under. Afternoon snack snorkel cruise (daily 2pm fall–spring) $79 adults, $49 children 4–12, free for children 3 and under. *Hula Kai* deluxe morning snorkel/dive cruise (daily 9:30am) $149 age 7 and up (younger not permitted). Manta ray snorkel/dive (daily 7:15pm) $109 age 7 and up (younger not permitted). Parking is on opposite side of Keauhou Bay, at end of King Kamehameha III Rd.

**Kamanu Charters ★★** The *Kamanu*, a sleek 38-foot sailing catamaran, provides a laidback **sail-and-snorkel cruise** from Honokohau Harbor to the marine preserve of **Pawai Bay.** The 3½-hour trip includes a tropical lunch (deli sandwiches, chips, fresh fruit, and drinks), snorkeling gear, and personalized instruction for first-time snorkelers; weather permitting, it sails at 9am and 1:30pm. It can hold up to 24 people but often has fewer, making it even more relaxed. Morning cruises include a **swim with spinner dolphins;** late-afternoon cruises include sunset cocktails and **snorkeling with manta rays.** Whale-watching is also offered in season. *Kamanu Elua,* a 31-foot, rigid-hull inflatable boat with seating, offers similar tours, but heads to **Kealakekua Bay** for snorkeling. *Note:* This Zodiac-style boat is not advised for children 7 or younger, pregnant women, or those with back or neck injuries.

Honokohau Harbor, 74-7380 Kealakehe Pkwy. (off Hwy. 19), Kailua-Kona. www.kamanu.com. *©* **800/348-3091** or 808/329-2021. Snorkel cruises 9am daily, $95 adults, $50 children 12 and under; 1:30pm, $85 adults. Dolphin swim and snorkel (times/days vary) $139 all ages. Sunset manta ray snorkel (times/days vary) $95. Whale-watching Dec 15–Apr 15 (times/days vary) $75 adults, $65 children. Check website for online discounts.

**Sea Quest ★** With a head start from Keauhou Bay, Sea Quest's four **rigid-hull inflatable rafts** offer three varieties of **Kealakekua Bay snorkeling**

## High & Dry: Glass-Bottomed Boats

If you're not a swimmer, you don't have to forgo seeing the multi-hued marine life for which the Kona and Kohala coasts are justly famous. Of the Big Island's several glass-bottomed boat cruises, **Kailua Bay Charters'** tour on the 36-foot *Marian*, which has comfy benches and shade, is well-suited to families. The trip is just an hour long, with a naturalist on board to explain what you're seeing. If you tire of staring down, head to the bow to scan for dolphins or humpback whales. Tours leave Kailua Pier at 11:30am

Thursday to Tuesday and 12:30pm Wednesday (www.konaglassbottomboat.com; ☎ **808/324-1749;** $40 adults, $20 children under 12; reservations required). See the underwater sights of Anaehoomalu Bay on **Ocean Sports'** 26-foot glass-bottom boat; it too has benches, shade, and a naturalist. Half-hour tours depart from the beach six times daily (www.hawaiioceansports.com; ☎ **888/724-5924,** ext. 103, or 808/886-6666, ext. 103; $27 adults, $14 children 6 to 12, and free children under 6).

**cruises** and one excursion to **swim with spinner dolphins,** which may also include a Kealakekua snorkel. The Zodiac-style rafts hold 18 passengers, but Sea Quest takes just 14; rafts on longer tours include shade. Both the 5-hour Expedition South Kona and 4-hour Deluxe Morning Adventure depart in the mornings and include snorkeling among the incredibly diverse marine life of **Honaunau Bay,** within view of the towering wood tikis and restored cultural sites at **Puuhonua o Honaunau National Historical Park** (p. 36); the Expedition includes a third site and deli lunch. The aptly named 3-hour Captain Cook Express heads straight to Kealakekua; all three tours explore Kona Coast lava tubes and sea caves that larger boats can't maneuver. Operating under the name **Blue**

**Ocean Dolphin Encounters,** Sea Quest also offers a 5-hour tour that starts by locating a pod of wild spinner dolphins to swim with, under the tutelage of a certified divemaster, before their late-morning sleep (which is why they're often spotted closer to shore that time of day). Afterward, it's off to Kealakekua or another Kona Coast reef for snorkel and lunch.

Keauhou Bay Pier, 78-7128 Kaleiopapa St., Kailua-Kona. www.seaquesthawaii.com. **℃ 808/329-7238.** Morning snorkel tour (daily 8am) $96 adults, $78 children 5–12. Afternoon snorkel tour (daily 12:30pm) $76 adults, $65 children 5–12. South Kona snorkel tour (weekdays 8am year-round; also weekends in summer and holiday periods) $114 adults, $93 children 5–12. Children under 6, pregnant women, and people with bad backs not allowed. Dolphin tours (ages 10 and older) 8am daily, $139. Discounts for booking online. Park in lot at end of King Kamehameha III Rd., across from pier.

## HILO, THE HAMAKUA COAST & PUNA DISTRICT

**Lava Ocean Tours ★★**   The unpredictability of Pele, at least as evidenced by the on-again, off-again lava flows into the sea from Kilauea, means there may or may not be **sunset lava-viewing tours** aboard the *Lava Kai* catamaran (34 ft. long; 24-passenger capacity but limited to 12) or the smaller *Kuewa* (27 ft.; six passengers). But Capt. Shane Turpin's **Volcano Boat Tour** departing from Pohoiki (Isaac Hale Beach Park) near Pahoa still offers a close look unique at volcanic formations (sea arches, hardened lava "waterfalls") along the coast. It's not quite as exhilarating as seeing molten rock pour into a hissing ocean, but it's still adventurous, given the open waters.

Departures from Wailoa Harbor, off Hwy. 11, Hilo, and Pohoiki (Isaac Hale Beach Park), Pahoa. www.seelava.com. **℃ 808/966-4200.** Volcano boat tours 4:30pm Sun and Wed, $145 adults, $119 children 12 and under.

# Body Boarding (Boogie Boarding) & Bodysurfing

As with other watersports, it's important to stay out of rough surf in winter or during storms that bring big surf. In normal conditions, the best beaches for body boarding and bodysurfing on the Kona side of the island are **Hapuna Beach** on the Mauna Kea Resort, **Laaloa Beach (White Sand/Magic Sands Beach) ★★** in Kailua-Kona, and **Kua Bay** (Maniniowali Beach) in **Kekaha Kai State Park,** north of the airport. Experienced bodysurfers may want to check out South Kona's **Hookena Beach Park.** On the Hilo side, try **Leleiwi Beach Park.** See "Beaches" (p. 82) for details.

Hotel beach concessions and most surf shops (see "Surfing" on p. 114) rent body boards, but you can also find inexpensive rentals at **Snorkel Bob's,** in the parking lot of Huggo's restaurant, 75-5831 Kahakai St. at Alii Drive, Kailua-Kona (www.snorkelbob.com; ✆ **808/329-0770**), and on the Kohala Coast in the Shops at Mauna Lani, 68-1330 Mauna Lani Dr., facing the road on the Mauna Lani Resort (✆ **808/885-9499**). Both stores are open 8am to 5pm daily.

# Kayaking

Imagine sitting at sea level, eye to eye with a turtle, a dolphin, even a whale—it's possible in an ocean kayak. After a few minutes of instruction and a little practice in a calm area (like **Kamakahonu Cove** in front of the Courtyard King Kamehameha Kona Beach Hotel), you'll be ready to explore. Beginners can practice their skills in **Kailua Bay;** intermediate kayakers might try paddling from **Honokohau Harbor** to **Kekaha Kai State Park;** while the more advanced can tackle the

5 miles from **Keauhou Bay** to **Kealakekua Bay** or the scenic but challenging **Hamakua Coast.** You can also rent kayaks, including a clear "peekaboo" version that allows you to view sea life, at **Hookena Beach Park** (p. 88) for $40 to $50 a day.

**KEALAKEKUA BAY GUIDED TOURS & RENTALS**
Although technically you can rent kayaks for exploring Kealakekua Bay on your own (and even land near the Captain Cook Monument, if you follow the arduous process of snagging one of 10 daily state permits), it's best to go with a guided tour. Only three kayak companies are allowed to offer guided tours in Kealakekua Bay that land at the Cook monument (Kaawaloa), all launching from Napoopoo Wharf. Tours include equipment, snorkeling gear, snacks or lunch, and drinks and should be booked in advance, due to the tight limit on permits. Note that Napoopoo is a residential area, where parking can be difficult if you're not on a tour.

**Kona Boys** ★★ (www.konaboys.com; © **808/ 328-1234**) was the first outfit to offer kayak rentals in Kona, and is still widely regarded as the best. Its Kealakekua Bay tours, held daily by reservation, meet at the shop at 79-7539 Mamalahoa Hwy. (Hwy. 11), Kealakekua, at 7:15am, and finish at 1pm. Tours cost $169 for adults $149 for children. You can also rent gear from Kona Boys' **beach shack** at Kamakahonu Bay (© **808/329-2345**), the only one of its two sites to offer kayaks by the hour, not just by the day or week. Rentals include kayak, paddles, backrests, cooler, life jackets, dry bag, and a soft rack to carry kayaks on top of your car (including convertibles). Hourly rates are $19 single kayak, $29 double, with daily rates $54 and $74, respectively (weekly $174/$249).

Owned by a Native Hawaiian family, **Aloha Kayak** ★★ (www.alohakayak.com; © 877/322-1444 or 808/322-2868) offers two tours of different lengths to Kealakekua Bay and Kaawalao Flats, where the memorial to Captain Cook stands. The 3½-hour tour (add an hour for check-in/check-out) departs at 8am and noon daily and costs $99 for adults and $50 for children 11 and under. The 5-hour tour, which allows more time at Kaawaloa and its cultural sites, departs at 7:15am Sunday, Tuesday, and Thursday; it's $129 for adults and $70 for children (check website for $20-off coupon). Half-day rental rates are $25 for a single and $45 for a double; full-day rates are $35 for a single and $60 for a double, with triple kayaks and discounts for longer periods also available. Aloha Kayak's original shop is in Honalo, about 8½ miles south of Kailua-Kona, at 79-7248 Mamalahoa Hwy. (Hwy. 11), just south of its intersection with Highway 180. In 2015 the family opened a second site, including a shave ice stand and other beach gear rentals, on Napoopoo Road, just below the Kona Pacific Farmers Cooperative mill.

The environmentally conscious **Adventures in Paradise** ★★ (www.bigislandkayak.com; © 888/210-5365 or 808/447-0080) has a small office at 82-6020 Mamalahoa Hwy. (Hwy. 11) in Captain Cook, but generally meets clients at Napoopoo for its 3½-hour Kealakekua tours ($90–$100 for ages 5 and up), departing at 7 and 11:30am daily. (*Tip:* Book the early tour for the least crowded snorkeling.)

## Parasailing

Get a bird's-eye view of Hawaii's pristine waters with **UFO Parasail** (www.ufoparasail.net; © 800/FLY-4-UFO or 808/325-5836), which offers parasail rides daily between 8am and 5:30pm from Kailua Pier. The cost is $65 for the standard flight of 8 minutes of air time at 800 feet, and $75 for a deluxe 10-minute ride at 1,200 feet. You can go up alone or with a friend (or two); no experience is necessary, but single riders must weigh at least 130 pounds, and groups no more than 450 pounds. The boat may carry up to eight passengers (observers pay just $35), and the total time in the boat, around an hour, varies on the rides they've booked. *Tip:* Save $5 by booking online per ride.

## Scuba Diving

The Big Island's leeward coast offers some of the best diving and snorkeling in the world; the water is calm, warm, and clear. Want to swim with fast-moving game fish? Try **Ulua Cave,** at the north end of the Kohala Coast, from 25 to 90 feet deep; dolphins, rays, and the occasional Hawaiian monk seal swim by. And don't forget to book a night dive to see the majestic **manta rays,** regularly seen in greater numbers here than anywhere else in Hawaii (or most of the world, for that matter). More than 2 dozen dive operators on island offer everything from scuba-certification courses to guided dives to snorkeling cruises.

Founded in 1984, **Kohala Divers** (www.kohala divers.com; ✆ **808/882-7774**) has daily two-tank dives ($139–$149) to spectacular sites off North and South Kohala, including a 30-foot-high lava dome covered in plate and knob coral that attracts huge schools of fish, and several spots off Puako frequented by green sea turtles. Snorkelers (gear included) and ride-alongs pay $85 to join these and other charters aboard the 42-foot dive boat, which books just 15 of its 24-passenger capacity. You can also rent scuba and snorkel gear at its shop in Kawaihae Harbor Shopping Center, 61-3665 Akoni Pule Hwy. (Hwy. 270), about a mile north of its intersection with Highway 19. It's open daily 8am to 6pm.

"This is not your mother or father's dive shop," says owner Simon Key of the **Kona Diving Company,** in the Old Industrial area, 74-5467 Luhia St. (at Eho St.), Kailua-Kona (www.konadivingcompany.com; © **808/331-1858**). "This is a dive shop for today's diver." What sets Kona Diving Company apart, Simon claims, is its willingness to take its 34-foot catamaran (complete with showers, TV, and restrooms) to unusual dive sites, and "not those sites just 2 minutes from the mouth of the harbor." Kona Diving also offers introductory dives ($205), two-tank morning dives ($130), and one- and two-tank manta ray night dives from Honokohau Harbor ($120–$140). Snorkelers and ride-alongs pay $80 to $115, gear included, depending on the trip; scuba gear cost $30 a day.

One of Kona's oldest and most eco-friendly dive shops, **Jack's Diving Locker,** in the Coconut Marketplace, 75-5813 Alii Dr., Kailua-Kona (www.jacks divinglocker.com; © **800/345-4807** or 808/329-7585), boasts an 8,000-square-foot dive center with solar-heated swimming pool (and underwater viewing windows), classrooms, and full-service rentals and sports-diving and technical-diving facility. It offers the classic two-tank dive for $125 ($65 snorkelers) and a two-tank manta-ray night dive for $155 ($125 snorkelers), on four roomy boats taking 10 to 18 divers (split into groups of six). Another night dive: "Pelagic Magic," a one-tank descent into dark water that reveals iridescent jellies and evanescent zooplankton ($175), offered Tuesday and Thursday.

# Snorkeling

If you come to Hawaii and don't snorkel, you'll miss half the fun. The clear waters along the dry Kona and Kohala coasts, in particular, are home to spectacular marine life, including spinner dolphins by day and giant manta rays by night. You'll want to take an evening **boat tour** (p. 95) or **kayak tour** (p. 104) to see the latter (and please heed instructions to just watch the mantas and not touch them, which harms their skin). For dolphins and reef denizens, go in the mornings, before afternoon clouds and winds lessen visibility. At all snorkeling sites, please be very careful not to stand on, kick, or touch the live coral, which takes years to grow. *Tip:* Rent your gear the night before you plan to snorkel, so you won't be tempted to rush the fitting process.

**GEAR RENTALS** If you're staying at a Kona or Kohala resort, the hotel concession should have basic gear for hourly rental. If you're thinking of exploring more than the beach outside your room, an inexpensive place to get basic rental equipment ($9 per week) is **Snorkel Bob's,** in the parking lot of Huggo's restaurant, 75-5831 Kahakai St. at Alii Drive, Kailua-Kona (www.snorkel bob.com; ✆ **808/329-0770**), and on the Kohala Coast in the Shops at Mauna Lani, 68-1330 Mauna Lani Dr., facing the road on the Mauna Lani Resort (✆ **808/ 885-9499**). Higher-quality gear costs $35 a week for adults, $22 for children ($44/$32 for prescription masks). Both stores are open 8am to 5pm daily.

You can also rent high-quality gear from **Jack's Diving Locker,** Coconut Grove Shopping Center (next to Outback Steak House), 75-5813 Alii Dr., Kailua-Kona (www.jacksdivinglocker.com; ✆ **800/345-4807** or 808/329-7585), open 8am to 8pm Monday to

Saturday, until 6pm Sunday. Snorkel sets cost $9 a day. On the Kohala Coast, visit **Kohala Divers** (www. kohaladivers.com; © **808/882-7774**) in the Kawaihae Shopping Center, 61-3665 Akoni Pule Highway (Hwy. 270), in Kawaihae, a mile north of the intersection with Highway 19. It's open 8am to 6pm daily, with snorkel sets starting at $10 a day.

On the island's east side, **Nautilus Dive Center,** 382 Kamehameha Ave. at Nawahi Lane (next to the Shell gas station) in Hilo (www.nautilusdivehilo. com; © **808/935-6939**), has daily snorkel packages for $6.

**TOP SNORKEL SITES** If you've never snorkeled in your life, **Kahaluu Beach ★★** (p. 82) is the best place to start, as long as the crowds don't throw you off. Just wade in on one of the small, sandy paths through the lava-rock tide pools and you'll see colorful fish. Even better, swim out to the center of the shallow, well-protected bay to see schools of surgeonfish, Moorish idols, butterflyfish, and even green sea turtles. The friendly and knowledgeable volunteers of the **Kahaluu Bay Education Center** (**KBEC;** www. kahaluubay.org; © **808/640-1166**) are on-site daily from 9:30am to 4:30pm to explain reef etiquette—essentially: "Look, but don't touch"—and answer questions about its marine life. The KBEC even rents snorkel gear ($14) from Jack's Diving Locker and boogie boards with viewing windows ($10), if you don't want to put your face underwater; proceeds benefit conservation at this popular spot, visited annually by some 400,000 snorkelers, swimmers, and surfers.

**Kealakekua Bay ★★★** may offer the island's best overall snorkeling (coral heads, lava tubes, calm waters, underwater caves and more), but because it's a marine life conservation district and state historical park (p. 34), access is restricted to preserve its treasures. The best way to snorkel here is via permitted **boat tours** (p. 95), generally departing from Kailua Pier or Keauhou Bay, or **kayak tours** (p. 104) with permits to launch from Napoopoo Wharf and land near the Captain Cook Monument. You can paddle a rental kayak, canoe, or stand-up paddleboard from Napoopoo on your own, if the company has acquired a special permit; otherwise, it's about a 10-mile round-trip paddle from Keauhou. Carrying your snorkel gear down and up the steep 5-mile trail from the highway is possible but not recommended. Watch out for spiny urchins as well as fragile coral when entering the water from lava rocks along the shore.

Much more easily accessible snorkeling, with a terrific display of aquatic diversity, can be found at **Honaunau Bay,** nicknamed "Two Step" for the easy entry off flat lava rocks into the crystalline waters just before **Puuhonua O Honaunau National Historical Park** (p. 36). Snorkeling is not permitted in the park itself, but you can pay the entrance fee to park your car there and walk to the bay, if the 25 or so spaces on the bayfront road—look for the coastal access sign off Highway 160—are taken.

North of the Kohala resort, the well-protected waters of Ohaiula Beach at **Spencer Park** (p. 90) are a great site for families to snorkel, with convenient facilities (restrooms, showers, picnic tables), not to mention a lifeguard on weekends and holidays, and a reputation for attracting green sea turtles. (Remember to look but don't touch or approach turtles.) It can get windy, so mornings are again your best bet here.

## Sport Fishing: The Hunt for Granders ★★

Big-game fish, including gigantic blue marlin and other Pacific billfish, tuna, sailfish, swordfish, ono (aka wahoo), and giant trevallies (*ulua*), roam the waters of the Kona Coast, known as the marlin capital of the world. When anglers catch marlin weighing 1,000 pounds or more, they call them "granders"; there's even a "wall of fame" in Kailua-Kona's Waterfront Row shopping mall honoring those who've nailed more than 20 tons of fighting fish. Nearby photos show celebrities such as Sylvester Stallone posing with their slightly less impressive catches. The celebrities of the fishing world descend on Kailua-Kona in August for the 5-day **Hawaiian International Billfish Tournament** (www.hibtfishing.com), founded in 1959. Note that it's not all carnage out there: Teams that tag and release marlin under 300 pounds get bonus points.

Nearly 100 charter boats with professional captains and crew offer fishing charters out of **Keauhou, Kawaihae, Honokohau,** and **Kailua Bay** harbors. If

Wahoo caught in Big Island waters.

you're not an expert angler, the best way to arrange a charter is through a booking agency like the **Charter Desk at Honokohau Marina** (www.charterdesk.com; © **888/566-2487** or 808/326-1800), which can sort through the more than 60 different types of vessels and fishing specialties to match you with the right boat. Prices range from $750 to $3,500 or so for a full-day exclusive charter (you and up to five friends have an entire boat to yourselves) or $450 to $600 for a half-day. One or two people may be able to book a "share" on boats that hold four to eight anglers, who take turns fishing—generally for smaller catch, to increase everyone's chances of hooking something. Shares start at $95 to $150 per person for half-day trips, $250 for a full day.

*Note:* Most big-game charter boats carry six passengers max, and the boats supply all equipment, bait, tackle, and lures. No license is required. Many captains now tag and release marlins; other fish caught belong to the boat, not to you—that's island style. If you want to eat your catch or have your trophy mounted, arrange it with the captain before you go.

## Stand-up Paddleboarding (SUP)

Anywhere the water is calm is a fine place to learn stand-up paddleboarding (SUP), which takes much less finesse than traditional surfing but offers a fun alternative to kayaking for exploring the coast. Numerous hotel concessions offer rentals and lessons, as do traditional surf shops.

**Kona Boys** ★★ (www.konaboys.com; © **808/328-1234**) has the best locale in Kailua-Kona to try your hand at SUP: **Kamakahonu Cove,** next to Kailua Pier and King Kamehameha's royal (and sacred) compound. The spring water in the well-protected cove is a little too cool and murky for snorkeling, but just right for getting your bearings. The 90-minute lessons costs $99 in a group setting, $149 private; once you've got the hang of it, you can also join one of Kona Boys' 90-minute tours ($99 group/$149 private) or just pick up a rental ($29 hourly, $74 daily). It also offers lessons and rentals at its Kealakekua location, 79-7539 Mamalahoa Hwy. (Hwy. 11), 1¼ miles south of its intersection with Highway 180. Both sites are open daily until 5pm; the Kamakahonu beach shack opens at 8am, Kealakekua at 7:30am.

Another good option in North Kona is at Keauhou Bay, where **Ocean Safaris** (www.oceansafariskayaks. com; © **808/326-4699**) offers 2-hour lessons and tours, each $79; rentals are $25 for 2 hours, but paddlers must stay within Keauhou Bay.

On the Kohala Coast, the smooth crescents of **Anaehoomalu Bay** and **Puako Bay** are also well-suited to exploring via SUP. **Ocean Sports** (www. hawaiioceansports.com) rents boards for $30 a half-hour ($50 hourly) from its kiosk on the sand in front of the Waikoloa Beach Marriott; see website for details on its other Kohala locations. **Hulakai** rents all kinds of beach gear from its outlet in the Shops at Mauna Lani (http://hulakai.com; © **808/896-3141**). Open 10am–4pm daily, it offers 1-hour SUP lessons ($68) and 90-minute "adventures" ($98), plus rentals for $75 a day, $295 a week.

## Surfing

Most surfing off the Big Island is for the experienced only, thanks to rocks, coral reef, and rip currents at many of the reliable breaks. As a general rule, the beaches on the north and west shores of the island get northern swells in winter, while those on the south and east shores get southern swells in summer. You'll also need to radiate courtesy and expertise in the lineup with local surfers, understandably territorial about their challenging breaks.

In Kailua-Kona, experienced surfers should check out the two breaks in **Holualoa Bay,** off Alii Drive between downtown Kailua-Kona and Keauhou: **Banyans** near the northern point and **Lyman's** near the southern point, once home to a surfers' temple. If you don't have the chops, don't go in the water; just enjoy the show. Another surfing shrine, its black-lava rock walls still visible today, stands near **Kahaluu Beach ★★** (p. 82), where the waves are manageable most of the year and there's also a lifeguard. Less-experienced surfers can also try **Pine Trees** north of town, at **Kohanaiki Beach ★★** (p. 86), where it's best to avoid the busy weekends.

Surf breaks on the east side of the island are also generally best left to skilled surfers. They include **Honolii Point,** north of Hilo; **Richardson's Point** at **Leleiwi Beach Park** (p. 91); **Hilo Bay Front Park;** and **Pohoiki Bay,** home to **Isaac Hale Beach Park,** near Pahoa.

**PRIVATE & GROUP LESSONS** You can have a grand time taking a surf lesson, especially with instructors who know where the breaks are best for beginners and who genuinely enjoy being out in the waves with you. The Native Hawaiian–owned **Hawaii Lifeguard Surf Instructors** (www.surflessonshawaii.com; ✆ **808/ 324-0442**), which gives lessons at Kahaluu Beach, has an especially good touch with kids and teens. For $110, adults and children as young as 3 can take a 90-minute private lesson (little ones under 55 pounds ride on the same board as their lifeguard/teacher). Lessons for ages 11 and up cost $75 per person for small groups (no more than three students per instructor) and $185 for a group of just two. On days when the waves are tame, HLSI offers the same lessons with stand-up paddleboards. Classes are three times a day, Monday through Saturday.

**BOARD RENTALS** You're never going to rent a board as good as your own, but you'll enjoy getting to know the local vibe at the appropriately named **Pacific Vibrations,** 75-5702 Likana Lane, tucked off Alii Drive just north of Mokuaikaua Church (© **808/329-4140**), founded in 1978 by the McMichaels, a Native Hawaiian family with deep ties to surfing and the Ironman triathlon. It's a trip just to visit the densely stocked surf shop in downtown Kailua-Kona. Surfboards rent for $10 to $20 a day, and body boards for just $5. Stand-up paddleboards go for $15 an hour. The staff is happy to help steer you to waves to match your skills.

Founded in Puako in 1997, surfboard shaper **Hulakai** (http://hulakai.com) also rents surfboards for $40 a day ($150 a week) from two locations: the Shops at Mauna Lani (© **808/896-3141**) on the Mauna Lani Resort and in downtown Hilo (© **808/315-7497**), at 1717 Kamehameha Ave. (at Banyan Drive), near the intersection of highways 11 and 19. You can also sign up for 2-hour private and semiprivate surfing lessons ($150 and $125 per person, respectively).

# OTHER OUTDOOR ACTIVITIES
## Biking

*Note:* In addition to the rental fees mentioned below, expect to put down a deposit on a credit card, or leave your credit card number on file.

## KONA & KOHALA COASTS

When you're planning to spend a fair amount of time in Kailua-Kona, where parking can be at a premium, consider renting a bicycle for easy riding and sightseeing along flat, often oceanview Alii Drive. A cruiser can also be handy if you're staying at a Kohala Coast resort and want an easy way to shuttle around shops, beaches, and condos without having to jump in the car. Experienced cyclists may also want to trace part of the Ironman course (112 miles round-trip) along the wide-shouldered "Queen K" and Akoni Pule highways from Kailua-Kona to Hawi, or join in one of the weekly group rides of the **Hawaii Cycling Club** (www.hawaiicyclingclub.com).

For simple cruisers, head to **Hawaiian Pedals,** Kona Inn Shopping Village, 75-5744 Alii Dr., Kailua-Kona (www.hawaiianpedals.com; ✆ **808/329-2294**), which has 7-speed hybrid bikes for $25 a day and $91 a week; a 24-speed city bike is $30 a day, $112 a week. Pros and amateurs alike flock to its sister store, **Bike Works,** Hale Hana Centre, 74-5583 Luhia St., Kailua-Kona (www.bikeworkskona.com; ✆ **808/326-2453**) for an even bigger selection of bikes, including mountain bikes ($17 a day), triathlon bikes ($28), and even electric bikes ($6), all with discounts for longer bookings. Bike Works also has a shop in **Queens' MarketPlace,** Waikoloa Beach Resort (www.bikeworkshawaii.com; ✆ **808/886-5000**), with road and city bike rentals ($25–$75 daily). Both locations offer weekly group rides open to all.

**Note:** Reserve well in advance for rentals in the first 2 weeks of October, during the leadup to the Ironman World Championship.

## HAWAII VOLCANOES NATIONAL PARK

The national park has miles of paved roads and trails open to cyclists, from easy flat rides to challenging ascents, but you'll need to watch out for cars and buses on the often winding, narrow roads, and make sure you carry plenty of water and sunscreen. Download a cycling guide on the park's website (www.nps.gov/havo/planyourvisit/bike.htm) or pick one up at the Kilauea Visitor Center. The closest bike-rental shops are in Hilo, including **Mid-Pacific Wheels,** 1133 Manono St. (www.midpacificwheelsllc.com; *©* **808/935-6211**), which has mountain and road bikes for $25 to $45 a day, including a helmet; bike racks are $10 a day. Opened in 2014, **Hawaii Rentals & Adventures** (www.hilobikerentals.com; *©* **808/364-0840**), at the corner of Kamehameha Avenue and Kalakaua Street, will let you take a spin for an hour for just $5; 24-hour rentals are $25, including helmet and lock.

Or leave the planning to **Volcano Bike Tours** (www.bikevolcano.com; *©* **888/934-9199** or 808/934-9199), which offers fully supported half- and full-day guided tours ($110–$134) in the national park that include some off-road riding and, on the longer tour, a van trip down to the end of Chain of Craters Road.

## Golf

All greens fees below are for visitors; those with Hawaii state ID (*kama'āina*) may receive substantial discounts. Rates include carts unless noted.

### THE KONA COAST

The fabulous **Hualalai Golf Course ★★★** at the Four Seasons Resort Hualalai (p. 145) is open only to resort guests—but for committed golfers, this Jack Nicklaus–designed championship course is reason enough to book a room and pay the sky-high greens fee of $275 ($150 for kids 13–18, free for children 12 and under with paying guest).

**Big Island Country Club ★★** Designed by Perry Dye, this par-72, 18-hole course offers sweeping views of towering Mauna Kea and the bright blue coastline from its perch 2,000 feet above sea level. Although it's not on the ocean, water features wind around nine of the holes, including the spectacular par-3 No. 17. Waterfalls, tall palms, and other lush greenery add to the tropical feel; look for native birds such as the nene (Hawaiian goose), hawks, stilts, and black-crowned night herons. The wide fairways and gently rolling terrain make it appropriate for players of every level. Facilities include club rentals, driving range, pro shop, lounge, and snack bar.

71-1420 Mamalahoa Hwy. (Hwy. 190), Kailua-Kona. www.big islandcountryclub.com. © **808/325-5044.** Greens fees $95 before noon; $79 after noon. 9 holes after 3pm, $66.

**Kona Country Club ★★** Although the 18-hole Mountain Course has permanently closed, the Keauhou club's newly renovated Ocean Course was expected to reopen in summer of 2015, after several delays. The extensive renovations to William Bell's original links are said to include expanded greens, new cart paths and bunkers, and a new irrigation system. The always-enticing views of pounding waves on lava rock—also visible from the well-stocked pro shop—will no doubt remain the biggest draw. Other facilities include club rentals, driving range, pro shop, locker rooms, and putting and chipping greens.

78–7000 Alii Dr., Kailua-Kona. www.konagolf.com. © **808/322-3431.** Greens fees $165 ($145 Keauhou Resort guests) before noon; $112 after noon. 9 holes after 3pm $60.

**Makalei Golf Club** ★   This par-72, 18-hole upcountry course—some 1,800 to 2,850 feet in elevation—goes up and down through native forests, cinder cones, and lava tubes over its championship length of 7,091 yards. The signature hole is the par-3 No. 15, offering a distant view of Maui and the best chance for a hole-in-one. A local favorite, Makalei is visited by wild peacocks, pheasants, and turkeys. Facilities include a golf shop, driving range, putting greens, club rentals (drop-off and pickup available), and the **Peacock Grille** restaurant, offering a full bar and a menu of burgers, salads, and snacks such as Spam musubi.

72-3890 Hawaii Belt Rd. (Mamalahoa Hwy./Hwy. 190), Kailua-Kona. www.makalei.com. ✆ **808/325-6625.** Greens fees $99 before noon; $79 after noon. From the intersection of Palani Rd. and Hwy. 11 in Kailua-Kona, take Palani Rd. (which becomes Hwy. 190) east 7¼ miles, and look for green gates and small white sign on right.

## THE KOHALA COAST

**Hapuna Golf Course** ★★★   Since its opening in 1992, this 18-hole championship course has been named the most environmentally sensitive course by "Golf" magazine, as well as "Course of the Future" by the U.S. Golf Association. Designed by Arnold Palmer and Ed Seay, the links-style course extends nearly 6,900 yards from the shoreline to 700 feet above sea level, with views of the pastoral Kohala Mountains and the Kohala coastline; look for Maui across the channel from the signature 12th hole. The elevation changes on the course keep it challenging (and windy the higher you go). There are a few elevated tee boxes and only 40 bunkers. Facilities include putting and chipping greens, driving range, practice bunker, lockers, showers, a pro shop, rental clubs, fitness center, and spa.

At the Hapuna Beach Prince Hotel, Mauna Kea Resort, off Hwy. 19 (near mile marker 69). www.princeresortshawaii.com. © **808/ 880-3000.** Greens fees $150 ($125 hotel guests) before 1pm; $80 after 1pm. Second round same day, $45. Ages under 18 $50.

**Mauna Kea Golf Course ★★★**  This breathtakingly beautiful, par-72, 7,114-yard championship course, designed by Robert Trent Jones, Jr., and recently updated by son Rees Jones, is consistently rated one of the top golf courses in the United States. The signature 3rd hole is 175 yards long; the Pacific Ocean and shoreline cliffs stand between the tee and the green, giving every golfer, from beginner to pro, a real challenge. Another par-3 that confounds duffers is the 11th hole, which drops 100 feet from tee to green and plays down to the ocean, into the steady trade winds. When the trades are

**Manua Kea Golf Course.**

blowing, 181 yards might as well be 1,000 yards. Book ahead; the course is very popular, especially for early weekend tee times. Facilities include a pro shop and clubhouse with restaurant, named **Number 3** for the hole Jones, Sr., once called "the most beautiful in the world."

At the Mauna Kea Beach Hotel, Mauna Kea Resort, off Hwy. 19 (near mile marker 68). www.princeresortshawaii.com. © **808/ 882-5400.** Greens fees $255 ($230 hotel guests) before 11am; $185 11am–1:30pm; $165 after 1:30pm. Back 9 holes or second round same day, $125. Ages under 18 $95.

**Mauna Lani Francis H. I'i Brown Championship Courses ★★★** Carefully wrapped around ancient trails, fish ponds, and petroglyphs, the two 18-hole courses here have won "Golf" magazine's Gold Medal Award every year since the honor's inception in 1988. The **South Course,** a 7,029-yard, par-72, has two unforgettable ocean holes: the over-the-water 15th hole and the downhill, 221-yard, par-3 7th, which is bordered by the sea, a salt-and-pepper sand dune, and lush kiawe trees. The **North Course** may not have the drama of the oceanfront holes, but because it was built on older lava flows, the more extensive indigenous vegetation gives the course a Scottish feel. The hole that's cursed the most is the 140-yard, par-3 17th: It's beautiful but plays right into the surrounding lava field. Facilities include two driving ranges, a golf shop (with teaching pros), a restaurant, and putting greens. Mauna Lani also has the island's only *keiki* (children's) course, a 9-hole walking course for juniors, beginners, and families (golfers under 14 must be with an adult).

At the Mauna Lani Resort, Mauna Lani Dr., off Hwy. 19 (20 miles north of Kona Airport). www.maunalani.com. © **808/885-6655.** Greens fees vary by time and season: $225 ($160–$170 for hotel guests) before 10am; $195 ($145–$155 hotel guests) 10am–noon; $145 ($120–$125 hotel guests) after noon. Keiki course: $25 children, including clubs; $35 adults ($15 clubs).

## Waikoloa Beach Resort Courses ★★ Two
18-hole courses beckon here. The pristine 18-hole, par-70 Beach Course certainly reflects the motto of designer Robert Trent Jones, Jr.: "Hard par, easy bogey." Most golfers remember the par-5, 505-yard 12th hole, a sharp dogleg left with bunkers in the corner and an elevated tee surrounded by lava. The Kings' Course, designed by Tom Weiskopf and Jay Morrish, is about 500 yards longer. Its links-style tract has a double green at the 3rd and 6th holes, and carefully placed bunkers see a lot of play, courtesy of the ever-present trade winds. Facilities include a golf shop, 15-acre practice range (with complimentary clubs and unlimited balls for just $15), and the affordable, Scottish-themed **Kings' Grille** restaurant; call for a free shuttle within the resort.

At the Waikoloa Beach Resort, 600 Waikoloa Beach Dr., Waikoloa. www.waikoloabeachgolf.com. ℂ **808/886-7888.** Greens fees: $145–$180 ($145 for resort guests) before 11:30am; $125 ($120 resort guests) 11:30am–1pm; $115 ($110 resort guests) 1–2pm; $95 after 2pm. 9 holes after 8:30am, $69. Children 6–17, $60. Second round same day, $55.

## Waikoloa Village Golf Course ★ This semipri-
vate 18-hole course, with a par-72 for each of the three sets of tees, is hidden in the town of Waikoloa, next to the Paniolo Greens timeshare resort. Overshadowed by the glamorous resort courses of the Kohala Coast, it's nevertheless a beautiful course with terrific views and some great golfing. The wind can play havoc with your game here (like most Hawaii golf courses). Robert Trent Jones, Jr., in designing this challenging

course, inserted his trademark sand traps, slick greens, and great fairways. The par-5, 490-yard 18th hole is a thriller: It doglegs to the left, and the last 75 yards up to the green are water, water, water. Enjoy the fabulous views of Mauna Kea and Mauna Loa, and—on a very clear day—Maui's Haleakala in the distance.

In Waikoloa Village, 68-1793 Melia St., Waikoloa. www.waikoloa villagegolf.com. © **808/883-9621.** Greens fees $98 ($72 Paniolo Greens guests) before 2pm; $60 after 2pm. Children 7–17 $45 before 2pm; $40 after 2pm. From the airport, turn left on Hwy. 19, head 18 miles to stoplight at Waikoloa Rd. Turn right, drive uphill 6½ miles to left on Paniolo Ave. Take 1st right onto Lua Kula St. and follow ½-mile to Melia St.

## HILO

**Hilo Municipal Golf Course** ★ This 146-acre course is great for the casual golfer: It's flat, scenic, and often fun. Just don't go after a heavy rain (especially in winter); the fairways can get really soggy and play can slow way down. The rain does keep the course green and beautiful, though. Wonderful trees (monkeypods, coconuts, eucalyptus, banyans) dot the grounds, and the views—of Mauna Kea on one side and Hilo Bay on the other—are breathtaking. There are four sets of tees, with a par-71 from all; the back tees give you 6,325 yards of play. It's the only municipal course on the island, and in the state's second largest city, so getting a tee time can be a challenge; weekdays are the best bet. Facilities include driving range, pro shop, club rentals, restaurant, and snack bar.

340 Haihai St. (btw. Kinoole and Iwalani sts.), Hilo. www.hawaii county.gov/pr-golf. © **808/959-7711.** Greens fees $34 Mon–Fri, $45 Sat–Sun and holidays; carts $16.

**Naniloa Country Club** ★ At first glance, this semi-private 9-hole course just off Hilo Bay looks pretty flat and short, but once you get beyond the 1st hole—a wide, straightforward 330-yard par-4—things get challenging. The tree-lined fairways require straight drives, and the huge lake on the 2nd and 5th holes is sure to haunt you. This course is very popular with locals and visitors alike. Facilities include driving range, putting green, pro shop, and club rentals.

120 Banyan Dr. (at the intersection of hwys. 11 and 19), Hilo. © **808/935-3000.** Greens fees: 9 holes, $10 adults ($9 seniors 62 and over, $5 children under 17); 18 holes, $15 adults ($12 seniors 62 and over, $9 children under 17). Cart $10 ($15 for 18 holes).

## Hiking

Trails on the Big Island wind through fields of coastal lava rock, deserts, rainforests, and mountain tundra, sometimes covered with snow. It's important to wear sturdy shoes, sunscreen, and a hat, and take plenty of water; for longer hikes, particularly in remote areas, it may also be essential to bring food, a flashlight, and a trail map—not one that requires a cellphone signal to access (coverage may be nonexistent). Hunting may be permitted in rural, upcountry, or remote areas, so stay on the trails and wear bright clothing.

The island has 16 trails in the state's **Na Ala Hele Hawaii Trail & Access System** (www.hawaiitrails.org; © **808/974-4382**), highlights of which are included below; see the website for more information. For an even greater number of trails on a variety of public lands, see the detailed descriptions on **www.bigislandhikes.com**.

### KONA & KOHALA COASTS

The **Ala Kahakai National Historic Trail** (www.nps.gov/alka; © **808/326-6012,** ext. 101) is the designation for an ancient, 175-mile series of paths through coastal lava rock, from Upolu Point in North Kohala along the island's west coast to Ka Lae (South Point) and east to Puna's Wahaula Heiau, an extensive temple complex. Some were created as long-distance trails, others for fishing and gathering, while a few were reserved for royal or chiefly use. There's unofficial access through the four national park sites—Puukohola Heiau, Kaloko-Honokoau, Puuhonua O Honaunau, and Hawaii Volcanoes (see "Attractions & Points of Interest" on p. 26)—but it's easy, free, and fun to walk a portion of the 15.4-mile stretch between Kawaihae and Anaehoomalu Bay, part of the state's **Na Ala Hele** trails system (www.hawaiitrails.org; ✆ **808/974-4382**). Signs mark only the 8-mile portion of Ala Kahakai between the northern terminus of Ohaiula Beach at **Spencer Park** (p. 20) through Puako to **Holoholokai Beach Park,** near the petroglyph field on the Mauna Lani Resort, but it's fairly easy to follow farther south by hugging the shoreline, past resort hotels and multimillion-dollar homes, anchialine ponds, and jagged lava formations.

For those not satisfied with the view from the **Pololu Valley Lookout** (p. 42), the steep, 1-mile **Pololu Valley Trail** will lead you just behind the black-sand beach (beware of high surf and riptides). In addition to a 420-foot elevation change, the trail's challenges can include slippery mud and tricky footing over ancient cobblestones. As with all windward (that is, rainy) areas, be prepared for pesky mosquitos and/or cool mist.

If you're willing to venture on Saddle Road (Hwy. 200), which some rental-car companies still forbid, the **Puu Huluhulu Trail** is an easy, .6-mile hike that gradually loops around both crests of this forested cinder cone, with panoramic views of Mauna Kea and Mauna Loa between the trees. There's a parking lot in front of the hunter check-in station at the junction of the Mauna Loa observatory access road and Saddle Road.

## THE HAMAKUA COAST

The 25% grade on the 1-mile "hike" down the road to **Waipio Valley** (p. 53) is a killer on the knees, and no picnic coming back up, but that's just the start of the epic, 18-mile round-trip adventure involving the **Muliwai Trail,** a very strenuous hike to primeval, waterfall-laced **Waimanu Valley.** This trail is the island's closest rival to Kauai's **Kalalau Trail**, and so is only worth attempting by very physically fit and well-prepared hikers. Once in Waipio Valley, you must follow the beach to Wailoa Stream, ford it, and cross the dunes to the west side of the valley. There the zig-zag Muliwai Trail officially begins, carving its way some 1,300 feet up the cliff; the reward at the third switchback is a wonderful view of Hiilawe Falls. Ahead lie 5 miles of 12 smaller, tree-covered gulches to cross before your first view of pristine Waimanu Valley, which has nine campsites (see "Camping" on p. 166) and two outhouses, but no drinking water. The trail is eroded in places and slippery when wet—which is often, due to the 100-plus inches of rain, which can also flood streams. This explains why the vast majority of those who see Waimanu Valley do so via helicopter (p. 76).

## HAWAII VOLCANOES NATIONAL PARK

This magnificent national treasure and Hawaiian cultural icon (p. 68) has more than 150 miles of trails, including many day hikes, most of which are well-maintained and well-marked; a few are paved or have boardwalks, permitting strollers and wheelchairs. **Warning:** If you have heart or respiratory problems or if you're pregnant, don't attempt any hike in the park; the fumes will bother you. Also: Stacked rocks known as *ahu* mark trails crossing lava; please do not disturb or create your own.

Plan ahead by downloading maps and brochures on the park website (www.nps.gov/havo), which also lists areas closed due to current eruptions. Always check conditions with the rangers at the Kilauea Visitor Center, where you can pick up detailed trail guides. **Note:** All overnight backcountry hiking and camping requires a free permit, available only the day of or the day before your hike, from the park's **Backcountry Office (© 808/985-6178)**.

In addition to sights described on the **Crater Rim Drive** tour (p. 69) and **Chain of Craters Road** tour (p. 72), here are some of the more accessible highlights for hikers, all demonstrating the power of Pele:

**KILAUEA IKI TRAIL**  The 4-mile loop trail begins 2 miles from the visitor center on Crater Rim Road, descends through a forest of ferns into still-fuming Kilauea Iki Crater, and then crosses the crater floor past the vent where a 1959 lava blast shot a fountain of fire 1,900 feet into the air for 36 days. Allow 2 hours for this fair-to-moderate hike, and look for white-tailed tropicbirds and Hawaiian hawks above you.

**DEVASTATION TRAIL ★★**  Up on the rim of Kilauea Iki Crater, you can see what an erupting volcano did to a once-flourishing ohia forest. The scorched earth with its ghostly tree skeletons stands in sharp contrast to the rest of the lush forest. Everyone can take this 1-mile round-trip hike on a paved path across the eerie bed of black cinders. The trailhead is on Crater Rim Road at Puu Puai Overlook.

**KIPUKA PUAULU (BIRD PARK) TRAIL**   This easy 1.2-mile round-trip hike lets you see native Hawaiian flora and fauna in a little oasis of living nature in a field of lava, known as a *kipuka*. For some reason, the once red-hot lava skirted this mini-forest and let it survive. Go early in the morning or in the evening (or, even better, just after a rain) to see native birds like the *'apapane* (a small, bright-red bird with black wings and tail) and the *'i'iwi* (larger and orange-vermilion colored, with a curved salmon-hued bill). Native trees along the trail include giant ohia, koa, soapberry, kolea, and mamane.

**PUU HULUHULU**   This moderate 3-mile round-trip to the summit of a cinder cone (which shares its name with the one on Saddle Rd., described above) crosses lava flows from 1973 and 1974, lava tree molds, and

Devastation Trail hiking path.

# GUIDED hikes

A guided day or night hike is a safe but stimulating way for city slickers to explore natural Hawaii. Book one of these excursions before you arrive; trips fill up quickly.

A longtime resident of Hawaii, Dr. Hugh Montgomery of **Hawaiian Walkways** ★ (www.hawaiianwalkways. com; ✆ **800/457-7759** or 808/775-0372), one-time winner of "Tour Operator of the Year" by the Hawaii Ecotourism Association of Hawaii, offers a variety of options, from excursions that skirt the rim of immense valleys to hikes through the volcano clouds. Hikes range from $129 to $190 for adults, and $99 to $130 for kids. Guides also lead hikes with tent camping in **Waipio Valley** and, via the **Muliwai Trail** (p. 172), Waimanu Valley, for $350–$525 for 1 night ($800 for 2), all gear and meals provided. Custom hikes are also available.

Naturalist and educator Rob Pacheco of **Hawaii Forest & Trail** ★★★ (www.hawaii-forest.com;

*kipuka.* At the top is a panoramic vista of Mauna Loa, Mauna Kea, the coastline, and the often steaming vent of Puu Oo. The trailhead is 8 miles from the visitor center, in the Mauna Ulu parking area on Chain of Craters Road. (Sulfur fumes can be stronger here than on other trails.)

For avid trekkers, several long, steep, unshaded hikes lead to the beaches and rocky bays on the park's remote shoreline; they're all considered overnight backcountry hikes and, thus, require a permit. Only hiking diehards should consider attempting the **Mauna Loa Trail,** perhaps the most challenging hike in all of Hawaii. Many hikers have had to be rescued

© 800/464-1993 or 808/331-8505) offers fully outfitted day trips to some of the island's most remote, pristine areas, including lands to which his company has exclusive access. His well-trained guides narrate the entire trip, offering extensive ecological, geological, and cultural commentary (and more than a little humor). Tours are limited to 12 to 14 people and are highly personalized to meet the group's interests and abilities. Options include my personal favorite, the 8-hour **Kohala Waterfalls Adventure ★★★** ($169 for adults, $139 for children 12 and under), which you can pair with ziplining (p. 135); exceptionally well-run, all-day **birding tours,** for ages 8 and older ($179–$189); all-day trips to **Hawaii Volcanoes National Park ★★★**, some 300 miles round-trip ($179–$189 for adults, $159 for children) and some shorter (6–7 hr.); and stargazing atop **Mauna Kea ★★★** ($199; for ages 16 and up only).

over the years due to high-altitude sickness or exposure, after becoming lost in snowy or foggy conditions. From the trailhead at the end of scenic but narrow Mauna Loa Road, about an hour's drive from the visitor center, it's a 7.5-mile trek to the Puu Ulaula ("Red Hill") cabin at 10,035 feet, and then 12 more miles up to the primitive Mauna Loa summit cabin at 13,250 feet, where the climate is subarctic and overnight temperatures are below freezing year-round. In addition to backcountry permits (see above), this 4-day round-trip requires special gear, great physical condition, and careful planning.

# Horseback Riding

Although vast Parker Ranch, the historic center of Hawaiian ranching, no longer offers horseback tours, several other ranches in upcountry Waimea provide opportunities for riding with sweeping views of land and sea. Picturesque Waipio Valley is also another focus of equestrian excursions. ***Note:*** Most stables require riders to be at least 8 years old and weigh no more than 230 pounds; confirm before booking.

The 11,000-acre Ponoholo Ranch, whose herd of cattle (varying between 6,000 and 8,000) is second only to Parker Ranch's, is the scenic home base for **Paniolo Adventures** (www.panioloadventures.com; ✆ **808/889-5354**). Most of its five rides are open-range style and include brief stretches of trotting and cantering, although the gorgeous scenery outweighs the equine excitement—all but the 4-hour Wrangler Ride ($175) are suitable for beginners. The tamest option is the 1-hour City Slicker ride ($69), but the 1½-hour Sunset Ride ($89) appears to be the most popular. Boots, light jackets, Australian dusters, chaps, helmets, hats, drinks, and even sunscreen are provided. Look for Paniolo Adventures' red barn on

**Horseback riders in the Waipio Valley.**

Kohala Mountain Road (Hwy. 250), just north of mile marker 13.

**Naalapa Stables** (www.naalapastables.com; © 808/889-0022) operates rides at Kahua Ranch, which also has an entrance on Kohala Mountain Road, north of mile marker 11. Riding open-range style, you'll pass ancient Hawaiian ruins, through lush pastures with grazing sheep and cows, and along mountaintops with panoramic coastal views. The horses and various riding areas are suited to everyone from first-timers to experienced equestrians. There are several trips a day: a 2½-hour tour at 9am and 1pm for $94 and a 1½-hour tour at 10am and 1:30pm for $73; check-in is a half-hour earlier.

Naalapa has another stable in Waipio Valley (© 808/775-0419), which offers the more rugged **Waipio Valley Horseback Adventure ★★**, a 2½-hour ride that starts with a 4WD van ride down to this little-inhabited but widely revered valley (p. 53). The horses are sure-footed in the rocky streams and muddy trails, while the guides, who are well-versed in Hawaiian history, provide running commentary. The cost is $94 for adults, with tours at 9:30am and 12:30pm Monday to Saturday. Don't forget your camera or bug spray; check in a half-hour earlier at **Waipio Valley Artworks,** 48-5415 Kukuihaele Road, off Highway 240, about 8 miles northwest of Honokaa.

Waipio Valley Artworks (see above) is also the check-in point for **Waipio Ridge Stables** (www.waipioridgestables.com; © 877/757-1414 or 808/775-1007), which leads riders on a 2½-hour Valley Rim Ride ($85), including views of the beach below and Hiilawe waterfall at the rear of the deep valley. The 5-hour Hidden Waterfalls Ride ($165) includes the sights along the rim ride, and then follows the stream that feeds Hiilawe through the rainforest to a picnic and swim in a bracingly cool waterfall pool, but it's rather long if you're not into riding. *Note:* Fog sometimes obscures views of Waipio Valley from the rim.

## Tennis

While some resorts only allow guests to use their tennis facilities, the Kohala Coast has several delightful exceptions. The 11-court **Seaside Tennis Club** (© **808/882-5420**) at the Mauna Kea Beach Hotel (p. 154) is frequently ranked among the world's finest, for good reason: Three of the courts ($25 per person) are right on the ocean, and all enjoy beautiful landscaping. The club also boasts luxurious locker rooms, a pro shop with racket and ball machine rentals, daily clinics, round robins, and lessons for ages 4 and up. Those not staying at the hotel just need to make a reservation for a court (open 8am–5pm daily) or lesson.

Just as highly ranked, the **Hawaii Tennis Center** © **808/887-7532**) at the Fairmont Orchid Hawaii (p. 150) offers 10 courts (including one stadium court), with evening play available until 9pm by reservation. It has a pro shop, rents rackets and ball machines, and offers lessons. Fees are $30 per court; check in at pro shop first. At Hilton Waikoloa Village (p. 153), **Palealea Ocean Sports Tennis** (www.hawaiioceansports.com; © **808/886-6666,** ext. 108) provides five cushioned courts and one stadium court, plus lessons, clinics, and racket and ball machine rentals. Court fees are $20 per hour ($30 per day if available).

You can also play for free at any Hawaii County tennis court; the easiest way to find one nearest you is to visit **www.tennisinhawaii.com**. For those in Kailua-Kona, the four courts at **Old Kona Airport Park** (p. 87) offer the best experience.

## Ziplining

Ziplining gives Big Island visitors an exhilarating way to view dramatic gulches, thick forests, gushing waterfalls, and other inspiring scenery—without significantly altering the landscape. Typically, the pulley-and-harness systems have redundant safety mechanisms, with lines and gear inspected daily and multiple checks of your equipment during the tour; your biggest worry may be losing your cellphone or anything not in a zipped pocket. Most outfitters also rent GoPro video cameras that attach to your helmets, so you can relive your whizzing rides at home.

*Note:* For safety reasons, tours have minimum ages (listed below) and/or minimum and maximum weights; read the fine print carefully before booking. Outfitters also go out several times a day, rain or shine, which on the Hilo side is likely to include both on any given day; dress accordingly. Most excursions last 2 to 3 hours, but the exact length of your tour varies based on number of riders, so don't schedule your day too tightly.

**NORTH KOHALA** The Australian eucalyptus and native kukui trees on **Kohala Zipline's Canopy Tour** ★★ (www.kohalazipline.com; © **800/464-1993** or 808/331-3620) might not provide the most colorful panoramas, but this nine-line adventure ($169 adults, $139 kids 8–12) emphasizes environmental awareness and cultural history in a compelling way—and the extra-quiet ziplines and multiple suspension bridges are a hoot, too. You'll fly from platform to platform in a sylvan setting that includes ancient taro terraces believed to have been farmed by Kamehameha before he became king. Tours ($169) depart from the zip station on Highway 270 between Hawi and Kapaau up to 16 times daily; shuttle service is also available from South Kohala and North Kona resorts for the 8:30am and 1pm tours ($209 adults, $179 children 8 to 12, lunch included). For a very special splurge, take the outfitter's 8-hour **Kohala Zip & Dip** ★★★ which combines the Canopy Tour with Hawaii Forest & Trail's fascinating Kohala Waterfalls Adventure (p. 131), including a waterfall swim and picnic overlooking beautiful Pololu Valley. The Zip & Dip tours ($249, for ages 8 and older) depart from Queens' MarketPlace in Waikoloa Beach Resort and Hawaii Forest & Trail headquarters on Highway 19 in Kailua-Kona, 74-5035 Queen Kaahumanu Hwy. (north of Kealakehe Parkway).

**THE HAMAKUA COAST**   I don't like the misleading name, but I can't begrudge the thrills involved on the **Akaka Falls Skyline Adventure** ★★ (www.zipline.com/bigisland; ⓒ **888/864-6947**), which actually zips past the nearly 250-foot-tall **Kolekole Falls,** downstream from the taller and more famous **Akaka Falls** (p. 47) in Honomu, about 12 miles north of Hilo. The seven-line course builds in length and speed, while the well-informed guides share insights into local flora and fauna—including banana, taro, and wild pigs—and the area's history as a sugar plantation. The 2½- to 3-hour tour costs $170 (ages 10 and older), with 10% off for online bookings.

The **Umauma Falls Zipline Tour** ★★★ (www.ziplinehawaii.com; 𝄐 **808/930-9477**) lives up to its name, where you see the captivating, three-tiered falls (p. 51) along with 13 other smaller cascades as you zip along its two-mile, nine-line course ($189) in Hakalau, about 16 miles north of Hilo. The Zip & Dip option ($239) includes an hour of kayaking and swimming under a waterfall, next to the Hilo side's only known petroglyph; for a four-line option, contact the company directly. There's no age limit, but children under 18 must be accompanied by a parent or guardian.

# WHERE TO STAY

by Jeanne Cooper

**4**

For additional **bed-and-breakfasts,** visit the website of **Hawaii Island B&B Association** (www.stayhawaii.com), which only allows licensed, inspected properties to become members; 34 are currently listed. **Vacation rentals,** which Hawaii County does not regulate the way it does B&Bs and hotels, are currently less of a hot-button issue here than on other islands. You'll find numerous listings of condos and houses on sites such as VRBO.com and airbnb.com. To help you more easily compare units and complexes, as well as guarantee rapid assistance should issues arise during your stay, though, consider booking vacation rentals through an island-based company, such as those listed for specific regions below.

All rooms listed below come with a private bathroom and free parking unless otherwise noted; all pools are outdoors. Rates do not include Hawaii's 13.41% tax, while cleaning fees refer to one-time charges, not daily service.

## The Kona Coast

Many of the lodgings in Kailua-Kona and Keauhou are timeshares or individually owned condos; rates, decor, and amenities in the latter may vary widely by unit. For a broad selection of well-managed condos and a smaller selection of homes (most with pools), contact **Kona Rentals** (www.konarentals.com; ✆ **800/799-5662**) or **Kona Hawaii Vacation Rentals** (www.konahawaii.com; ✆ **809/244-4752** or 808/329-3333). *Note:* Prices and minimum-stay requirements may be significantly higher during the week before and after the Ironman World Championship (usually the second Sat in Oct), as well as during holidays.

## CENTRAL KAILUA-KONA

In addition to the lodgings below, consider booking a condo at the **Royal Sea Cliff ★★**, on the ocean side of Alii Drive about 2 miles south of the Kailua Pier. There's no beach, but it has two oceanfront pools, often the site of free entertainment, and a tennis court. **Outrigger Hotels & Resorts** (www.outrigger.com; ✆ **800/688-7444** or 808/329-8021) manages 62 of the 148 large units, ranging from studios (650 sq. ft.) up to two-bedroom, two-bathroom units (1,100–1,300 sq. ft.), all with full kitchens and washer-dryers. Outrigger charges $129 to $399, plus cleaning fees of $75 to $115, for its well-appointed accommodations.

### Moderate

**Courtyard King Kamehameha Kona Beach Hotel ★★★** Long a somewhat shabby hotel in a premium setting—in front of King Kamehameha's royal compound on Kailua Bay—King Kam is shabby no more. Rooms and public spaces have not only been revitalized with flatscreen TVs, new bathrooms, and modern furnishings but also imbued with a new sense of history and place. Subtle patterns in the stylish guest rooms reflect lava, native plants, and traditional

# Hotels & Restaurants on the Kona Coast

## Kailua-Kona

**RESTAURANTS**

Akule Supply Co. **18**
Big Island Grill **4**
Caffe Florian **22**
Da Poke Shack **14, 25**
Daylight Mind **7**
Hono's on the Beach **3**
Huggo's/On the Rocks **9**
Island Lava Java **8**
Kenichi **17**
Kona Brewing Co. **2**
Kona Coast Coffee Shack **24**
Lemongrass Bistro **6**
Manago Hotel **23**
Mi's Italian Bistro **21**
Peaberry & Galette **17**
Rays on the Bay **9**
Sam Choy's Kai Lanai **17**
Ulu Ocean Grill & Sushi Lounge **1**

**HOTELS**

Areca Palms Estate B&B **20**
Courtyard King Kamehameha
  Kona Beach Hotel **3**
Four Seasons Resort Hualalai **1**
Holiday Inn Express Kailua-Kona **5**
Holualoa Inn **12**
Horizon Guest House **26**
Kona Magic Sands **15**
Kona Seaspray **16**
Kona Tiki Hotel **11**
Manago Hotel **22**
Royal Sea Cliff **13**
Sheraton Kona Resort & Spa **19**
Silver Oaks Guest Ranch **10**

The Courtyard King Kamehameha Beach Hotel.

tattoo designs, while colors suggest sand, coffee, and rainforest ferns. The high-ceilinged, bright-toned lobby is home to a gallery of royal portraits and Hawaiian cultural scenes by the late Herb Kawainui Kane. More recently, the hotel restored its two tennis courts and pro shop, and expanded the food offerings and music (including sushi and jazz) at **Honu's on the Beach ★★**, its popular indoor/outdoor restaurant. *Note:* For a week or so in early October, this is Ironman central, full of buff bodies, many belonging to international triathletes, all abuzz about the world championship that starts and ends just outside the "King Kam's" door.

75-5660 Palani Rd., Kailua-Kona. www.konabeachhotel.com. © **800/367-2111** or 808/329-2911. 460 units. $151–$539 up to 4 people; from $394 one-bedroom suite. Check for online discounts and packages. Parking $14. **Amenities:** 2 restaurants; poolside bar; convenience store; fitness center; coin-operated laundry; luau; infinity pool; hot tub; Dollar and Hertz rental-car agencies; room service; spa; 2 lighted tennis courts and pro shop; watersports equipment rentals; Wi-Fi (free).

**Holiday Inn Express Kailua-Kona** ★   Its neutral-toned, modern "chain hotel" decor may seem out of place in Hawaii, but this 75-room hotel, opened in late 2014, is nevertheless a very welcome addition to the area. Tucked on a one-way street between Alii Drive and Kuakini Highway, the three-story building offers surprisingly quiet rooms, some with a glimpse of the ocean, including suites with a sofa sleeper. All have 42-inch flatpanel TVs, ample desk space, and gleaming bathrooms; the pool, hot tub, and fitness center are compact but also immaculate. The hot breakfast buffet may lacks tropical touches, but it's free. The only downside: The hotel has just 55 parking spaces ($10) in a shared lot. Luckily, the very hospitable staff will tell you where to nab another spot.

77-146 Sarona Rd., Kailua-Kona. www.hiexpress.com/kailua-kona. © **855/373-5450** or 808/329-2599. 75 units. $135–$199, $161–$219 suite, $178–$239 oceanview suite with king or two queens, plus sofa sleeper; rates include up to 4 people per room. Parking $10. **Amenities:** Free breakfast buffet; business center; fitness center; hot tub; pool; Wi-Fi (free).

**Kona Magic Sands** ★   With Kailua-Kona's largest (if somewhat fickle) sandy beach next door, and oceanfront lanais on every unit to soak in the sunsets and let in the sound of pounding waves, this location is ideal for couples who don't want to spend a bundle at a resort. All the units are studios, with the living/sleeping area bracketed by the lanai on one end and the kitchen on the other; because they're individually owned (and some managed by other companies than the one listed below), furnishings vary greatly unit to unit. Try to book a corner unit, since those have larger lanais, or spring for the luxuriously remodeled No. 302, which comes with granite counters, travertine tile floors, and gorgeous hardwood cabinets, including one that hides a Murphy bed with Tempurpedic mattress. The pool is also right on the ocean. ***Note:*** The ground-floor restaurant remained closed at press time, but units above it can expect to hear noise if it reopens.

77-6452 Alii Dr. (next to Laaloa/Magic Sands Beach Park), Kailua-Kona. Reservations c/o Hawaii Resort Management. www.kona hawaii.com. ℂ **800/244-4752** or 808/329-3333. 37 units, all with shower only. Apr 15–Dec 15: $115, $125–$150 corner, $159 No. 302. Dec 16–Apr 14: $150, $160–$195 corner, $179 No. 302. Higher rates for stays less than 3 nights; weekly and monthly discounts available. Cleaning fee $85 for 3-night or longer stays. **Amenities:** Pool; Wi-Fi (free).

### Inexpensive

**Kona Tiki Hotel** ★★  How close are you to the ocean here? Close enough that waves occasionally break on the seawall, sending seaspray into the ocean-front pool, and close enough that their constant crashing drowns out all or most of the traffic noise from nearby Alii Drive. The small, simply furnished rooms (no TV or phones) feature homey decor, such as pastel tropical print bedspreads. All come with oceanfront lanais, mini-fridges, and ceiling fans (you'll need them); upper-story units have kitchenettes so you can make light meals in addition to the basic continental breakfast (bagels, fruit, coffee) served by the pool. The warm, helpful staff members are quick to lend beach gear and give travel tips; they also make every sunset a special occasion, enlisting guests to help light the tiki torches and blow a conch shell. With no fees for parking, Wi-Fi, or cleaning, this is a true bargain.

75-5968 Alii Dr., Kailua-Kona (about a mile from downtown). www.konatikihotel.com. ℂ **808/329-1425.** 15 units. $89–$95 queen; $108-$115 queen with single bed; $119–$125 queen or king with single bed and kitchenette; $179 suite with king bed

(2 adults max). Rates include continental breakfast. 3-night minimum. Extra person $15 per adult ($18 in high season, Dec 15–Mar 31 and Ironman week), $7 per child 6–11. Futon $6 per night, crib $6 for 3 nights. Deposit required; credit cards accepted for amounts over $350; PayPal for lesser amounts. **Amenities:** Pool; Wi-Fi (free).

## NORTH KONA

The cool, rural uplands above central Kailua-Kona are home to two distinctive lodgings. Part of a 30-acre coffee farm in quaint Holualoa, owner Sandy Hazen's **Holualoa Inn** ★★ (www.holualoainn.com; © **800/ 392-1812** or 808/324-112) offers an ocean-view pool, six immaculate suites ($365–$465) and a handsome cottage with full kitchen ($525–$595); rates include a gourmet breakfast. At **Silver Oaks Guest Ranch** (www.silveroaksranch.com; © **808/325-2000**), guests in the three cottages ($120–$195 double) enjoy meeting miniature donkeys and other animals on the 10-acre working ranch, as well as sunsets from the pool and hot tub.

### Expensive

**Four Seasons Resort Hualalai at Historic Kaupulehu** ★★★ Sometimes, you do get what you pay for—and that's just about anything you could desire at this serenely welcoming resort, only a 15-minute drive from the airport but definitely worlds away from anything resembling hustle and bustle. Rooms in the small clusters of two-story guest-room buildings and villa start at 635 square feet, with private lanais and large bathrooms outfitted with glass-walled showers and deep soaking tubs; ask for one with an outdoor lava-rock shower. All have views of the ocean or one of seven swimming pools; the newest is the adults-only Palm Grove Pool, with a swim-up bar and daybeds, but

The Four Seasons Resort Hualalai at Historic Kaupulehu.

snorkeling in Kings' Pond amid rays and tropical fish remains a top draw. Dinner at **Ulu Ocean Grill ★★★** (p. 174) or the **Beach Tree ★★** are consistently excellent, if costly; it can be hard to tear yourself away in search of cheaper options nearly a half-hour away. Kudos to the Four Seasons for continuing to buck the resort-fee trend, for not charging for its children's or cultural programs, and for committing to numerous environmental measures, including the support of the Hawaiian Legacy Hardwoods' koa reforestation (see "Organized Tours," p. 76). *Note:* The 18-hole Jack Nicklaus signature golf course and award-winning spa and fitness center are open only to hotel guests and members.

72-100 Kaupulehu Dr., Kailua-Kona. www.fourseasons.com/hualalai. ✆ **888/340-5662** or 808/325-8000. 243 units. $695–$1,480 double; from $1,595 suite. Children 18 and under stay free in parent's room (maximum occupancy in guest rooms is 3 people; couples with more than 1 child must get a suite or 2 rooms). Self-parking free, valet parking $20 per day. **Amenities:** 5 restaurants and lounges; 2 bars; babysitting; complimentary children's program; concierge; cultural center; fitness center;

18-hole golf course, 7 pools; room service; spa; 8 tennis courts (4 lit for night play); watersports rentals; Wi-Fi (free).

## KEAUHOU

### Expensive

**Sheraton Kona Resort & Spa at Keauhou Bay ★★★** The name and look have changed several times over the years, but this excellently priced resort overlooking Keauhou Bay and the ocean just keeps getting better. A $20-million makeover, completed in late 2012 and overseen by cultural expert and textile designer Sig Zane (see "Big Island Shopping," p. 194), has added more splashes of bright color, improved landscaping, and highlighted the area's rich cultural history with new signage and tours. In addition to the sandy-bottomed pool, water slide, and kid-pleasing fountain play area, there's a lounge just for teens, with Xbox, Wii, and table tennis. The vast majority of rooms have lanais, most with full or partial oceanview—all the better to ogle the manta rays that frequent this area. You can also spot rays from the lanai off **Rays on the Bay ★**, a vivacious restaurant/lounge with firepits and tasty cocktails. *Note:* Check online for one of the frequent deals with prices at the "moderate" level, even with the $31 daily resort fee.

78-128 Ehukai St., Kailua-Kona. www.sheratonkona.com. **© 888/ 488-3535** or 808/930-4900. 509 units. $179–$530 double; from $399 two-room suite with king and sofabed. Online packages available. Daily resort fee $31, includes self-parking (valet $7 additional per day), bottled water, local calls, Kona Trolley, yoga, cultural tours, Wi-Fi, and more. Extra person or rollaway $65. Children 18 and under stay free in adult's room using existing bedding. **Amenities:** 3 restaurants; 1 cafe; 2 bars; babysitting; rental bikes; concierge; fitness center; weekly luau (p. 207); multilevel pool w/water slide; room service; spa; 2 tennis courts, basketball court, and sand volleyball court; whirlpool; Wi-Fi (included in resort fee).

## Moderate

**Kona Seaspray ★**  Pay close attention to the details when booking a unit here, across Alii Drive from bustling Kahaluu Beach, because the eight, spacious two-bedroom/two-bathroom units in the three-story main building have varying bedding configurations, views, and decor. All offer ocean views (best from the top two floors), full kitchens, and washer-dryers, but some have been recently remodeled with granite counters and stainless-steel sinks in the kitchen and slate tiles on the lanai. Two one-bedroom units in the adjacent, two-story Seaspray building share laundry facilities. A pretty, blue-tiled wall provides privacy for the ground-floor pool, with lounges and a hammock next to the covered grill and dining area.

78-6671 Alii Dr., Kailua-Kona. www.konaseaspray.com. **© 808/ 322-2403.** 10 units. Main building: $155–$195 1-bedroom for 2 (sleeps up to 4); $175–$205 2-bedroom for 4 (sleeps up to 6). Seaspray building: $155–$195 double (sleeps up to 4). 5% discount for weekly rentals, 10% discount May 1–Dec 1. Extra person $20. Cleaning fee $85 1-bedroom, $110 2-bedroom, plus $20 per 5th or more person. 3-night minimum. **Amenities:** Barbecue; pool; whirlpool spa; Wi-Fi (free).

## SOUTH KONA

This rural region of steeply sloping hills, often dotted with coffee and macadamia nut farms, is home to many unassuming B&Bs that may appeal to budget travelers who don't mind being far from the beach.

At the higher end, in every sense, **Horizon Guest House ★★** (www.horizonguesthouse.com; **© 808/ 938-7822**) offers four suites ($250–$350) with private entrances and lanais on a 40-acre property, including a spacious pool and whirlpool spa, at 1,100 feet of elevation in Honaunau, 21 miles south of Kailua-Kona.

Rates include a gourmet breakfast by host Clem Classen; children 13 and under are not allowed.

In a more residential area of Captain Cook, 12 miles south of Kailua-Kona, cozy **Areca Palms Estate Bed & Breakfast** ★ (www.konabedandbreakfast. com; © **808/323-2276**) has four rooms ($120–$145 double, 2-night minimum) in a cedar home that backs on to a nature reserve (with coqui frogs). Rates include co-owner Janice Glass's delicious full breakfast, Wi-Fi, and use of snorkel and beach gear; the hot tub is heated by request. *Tip:* Book the downstairs Lanai Room for the most privacy.

### Inexpensive

**Manago Hotel** ★   You can't beat the bargain rates at this plantation-era hotel, opened in 1917 and now run by the third generation of the friendly Manago family. Although clean, the original 22 rooms with shared bathrooms ($38 double) should be considered just above camping; they're ultra-spartan and subjected to highway noise. The newer, 42 rooms in the three-story wing at the rear also have rather bare walls, but they come with private bathrooms and views of the coast that improve with each floor. Book the third-floor corner Japanese room for a *ryokan* experience, sleeping on a futon and soaking in the *furo* (hot tub). *Note:* There's no elevator. Walls are thin, and sound can carry through jalousie windows used to let cooling breezes in, but neighbors tend to be considerate. If you want to watch TV, head to the lounge next to the **Manago Hotel Restaurant** ★★ (p. 178), the latter popular with locals for down-home cooking and friendly ambience. 82-6151 Mamalahoa Hwy., Captain Cook (Hwy. 11, *makai* side, between mile markers 109 and 110, 12 miles south of Kailua-Kona). www.managohotel.com. © **808/323-2642.** 64 units.

$38 double with shared bathroom; $62–$67 double with private bathroom; $83 double Japanese room with private bathroom. Extra person $3. 4-person maximum. **Amenities:** Restaurant; bar; Wi-Fi (free).

# The Kohala Coast
## SOUTH KOHALA

There's no way around it: The three hotel resorts here are very costly, but the beaches, weather, amenities, and services are among the best in the state. Although you'll miss out on fabulous pools and other resort perks, you can shave costs (and save money on dining) by booking a vacation rental. **South Kohala Management** boasts the most listings (100-plus) of condos and homes in the Mauna Lani, Mauna Kea, and Waikoloa Beach resorts (www.southkohala.com; ✆ **800/822-4252**). **Outrigger Hotels & Resorts** also manages well-maintained condos and townhomes in five complexes in the Mauna Lani and Waikoloa Beach resorts (www.outrigger.com; ✆ **866/956-4262**).

Right on the sand at Anaehoomalu Bay, the lively **Lava Lava Beach Club** restaurant and bar (www.lavalavabeachclub.com; ✆ **808/769-5282**) also offers four luxurious **beach cottages** ★ ($450–$675), with kitchenettes and king beds; just keep in mind the nearby bar is open until 10pm nightly, with live music until 9pm.

### Expensive

**Fairmont Orchid Hawaii** ★★★  The two guest wings at this polished but inviting sanctuary are set off the main lobby like two arms ready to embrace the well-manicured grounds and rugged shoreline; you may feel like hugging it, too, when you have to leave. Tucked among burbling waterfalls and lush greenery are 10 thatched-roof huts in the **Spa Without Walls,**

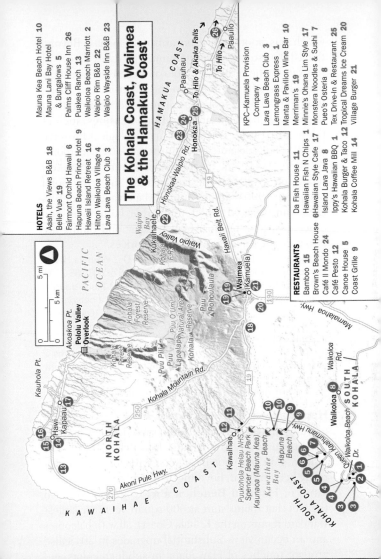

# The Kohala Coast, Waimea & the Hamakua Coast

## HOTELS

Aaah, the Views B&B **18**
Belle Vue **19**
Fairmont Orchid Hawaii **6**
Hapuna Beach Prince Hotel **9**
Hawaii Island Retreat **16**
Hilton Waikoloa Village **4**
Lava Lava Beach Club **3**
Mauna Kea Beach Hotel **10**
Mauna Lani Bay Hotel
  & Bungalows **5**
Palms Cliff House Inn **26**
Puakea Ranch **13**
Waikoloa Beach Marriott **2**
Waipio Rim B&B **22**
Waipio Wayside Inn B&B **23**

## RESTAURANTS

Bamboo **15**
Brown's Beach House **24**
Café Il Mondo **12**
Café Pesto **12**
Canoe House **5**
Coast Grille **9**
Da Fish House **11**
Hawaiian Fish N Chips **1**
Hawaiian Style Cafe **17**
Island Lava Java **1**
Ippy's Hawaiian BBQ **1**
Kohala Burger & Taco **12**
Kohala Coffee Mill **14**
KPC–Kamuela Provision
  Company **4**
Lava Lava Beach Club **3**
Lemongrass Express **1**
Manta & Pavilion Wine Bar **10**
Merriman's **19**
Minnie's Ohana Lim Style **17**
Monstera Noodles & Sushi **7**
Pueo's Osteria **8**
Tex Drive-In & Restaurant **25**
Tropical Dreams Ice Cream **20**
Village Burger **21**

151

which has another five oceanfront cabanas. Beyond the 10,000-square-foot swimming pool lies a cove of soft sand, where the Hui Holokai Beach Ambassadors make guests feel at home in the water and on shore, teaching all kinds of Hawaiiana and sharing their knowledge about the area's cultural treasures, such as the nearby Puako Petroglyph Archaeological Preserve (p. 39). The elegant, generously proportioned rooms (starting at 510 sq. ft.) with lanais were completely renovated in 2013—the largest redo since the hotel opened in 1990—adding subtle island accents such as rattan and carved wood to marble bathrooms and other luxurious fittings. Golf, tennis, and dining are also exceptional here, as befits the prices.

At the Mauna Lani Resort, 1 N. Kaniku Dr., Waimea. www.fairmont.com/orchid-hawaii. © **800/845-9905** or 808/885-2000. 540 units. $299–$869 double; $499–$779 Gold Floor double; from $699 suite. Check for online packages. Extra person $75. Children 17 and under stay free in parent's room. Daily resort fee $25, includes self-parking and Wi-Fi. Valet parking $22. **Amenities:** 6 restaurants; 3 bars; babysitting; bike rentals; year-round children's program; concierge; concierge-level rooms; 2 championship golf courses; fitness center; luau (p. 207); pool; room service; spa; theater; 10 tennis courts (7 lit for night play); watersports rentals; Wi-Fi (included in resort fee).

**Hapuna Beach Prince Hotel ★★★**   Now that an evening shuttle links this larger, more low-key hotel to its sister property, the Mauna Kea Beach Hotel, this hidden gem may not be a secret for long. It's never really been hidden, hovering as it does above the wide sands of **Hapuna Beach ★★★**. Cognoscenti relish the fact that rooms start at 600 square feet (the largest standard rooms on the Kohala Coast), all with balconies and an ocean view. Substantial upgrades in 2013 also brought touches of Hawaiiana in subdued colors and improved the deck around the long, large pool, great for lap swimming. The sprawling, terraced grounds host an 18-hole championship golf course (p. 120) and several open-air restaurants, among them the wonderful **Coast Grille ★★★** (p. 179) and a small cafe with affordable (for this area) takeout fare. The 8,000-square-feet Hapuna Villa, a four-bedroom residence with butler service and pool, is a truly hidden gem, albeit one that starts at a princely $7,000 a night. *Tip:* Rates dip sharply in the off season.

At the Mauna Kea Resort, 62-100 Kaunaoa Dr., Waimea. www.princeresortshawaii.com. *©* **800/882-6060** or 808/880-1111. 351 units. $225–$800 double; from $559 suite. Extra person $60. Children 17 and under stay free in parent's room using existing bedding. Valet parking $20; self-parking $15. **Amenities:** 3 restaurants; 2 bars; babysitting; cafe/gift shop; seasonal children's program; concierge; 18-hole championship golf course (p. 121); fitness center; pool; room service; spa; access to Mauna Kea Beach Hotel tennis center; watersports rentals; Wi-Fi ($12 per day).

**Hilton Waikoloa Village ★★**   It's up to you how to navigate this 62-acre oceanfront Disneyesque golf resort, laced with fantasy pools, lagoons, and a profusion of tropical plants in between three low-rise towers. If you're in a hurry, take the Swiss-made air-conditioned tram; for a more leisurely ride, handsome mahogany boats ply canals filled with tropical fish. Or just walk a half-mile or so through galleries of Asian and Pacific art on your way to the ample-sized rooms designed for families. In 2013, the resort unveiled the new Makai section of its Lagoon Tower: 161 rooms and eight suites, all ocean view, with upgraded bathrooms (including dual vanities), roomier closets, and high-end bedding, with a sophisticated palette evoking lava and sand. Kids will want to head straight to the 175-foot water slide and 1-acre pool, and will pester you to pony up for the DolphinQuest encounter with Pacific bottlenose dolphins. The actual beach is skimpy here, hence an enormous swimming and watersports lagoon that's home to green sea turtles and other marine life. There's also a separate lagoon for swimming with two black-tipped reef sharks for a fee; it's free to watch the daily feedings at noon. You won't want for places to eat here, either, although much more affordable options await at the two nearby shopping centers.

69-425 Waikoloa Beach Dr., Waikoloa. www.hiltonwaikoloa village.com. © **800/445-8667** or 808/886-1234. 1,241 units. $199–$409 double; $279–$478 Makai deluxe double; from $399 suite with king and sofabed; Daily resort fee $25, includes Wi-Fi, local/toll-free calls, cultural lessons, in-room PlayStation 3 with unlimited movies and games, and more. Extra person $50. Children 18 and under stay free in parent's room. Valet parking $25 self-parking $30. **Amenities:** 9 restaurants; 5 bars; babysitting; bike rentals; children's program; concierge; fitness center; 2 18-hole golf courses; luau (p. 207); 3 pools (1 adults-only); room service; spa; 6 tennis courts; watersports rentals; Wi-Fi (included in resort fee).

## Mauna Kea Beach Hotel ★★★

Old-money travelers have long embraced this golf-course resort, which began as a twinkle in Laurance Rockefeller's eye and in 1965 became the first hotel development on the rugged lava fields of the Kohala Coast. The 2006 earthquake provided the literal shakeup behind $150 million in renovations that reduced the number of rooms but expanded their size, creating spacious, modern bathrooms and closets. Further renovations in 2013 brightened the family-size rooms and suites in the Beachfront Wing, now with picture windows above the soaking tubs. Dining, golf, and tennis are all top-notch here, although the pool is small by today's standards. The true pearls are sandy **Kaunaoa Beach** ★★★ (p. 89), where manta rays skim the north point, and the gracious staff members, many of whom know several generations of guests by name. ***Note:*** The hotel is now part of Marriott's Autograph Collection, although management hasn't changed.

At the Mauna Kea Resort, 62-100 Mauna Kea Beach Dr., Waimea. www.princeresortshawaii.com. © **866/977-4589** or 808/882-7222. 252 units. $339–$1,150 double; from $1,000 suite. Extra person $75. 3-adult maximum. Valet parking $20; self-parking $15. **Amenities:** 4 restaurants; 3 bars; cafe; babysitting; seasonal children's program; concierge; 18-hole championship golf course (p. 121); fitness center; pool; hot tub; room service; 11 tennis courts; watersports rentals; Wi-Fi ($15 per day).

## Mauna Lani Bay Hotel & Bungalows ★★

After a $30-million renovation that wrapped up in late 2013, the posh guest rooms once again gleam with understated elegance, outfitted in new mahogany cabinets, stone-tiled bathrooms, quilted bedspreads, and ceiling fans behind the signature plantation shutters, also newly refinished. They're still angled for premium ocean views, all with private lanais; some look over the ancient fishponds and historic cottage where the popular "Twilight at Kalahuipua'a" monthly storytelling (p. 205)—one of many free cultural programs—takes place. Koi ponds and evening entertainment add life to the somewhat skeletal lobby. Although the opulent two-bedroom bungalows have also been updated, it's less costly to splurge on dining at the **Canoe House** ★★ (p. 179) or on a treatment at the thatched-hut spa, with a unique outdoor lava rock sauna. The two beach areas are small but popular with green sea turtles; some may have been raised by the hotel and released at the annual July 4th celebration. Aiding turtles is just one of the hotel's many environmental efforts, which include low-impact care of the two championship golf courses (p. 122).

At the Mauna Lani Resort, 68-1400 Mauna Lani Dr., Puako. www.maunalani.com. ✆ **800/367-2323** or 808/885-6622. 341 units. $260–$850 double; from $1,070 suite; $4,000–$4,500 bungalow (sleeps up to 4). Extra person $75. Daily resort fee $25, includes valet or self-parking, Wi-Fi, local calls, beach cabana, and more. **Amenities:** 3 restaurants; lounge; babysitting; free bike rentals; concierge; children's program; 2 18-hole golf courses; fitness center with lap pool; oceanfront pool; hot tub; room service; spa; access to 10 tennis courts at the Fairmont Orchid Hawaii; watersports rentals; Wi-Fi (free).

## Waikoloa Beach Marriott Resort & Spa ★★

Of all the lodgings in the Waikoloa Beach Resort, this hotel has the best location on **Anaehoomalu Bay ★★** (nicknamed "A-Bay"; p. 88), with many rooms offering views of the crescent beach and historic fishponds; others look across the parking lot and gardens toward Mauna Kea. Besides all kinds of watersports at the beach, kids will enjoy the sandy-entrance children's pool, while adults delight in the heated infinity-edge pool, the two-level **Mandara Spa,** and the spacious, well-equipped fitness center. The light-hued rooms are also enticing, with glass-walled balconies and plush beds with down comforters in crisp white duvets. Families should book one of the spacious corner rooms, which include king-size bed and sofa bed; despite the resort fee ($30 daily), this hotel typically offers the best prices of the Kohala Coast resorts, with access to nearby golf courses.

69-275 Waikoloa Beach Dr., Waikoloa. www.marriotthawaii. com. ✆ **888/236-2427** or 808/886-6789. 555 units. $179–$547 double; from $541 suite. Check for online packages. Daily $30 resort fee includes self-parking, local and mainland U.S./ Canada calls, cultural activities, and more. Extra person $45. Children 17 and under stay free in parent's room. Valet parking $21. **Amenities:** Restaurant; bar; babysitting; cafe; concierge; cultural activities; fitness center; Jacuzzi; luau; 3 pools; rental-car desk; room service; spa; watersports rentals; Wi-Fi (included in resort fee).

## NORTH KOHALA

This rural area, steeped in Hawaiian history and legend, has few overnight visitors, given its distance from swimmable beaches and other attractions. But it does include two luxurious accommodations that reflect its heritage in unique ways. At **Puakea Ranch ★★** (www. puakearanch.com; © **808/315-0805**), west of Hawi and 400 feet above the coast, three plantation-era bungalows and a former cowboy bunkhouse have been beautifully restored as vacation rentals ($289–$899; 3- to 7-night minimum). Sizes vary, as do amenities such as soaking tubs and swimming pools. On the ocean bluff between Hawi and Kapaau, hidden from the road, the "eco-boutique" **Hawaii Island Retreat ★★** (www.hawaiiislandretreat.com; © **808/889-6336**) offers 10 posh guest rooms with large bathrooms and balconies ($415–$490 double, 2-night minimum). Clustered near the spa and saltwater infinity pool are seven yurts (large tent-like structures with vaulted ceilings) with private bathrooms and shared indoor/ outdoor showers ($185 double). Rates include a sumptuous, homegrown organic breakfast.

## WAIMEA

As an economical alternative to the Kohala resorts, the cowboy town of Waimea offers a few very basic motels (not recommended) and several more comfortable options, all within a 20-minute drive of Hapuna Beach.

The two large suites ($179–$199 double) of **Aaah, the Views Bed & Breakfast ★★** (www.aaah theviews.com; ☏ **808/885-3455**) have plenty of windows so you can revel in the majestic views of Mauna Kea, ranchlands, or red skies at sunset; breakfast supplies are left in your kitchen or kitchenette. The two-room Treetop Suite, with four beds, is ideal for families. Closer to the center of town, the two-story, two-unit **Belle Vue ★** (www.hawaii-bellevue.com; ☏ **800/772-5044** or 808/885-7732) vacation rental has a penthouse apartment with high ceilings and views from the mountains to the distant sea, and a downstairs studio ($95–$175 double). Both sleep four and have private entrances and kitchenettes with breakfast fixings.

## The Hamakua Coast

This emerald-green, virtually empty coast is a far drive from resort-worthy beaches and Hawaii Volcanoes National Park, and so is less frequented by overnight visitors (other than coqui frogs). Those who do choose to spend a night or more, though, will appreciate getting away from it all. Two miles north of Honokaa off Hwy. 240, the **Waipio Wayside Inn Bed & Breakfast ★★** (www.waipiowayside.com; ☏ **800/833-8849** or 808/775-0275) perches on a sunny ocean bluff. A restored former plantation supervisor's residence, the inn has five antiques-decorated rooms with modern bathrooms ($110–$200 double) and a handsome living/dining room, where owner Jacqueline Horne serves hot organic breakfasts promptly at 8am. (You can sample some of the 30-plus teas she keeps in stock any time of the day.)

At the northern end of Hwy. 240, you'll find an amazing vista of Waipio Valley and privacy at **Waipio Rim B&B ★★** (www.waipiorim.com; ☏ **808/775-1727**). There's only one unit: a second-floor, detached studio ($200) with flatscreen TV, kitchenette, and Wi-Fi for when you tire of the panorama. The hot breakfast even comes to you, at 8am; enjoy it on the ocean-view deck.

Closer to Hilo, in rustic Honomu, the sprawling, Victorian-inspired **Palms Cliff House Inn ★** (www. palmscliffhouse.com; © **866/963-6076** or 808/963-6076) serves a full breakfast on its lanai overlooking. Pohakumanu Bay. Some of its eight large oceanview suites ($239–$449) come with air-conditioning and jetted tubs.

*Note:* You'll find these accommodations on "The Kohala Coast, Waimea & the Hamakua Coast" map on p. 151.

## Hilo

Although several hotels line scenic Banyan Drive, most fall short of visitors' expectations, with the exception of the **Hilo Naniloa ★★**, described below. You'll find more character in lodgings elsewhere in and around Hilo, but be aware you may hear coqui frogs throughout the night.

Jack London and Queen Liliuokalani are said to have stayed at the gracious Victorian mansion on Reed's Island now known as **Shipman House Bed & Breafast Inn ★★** (www.hilo-hawaii.com; © **800/ 627-8447** or 808/934-8025). The restored inn includes five rooms ($219–$249) with modern conveniences such as mini-fridges and fans tucked among the heirlooms, and lavish continental breakfast on the lanai. The **Old Hawaiian Bed & Breakfast ★** (www.the bigislandvacation.com; © **877/961-2816** or 808/961-2816) provides easy access to Rainbow Falls from a quaint 1930s house with three rooms ($85–$125, with full breakfast); children under 12 not permitted.

On a hilltop 22-acre compound boasting its own waterfall swimming pool, the **Inn at Kulaniapia Falls** ★★ (www.waterfall.net; © **808/935-6789**) offers a choice of 10 Asian- or Hawaiian-themed rooms ($179–$199, with full breakfast) or the Pagoda Cottage ($289, with kitchen stocked with breakfast supplies). Kayaks, paddleboards, yoga, and light lunches are also available.

*Note:* The lodgings in this section are on the "Hilo" map on p. 56.

### INEXPENSIVE

**Hilo Naniloa Hotel** ★★    The bright spot on somewhat rundown Banyan Drive is this 12-story oceanfront hotel (formerly the Naniloa Volcanoes Resort), which includes the 9-hole **Naniloa Golf Course** (p. 124) and wonderful views of Hilo Bay. New owners have undertaken extensive renovations, such as refurbishing rooms (312–330 sq. ft.) with new marble bathrooms and floors, 32-inch flatscreen TVs, and triple-sheet white bedding. Families should consider the oceanfront suite (660 sq. ft.; $238–$269), with two king beds, kitchenette, and living area. The pool can be a bit chilly, but it also overlooks the sparkling bay.
93 Banyan Dr., Hilo. www.hilonaniloa.com. © **855/747-0757** or 808/969-3333. 193 units. $94–$169 double; $238–$269 suite w/2 kings. Most rates include free golfing. **Amenities:** 9-hole golf course (free); pool; Wi-Fi in lobby (free).

## Puna

For vacation rentals in **Pahoa** and **Kapoho,** some on the ocean with their own thermal ponds, contact Joanie Lehr of **Hawaii Island Dreams** (www.hawaiiislanddreams.com; © **808/938-2996**). Yoga and nature lovers should investigate the variety of funky lodgings

($95–$245) and classes at the bohemian **Kalani Oceanside Retreat** ★ on Highway 137 about halfway between Kapoho and Kalapana (www.kalani.com; ✆ **800/800-6886**; 808/965-7828). Be prepared for the noise of coqui frogs.

In **Volcano Village,** the frogs don't like the misty, cool nights as much—the village is at 3,700 feet—but ask about heating when booking a rental. Joey Gutierrez of **Hawaii Volcano Vacations** (www.hawaii volcanovacations.com; ✆ **800/709-0907** or 808/967-7178) manages a great selection of cottages, cabins, and houses ranging from $95 to $200 a night. If you can climb its ship-style ladder to the sleeping loft, **Mahinui Na Lani** ★★ (www.mahinui.com; ✆ **510/965-7367**; $235) is a romantic, eco-friendly hideaway; the whimsical treehouse studio offers a kitchenette and cedar hot tub for two ($235).

*Note:* You'll find Mahinui Na Lani and the following accommodations on the "Hotels & Restaurants in the Volcano Area" map on p. 163.

## VOLCANO VILLAGE

### Expensive

**Volcano Village Lodge ★★★**   Built as an artists' retreat in 2004, the five romantic cottages in this leafy, 2-acre oasis offer gleaming hardwood floors and paneled walls, vaulted ceilings, fireplaces, kitchenettes, and endless walls of windows—the lush rainforest envelops the oh-so-peaceful lodge in privacy. Fixings for a full breakfast—fruit, baked goods, coffee, tea, and an entree to reheat in your microwave—are left in your room each night. Enjoy the communal hot tub in the gardens after a day of hiking in the national park. For true sumptuousness or extra guests, book the two-room Mauna Loa cottage, which includes a "meditation"

One of the cottages at Volcano Lodge.

loft under the eaves. ***Note:*** Families should also consider the lodge's **5th Street Ohana** (www.5thstohana. com; © **808/985-9500**). On the other side of Hwy. 11, this modern vacation rental offers a two-bedroom suite ($165) plus studio ($115), both with full kitchens, that can be combined as one unit ($280).

19-4183 Road E, Volcano. www.volcanovillagelodge.com. © **808/985-9500.** 5 units. $280–$375 double (up to 4 guests). Rates include full breakfast. From Hwy. 11, take Wright Rd. exit, head .8 mile north to right on Laukapu St.; it ends at Road E. Turn left; lodge is first driveway on the left. **Amenities:** Hot tub; DVD library; Wi-Fi (free).

#### Moderate

**Kilauea Lodge ★★**  This former YMCA camp, built in 1938, has served as a gracious inn since 1986. The 10-acre main campus has 11 units in two wings and two cottages; most have gas fireplaces, along with European-Hawaiian decor and thoughtful touches such as heated towel racks. Another four cottages lie within a walk or short drive of the lodge; my favorites are the

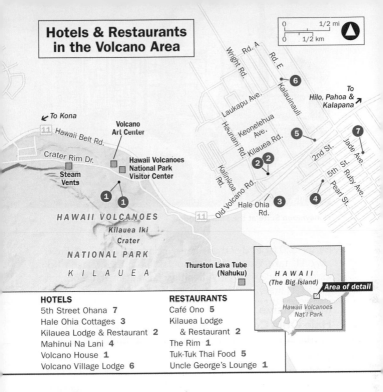

## Hotels & Restaurants in the Volcano Area

To Kona

Hawaii Belt Rd. 11

Crater Rim Dr.

Steam Vents

Volcano Art Center

Hawaii Volcanoes National Park Visitor Center

Wright Rd.

Rd. A

Rd. E

Kalauinauli

To Hilo, Pahoa & Kalapana

Laukapu Ave.

Haunani Rd.

Keonelehua Ave.

Kilauea Rd.

Kalinkoa Rd.

Old Volcano Rd.

Hale Ohia Rd.

11

2nd St.

5th St.

Ruby Ave.

Pearl St.

Jade Ave.

HAWAII VOLCANOES

Kilauea Iki Crater

NATIONAL PARK

K I L A U E A

Thurston Lava Tube (Nahuku)

HAWAII (The Big Island)

Area of detail

Hawaii Volcanoes Nat'l Park

0     1/2 mi
0     1/2 km

### HOTELS
5th Street Ohana **7**
Hale Ohia Cottages **3**
Kilauea Lodge & Restaurant **2**
Mahinui Na Lani **4**
Volcano House **1**
Volcano Village Lodge **6**

### RESTAURANTS
Café Ono **5**
Kilauea Lodge
   & Restaurant **2**
The Rim **1**
Tuk-Tuk Thai Food **5**
Uncle George's Lounge **1**

two-bedroom, two-bathroom Pii Mauna, overlooking the Volcano Golf Course, and the two-bedroom, one-bathroom Olaa Plantation House, an elegantly restored 1935 home with a huge kitchen, breakfast room, and living room with window seats. All rates include gourmet breakfast in the superb **Kilauea Lodge Restaurant** (p. 189). *Note:* The lodge and restaurant were both for sale at press time, although owners Albert and Lorna Jeyte planned to stay on until it was sold.
19-3948 Old Volcano Rd., Volcano. www.kilauealodge.com.
*(C)* **808/967-7366.** 11 units on main property, 4 cottages nearby. $190–$205 double room; $220–$295 cottage. Extra

Honeymoon Suite at the Kilauea Lodge.

person $20 (ages 2 and up). Rates include full breakfast. From Hwy. 11, take Wright Rd. exit to 1st left at Old Volcano Rd; lodge is .1 mile on right. **Amenities:** Restaurant; gift shop; hot tub; Wi-Fi (free).

### Inexpensive

**Hale Ohia Cottages ★★** Kentucky native Michael Tuttle, a former chef and historic building renovator, came across this secluded garden estate in the early 1990s and happily made this "old Volcano home." The quiet main lodge has two units, with a connecting hallway to create a family suite if desired. I recommend one of the three unique guest cottages, each with one to three bedrooms and greater privacy. The Ihilani Cottage, which dates from the 1920s, and Cottage 44, a transformed 1930s redwood water tank, have charming turret-shaped bedrooms and inviting nooks. Continental breakfast is included, except at two offsite properties: the newly built Laulani and the 1940s Cottage in the Woods, both two-bedroom, two-bathroom and divisible into smaller units.

11-3968 Hale Ohia Rd., Volcano. www.haleohia.com. ✆ **800/ 455-3803** or 808/967-7986. 10 units. $105–$220 double. Extra person $20. 3% surcharge for credit cards. Most rates include continental breakfast. 2-night minimum during peak periods; 1-night stays $20–$40 extra. **Amenities:** Wi-Fi (main property; free).

# HAWAII VOLCANOES NATIONAL PARK
## Expensive
**Volcano House** ★    Reopened in 2013 after extensive infrastructure renovations, this historic two-story wooden inn is extremely modest for its price, especially compared with Yosemite's Ahwahnee and the grand lodges of other national parks. Still, its location on the very rim of the Kilauea Caldera is nothing short of spectacular—to wake up to that view is very special indeed. Rooms are on the small and plain side and the vintage bathrooms downright tiny, so explore your surroundings during the day and then enjoy dinner and drinks at **The Rim ★★★** (p. 190) or **Uncle George's Lounge** downstairs, before falling into the comfy beds. Now that the crater-view rooms have risen to $335 to $385, this is a real splurge. The hotel also manages 10 cabins and 16 campsites in the park; see "Camping," below.

1 Crater Rim Dr., Hawaii Volcanoes National Park. www.hawaii volcanohouse.com. (C) **866/536-7972** or 808/756-9625. 33 units. $285–$385 double. Extra person $30. 1-time $10 park entrance fee. Check for online packages. **Amenities:** Restaurant; bar; bicycles; gift shop; Wi-Fi (free).

# Kau

As with the Hamakua Coast, few visitors overnight in this virtually undeveloped area, halfway between Kailua-Kona and Hawaii Volcanoes National Park, but there is one lodging that encourages guests to linger. In a tranquil setting above the road to South Point (Ka Lae), luxurious **Kalaekilohana ★★** (www.kau-hawaii.com;

*©* **808/939-8052**) has four large guest suites ($329) in a modern plantation-style home. After one night in a plush bed, with a beautifully presented breakfast on the lanai, and true Hawaiian hospitality from hosts Kenny Joyce and Kilohano Domingo, many guests kick themselves for not having booked a second night or more—and multi-night discounts start at $40 off a 2-night stay. Kenny's delicious dinners ($25–$40 per person) are a nightly option.

## Camping

Camping is available at **10 county beach parks, six state parks and reserves,** a few **private camp-grounds,** and **Hawaii Volcanoes National Park.** I don't recommend the county parks, due to noise at popular sites (such as **Spencer Beach Park,** p. 90) and security concerns at more remote ones (such as **Punaluu Beach,** p. 94). All county campsites require advance-purchase permits, which cost $20 a night per person for nonresidents (http://hawaiicounty.ehawaii.gov; *©* **808/961-8311**).

State campsites also require permits that must be booked in advance (http://camping.ehawaii.gov; *©* **808/961-9540**), the most desirable are at **Hapuna Beach** (p. 89), which offers six A-frame screened shelters with wooden sleeping platforms and a picnic table, plus communal restrooms and cold showers. Nonresidents pay $50 per shelter per night for permits; purchase at least a week in advance. Friday through Sunday nights, **Kiholo State Park Reserve** (p. 85) allows tent camping in a kiawe grove on a pebbly beach, with portable toilets but no water; nonresidents pay $18 per campsite per night. For hard-core backpackers, camping in the state preserve of remote

**Waimanu Valley** is the reward for tackling the arduous Muliwai Trail, but perhaps best attempted with a guide from **Hawaiian Walkways** (see "Guided Hikes," p. 130). Permits for nonresident campers cost $18 per site (for up to six people).

Now that a local "Aloha Patrol" provides security, the privately run campground at **Hookena Beach Park** (p. 88) in South Kona is one more option for those really wanting to pitch a tent by the waves. Reservations, though recommended, are not required; campsites cost $21 per person per night for ages 7 and older and $20 for younger campers (www.hookena. org; © **808/328-7321**). You can also rent tents, camping stoves, tables, and chairs.

In **Hawaii Volcanoes National Park** (p. 68), the only campground accessible by car is **Namakanipaio,** which has 10 cabins and 16 campsites managed by **Volcano House** (www.hawaiivolcanohouse. com, © **866/536-7972** or 808/441-7750). The recently refurbished one-room cabins sleep four apiece, with bed linens and towels provided, grills, and a community restroom with hot showers; the cost is $80 a night. Tent campers have restrooms but not showers; sites cost $15 a night, on a first-come, first-served basis, with a 7-night maximum stay. Call the hotel in advance to rent a tent set up for you with a comfy foam mattress, linens, cooler, lantern, and two chairs, for $55 a night.

Backpack camping is allowed at seven remote areas in the park, some with shelters and cabins, but you must register first at the **Backcountry Office** (www.nps.gov/havo; © **808/985-6178**), no more than 1 day in advance.

*Note:* No places rent camping gear on island, but you can buy some at the **Hilo Surplus Store,** 148 Mamo St., Hilo (www.hilosurplusstore.com; ✆ **808/935-6398**), or in one of the island's big-box stores such as **Kmart,** 74-5456 Kamaka Eha Ave., Kailua-Kona (✆ **808/326-2331**).

**Island RV & Safari Activities** (www.islandrv.com; ✆ **800/406-4555** or 808/960-1260) offers weekly rentals of a 22-foot, class-C motor home, which sleeps up to four, for $2,400. Included are airport transfers, linens, barbecue grill, a last night in a hotel, and help with itinerary planning; you must book county campsite permits in advance. Vehicle-only weekly rentals for a 20-foot, class-B motorhome are $1,400. *Note:* RV camping is not allowed in Hawaii state and national parks.

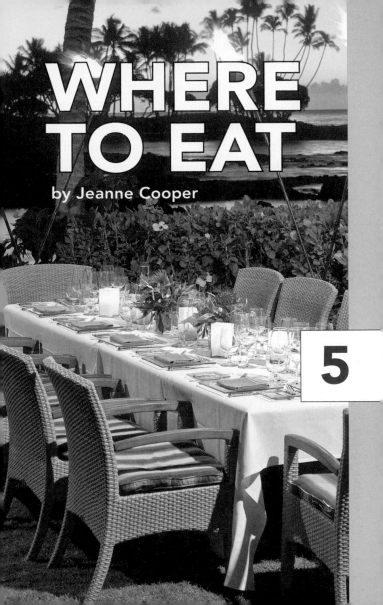

# WHERE
# TO EAT

by Jeanne Cooper

T hanks to its deep waters, green pastures, and fertile fields, the Big Island provides local chefs with a cornucopia of fresh ingredients. The challenge for visitors is finding restaurants to match their budgets. Don't be afraid to nosh at a roadside stand or create a meal from a farmer's market (see "Big Island Shopping," p. 193), as locals do, but indulge at least once on an oceanfront sunset dinner for the best of all the Big Island has to offer.

## The Kona Coast
### CENTRAL KAILUA-KONA

With few exceptions, this is a no-man's-land for memorable, sensibly priced dining; chains abound, and service is often inordinately slow. One bright spot: **Honu's on the Beach ★★** (daily 6–10:30am and 5:30–10pm), the indoor/outdoor restaurant at the Courtyard King Kamehameha Kona Beach Hotel (p. 140). Live jazz and sushi Sunday to Thursday nights attract both locals and visitors; well-prepared farm-to-table Hawaii Regional Cuisine is available nightly (main courses $15–$28), with a prime rib/seafood buffet ($45) Friday and Saturday nights.

In a less scenic setting, duck into **Lemongrass Bistro ★**, 75-5742 Kuakini Hwy. (*makai* side, at Hualalai Rd.), for fragrant curry and noodle dishes ($13–$18). It's open daily for lunch and dinner, and as late as

PREVIOUS PAGE: **Browns Restaurant at Fairmont Orchid**

10:30pm weekdays (www.lemongrass-bistro.webs.com; ✆ **808/331-2708**). Big appetites should head to the **Big Island Grill** ★, 75-5702 Kuakini Hwy. (*makai* side, south of Henry St.), for local and American classics ($5–$17 breakfast, $8–$20 lunch, $9–$24 dinner) in a strip mall, happily with parking. It's open 7am to 9pm daily except Sunday (✆ **808/326-1153**).

### Expensive

**Daylight Mind** ★★ HAWAII REGIONAL   Bakery, coffee bar, restaurant, coffee roaster, community center—this two-story complex with vaulted wooden ceilings and a large, wraparound oceanfront lanai tries to be many things to many people, and mostly succeeds. Many of the ingredients are locally sourced, of course, including Kona, Kau, and other Hawaiian coffees. The coffee bar also serves tropical kombucha (fermented tea), coffee cherry tisane, and other brews; check the bakery for fresh sourdough bread. In the restaurant, the eclectic brunch and dinner menu runs the gamut from trendily healthful (quinoa porridge with chia seed yogurt) to utterly rich (Keahole lobster BLT). *Note:* A second location was expected to open at the Queens' MarketPlace in the Waikoloa Beach Resort by 2016.

At rear of Waterfront Row, 75-5770 Alii Dr., Kailua-Kona. www.daylightmind.com. ✆ **808/339-7824.** Main courses $8–$16 brunch, $12–$31 dinner. Daily brunch 8am–3pm, bar 3–9pm, dinner 5–9pm.

**The famed lobster BLT of Daylight Mind**

**Huggo's** ★★ PACIFIC RIM/SEAFOOD  The setting doesn't get any better in Kailua-Kona than this, a covered wooden deck overlooking tide pools and the sweep of Kailua Bay. But executive chef Ken Schloss isn't content to rest on the visual laurels, frequently introducing new preparations, such as "mangospacho"— chilled mango with avocado, cucumber, and onions— stacked with fresh crab; native pohole ferns might appear in a salad, or kabocha pumpkin in risotto. Fresh catch with lemongrass haupia sauce is a must. Next door, even closer to the shore, is the more casual and moderately priced **On the Rocks** ★, helmed by chef de cuisine Carlos Nava; it's a pulsating nightclub after sunset. **Java on the Rocks** ★ occupies the same space from 6 to 11am, serving Kona coffee, bagels, papaya, and a few egg dishes on paper plates, all under the watchful eye of birds waiting for you to be distracted by the sea views.

75-5828 Kahakai Rd., Kailua-Kona. www.huggos.com. © **808/ 329-1493.** Reservations recommended. Main courses $28– $39. Sun–Thurs 5–9pm, Fri–Sat 5–10pm. On the Rocks: Main courses $11–$18. Daily 11:30am–midnight, happy hour 3–6pm. Java on the Rocks: Main courses $8–$12. Daily 6–11am.

### Moderate

**Da Poke Shack** ★★★ SEAFOOD  Nestled in an out-of-sight corner of an unassuming stretch of vacation rental condos, with just a couple of picnic tables for seating, Da Poke Shack has nevertheless put itself on the culinary (and social media) map with a lineup of eight or so *poke*—diced raw seafood with different marinades and seasonings—that are so fresh you may spot fishermen delivering their latest catch. Go early for the best selection, since it often sells out; the spicy Pele's Kiss and creamy avocado versions are first-rate. Prices vary daily and are on the high side for lunch plates and bowls with quinoa, rice, or potato salad; it's the seafood that's the star here, so spend your money on that. A second location, convenient for those en route to Puuhonua O Honaunau, opened in Captain Cook in 2014.

At the Kona Bali Kai, 76-6246 Alii Dr., Kailua-Kona. www.dapoke shack.com. © **808/329-7653.** Reservations not accepted. Market price, averaging $20 per pound, plates $21, bowls $11. Daily 10am–6pm. Also at 83–5308 Mamalahoa Hwy. (*mauka* side, at mile marker 106), Captain Cook. © **808/328-8862.** Daily 10am–6pm.

**Island Lava Java** ★ AMERICAN Residents of upcountry Waikoloa Village were thrilled when this perennial favorite opened a branch there in 2012, but there's no competing with the lively ambience and oceanview setting of the Kailua-Kona original. Founded in 1994, the former espresso bar has long since blossomed into a full-service cafe for breakfast, lunch, and

## TAPPING INTO kona brewing co.

Father and son Cameron Healy and Spoon Khalsa opened microbrewery and pub **Kona Brewing Co.** ★★ (www.konabrewingco.com; © **808/334-2739**) in an obscure warehouse in Kailua-Kona in 1998; now they also run two restaurants on Oahu (one at the Honolulu airport) and enjoy widespread Mainland distribution of their most popular brews, including Fire Rock Pale Ale and Longboard Lager. The Kona brewpub, 75-5629 Kuakini Hwy., still offers affordable lunch specials (pizzas, fish tacos), a palm-fringed patio, and short free tours daily at 10:30am and 3pm; it's open 11am to 9pm Sunday to Thursday, until 10pm Friday to Saturday.

dinner, with most tables on a patio overlooking the breakers across Alii Drive and a low seawall. Pluses: The coffee is 100% Kona; breads, pastries, and desserts are made in house; and organic salads, sandwiches, and pizzas feature mostly local ingredients. Minuses: With the exception of the Big Island grass-fed beef burger ($15) or pizzas to share ($21–$24), dinner plates are expensive, and service can be leisurely. Enjoy the people- and surf-watching while you wait, and bring your own beer or wine—there's no corkage fee.

75-5799 Alii Dr., Kailua-Kona. www.islandlavajava.com. © **808/ 327-2161.** Main courses $7–$18 breakfast; $10–$20 lunch; $15–$30 dinner. Daily breakfast 6:30am–11:30am, lunch 11:30am–5pm, dinner 5–9:30pm. Also in the Waikoloa Highlands Shopping Center, 68-1845 Waikoloa Rd., Waikoloa. © **808/ 217-7661.** Weekdays 5:30am–9pm; weekends 6:30am–9pm.

## NORTH KONA

**Ulu Ocean Grill & Sushi Lounge** ★★★ ISLAND FARM/SEAFOOD Now under the direction of executive chef Massimo Falsini, formerly of Harry's Bar in Rome, the Four Seasons' beachfront destination restaurant remains a superb showcase for the wares of 160 local fishermen and farmers. Refined yet approachable dishes include roasted pineapple mahi in a Thai chili black bean sauce, Kona coffee–crusted New York steak with kiawe-smoked potatoes, and Big Island wild boar in a poha berry chutney. Jewel-like sashimi and artful sushi rolls can be ordered in the oceanview lounge (with firepits) or the open-air dining room, behind roe-like curtains of glass balls. Browse the extensive wine list on an iPad, or simply ask the expert waitstaff for advice. On Saturday, sign up for the four-course, prix-fixe Farm-to-Table dinner ($95/$150 with wine), limited to 40 guests, who meet with the chef de

The bar at Ulu Ocean Grill & Sushi Lounge

cuisine and dine on a private lanai. *Note:* The breakfast menu is also locally sourced, but seems more exorbitant.

At the Four Seasons Resort Hualalai, 72-100 Kaupulehu Dr., Kailua-Kona (off Hwy. 19, 6 miles north of Kona airport). ℰ **808/325-8000.** www.uluoceangrill.com. Reservations recommended. Breakfast buffet $30–$44; dinner main courses $32–$55. Daily 6:30–11am (buffet 6:30–10:30am) and 5:30–9pm (sushi until 9:30pm).

## KEAUHOU

High above Alii Drive, Keauhou Shopping Center has several more affordable options than Sam Choy's Kai Lanai (below) and **Kenichi ★★** (www.kenichipacific. com; ℰ **808/322-6400**), a stylish but high-priced Asian fusion/sushi dinner spot, open daily 5 to 9:30pm. The best is **Peaberry & Galette ★** (www.peaberry-andgalette.com; ℰ **808/322-6020**), a small cafe with a wide selection of savory and sweet crepes, plus good coffee; it's open 7am to 7pm Monday to Thursday, until 8pm Friday to Saturday, and 8am to 6pm Sunday.

The newer, ultra-casual **Akule Supply Co.** ★★ (www.akulesupply.com; ✆ 808/498-4987) may not be a culinary rival to any of the above, but it can claim the best setting: Keauhou Harbor, at the end of Kaleiopapa St. Open 8am to 8pm daily, it serves local favorites like fish and eggs ($10) and Spam musubi ($4) at breakfast; sandwiches and burgers ($10–$14) at lunch and dinner; and a 10-ounce steak ($25) and market-rate fish plates at dinner only (5–8pm). At sunset, relax by the bayfront firepit until your order's ready.

**Sam Choy's Kai Lanai** ★ HAWAII REGIONAL The miles-long coastal views from this former Wendy's are spectacular—if only the service and food consistently measured up. When they're in top form, this aerie run by renowned Honolulu chef Sam Choy is hard to beat. Lunch offers bargains, with local dishes such as saimin (noodle soup), Portuguese bean soup, and beef stew omelet; the copious breakfast buffet ($15) is also a good value and features a changing lineup of American classics and Pacific Islander treats such as Samoan *pani popo* pancakes. Appetizers and dinner courses veer into the expensive category, but the fried poke ($12) and seafood *laulau* (fish and seafood in steamed ti leaves, $28) merit the expense. Go early to nab a happy-hour seat by the firepits or at the bar.

In Keauhou Shopping Center, 78-6831 Alii Dr., Kailua-Kona. ✆ **808-333-3434.** Reservations recommended for dinner. Lunch main courses $8–$14; dinner main courses $17–$36. Daily 11am–9pm (happy hour 3–5pm), breakfast buffet ($15) Sat–Sun 8–11am.

## SOUTH KONA

For pastries, breakfast, lunch, elevated ocean views, and of course, Kona coffee, consider two cafes on the *makai* side of Hwy. 11. **Kona Coffee Shack** ★,

83-5799 Mamalahoa Hwy. (between mile marker 108 and 109) in Captain Cook, serves plump if pricey sandwiches on fresh-baked bread ($12) and pizza ($14–$15); it's open daily 7:30am to 3pm (www.coffee shack.com; © **808/328-9555**). The more modern, Italian-themed **Caffe Florian** ★ offers counter service for a light menu that includes *panini*; it's open 6:30am to 4:30pm weekdays, 7am to 3pm Saturday, at 81-6637 Mamalahoa Hwy., Kealakekua (at Kee-Kee Rd.; © **808/238-0861**). For fresh seafood to go, don't forget the southern outpost of Kailua-Kona's **Da Poke Shack** ★★ (see p. 172 for details.)

### Expensive

**Mi's Italian Bistro** ★★★ ITALIAN   There's no fabulous view here, only superbly executed, thoughtfully created Italian dishes using fresh ingredients from chef Morgan Starr's own garden, local beef, handmade pasta, and off-the-hook ahi. Starr, formerly at Four Seasons Resort Hualalai, and wife Ingrid Chan opened their small, dark-toned restaurant in a drab shopping strip in late 2007 to rave reviews. They've maintained their commitment to top-notch, well-priced cuisine (and wine list) while raising two children, often at their mother's side. The ahi bolognese ($17) is a revelation, meaty without a hint of fishiness; porcini-crusted pork tenderloin ($23) with gnocchi comes with a velvety *pioppini* mushroom sauce. Grilled rack of lamb ($35) is worth the splurge, but save some calories for dessert, such as Meyer lemon crème brûlée or white pineapple sorbet.

81-6372 Mamalahoa Hwy. (Hwy. 11, *makai* side), Kealakekua; park in lot next to Captain Cook Mini Market. www.misitalian bistro.com. © **808/323-3880.** Main courses $14–$35. Daily 4:30–8:30pm.

### Inexpensive

**Manago Hotel Restaurant** ★★ AMERICAN
Like its clean but plainspun hotel, the family-run dining room with Formica tabletops and vinyl-backed chairs has changed little over the years. Service is friendly and fairly swift, with family-style servings of rice, potato salad, and fresh vegetables accompanying the generous portions of pork chops, teri chicken, and sautéed mahimahi, among other popular choices. Breakfast is a steal: papaya or juice, toast or rice, two eggs, breakfast meat, and coffee for $6.

At the Manago Hotel, 82-6151 Mamalahoa Hwy. (Hwy. 11), Captain Cook, between mile markers 109 and 110, *makai* side. www.managohotel.com/rest.html. *℃* **808/323-2642.** Reservations recommended for dinner. Breakfast $5–$6, lunch and dinner $6–$15. Tues–Sun 7–9am, 11am–2pm, and 5–7:30pm.

## The Kohala Coast

*Note:* You'll find the following restaurants on "The Kohala Coast, Waimea & the Hamukua Coast" map on p. 151.

### SOUTH KOHALA

For cheaper but still convenient alternatives to pricey hotel dining, don't snub the food court in the Queens' MarketPlace in Waikoloa Beach Resort: **Lemongrass Express** ★★ (*℃* 808/886-3400) is a compact version of Kailua-Kona's tasty **Lemongrass Bistro** (p. 170), with indoor-outdoor seating and seafood specials that rival those of resort chefs. **Hawaiian Fish N Chips** ★ (*℃* 808/886-1595) smokes its own fish and serves local delicacies such oxtail soup, while **Ippy's Hawaiian BBQ** ★ (*℃* 808/886-8600) prepares well-seasoned plate lunches with ribs, chicken, and fish, under the aegis of Food Network celebrity Philip "Ippy" Aiona.

# SORTING OUT THE resorts

There's no getting around sticker shock when dining at the South Kohala resort hotels, especially at breakfast and lunch. Dazzling sunsets help soften the blow at dinner, when chefs at least show more ambition. Here's a quick guide to help you distinguish between the top dinner-only hotel restaurants, all serving excellent (for the most part) yet costly variations on farm-to-table Hawaii Regional Cuisine:

o **Mauna Lani: Brown's Beach House** ★★ at the **Fairmont Orchid Hawaii** (p. 150) offers attentive service at tables on a lawn just a stone's throw from the water; at **Canoe House** ★★ in the **Mauna Lani Bay Hotel & Bungalows** (p. 165), chef Allen Hess personally presents each dish of his "Captain's Table" Blind Tasting Menu ($110; $160 with wine pairings), offered Thursday to Saturday by 24-hour reservation (🕾 **808/881-7911**).

o **Mauna Kea: Manta & Pavilion Wine Bar** ★★★ at the **Mauna Kea Beach Hotel** (p. 154) offers a sweeping ocean view, artful cuisine, and 48 high-end wines by the glass from the nifty Enomatic dispenser. Less elegant but still worthy, **Coast Grille** ★★ at the **Hapuna Beach Prince Hotel** (p. 152) also provides an expansive view, plus the best value of all the resorts: the $55 four-course Locavore Series menu, a monthly showcase of a local ingredient such as corn, mango or avocado.

o **Waikoloa Beach: KPC– Kamuela Provision Company** ★ at the Hilton Waikoloa Village (p. 153) has the oceanfront setting to rival other resorts' restaurants, although its culinary ambitions are not as high as its prices. Be sure to book an outdoor table for at least a half-hour before sunset.

Views of Anaehoomalu Bay, especially at sunset, never fail to please at **Lava Lava Beach Club ★★**, which serves fresh American and island food from 11am to 9pm daily on the beach. Owned by the team behind **Huggo's** (p. 172), it's at the end of Kuualii Place in the Waikoloa Beach Resort (www.lavalava beachclub.com; ✆ **808/769-5282**).

The commercial port of Kawaihae also harbors several inexpensive, homespun eateries, including **Kohala Burger and Taco ★**, upstairs in the Kawaihae Shopping Center (www.kohalaburgerandtaco. com; ✆ **808/880-1923**). Its burgers are made with local grass-fed beef, while buns and tortillas (used for fresh fish tacos, burritos, and quesadillas) are housemade. It's open daily hours vary widely by season. The lunch wagon next to **Da Fish House** fish market (p. 202) naturally has very fresh fish plates ($9), though little seating; it's open weekdays 10:30am to 3:30pm and takes cash only.

### Expensive

**Monstera Noodles & Sushi ★★** JAPANESE Master sushi chef Norio Yamamoto left his namesake restaurant (still called Norio's) at the Fairmont Orchid Hawaii to open this bright, less formal dining room in the Shops at Mauna Lani. No worries if you're not a fan of raw fish: His "sizzling plates" menu includes New York strip steak in a choice of sauces, boneless fried chicken in spicy garlic-sesame sauce, and pork loin stir-fried with kimchee. But it would be a shame to skip seafood specialties like his volcano roll (a combination of spicy tuna and shrimp tempura with local avocado), or ultra-fresh, silken sashimi such as Hawaiian fatty tuna (*chu toro*). Individual dishes are moderately priced but add up quickly, especially if ordering from the gourmet sake or tropical cocktail menu has stimulated your appetite.

In the Shops at Mauna Lani, 68-1330 Mauna Lani Dr., Waimea. www.monsterasushi.com. ℭ **808/887-2711.** Reservations recommended. Main courses $18–$30; sushi (3 pieces) $7–$16; rolls $10–$22; sashimi $17–$20. Daily 5:30–9:30pm. Restaurant is on upper level; access by stairs or elevator from patio.

## Moderate

**Café Pesto ★★** PIZZA/PACIFIC RIM  Locals may dart in and out for wood-fired pizzas to go, but there's something to be said for enjoying the capable service and cozy yet uncluttered atmosphere of the original Café Pesto, which opened in 1988, joined by a Hilo branch (p. 187) 4 years later. More local produce and proteins appear on the menu now, but otherwise the pizzas, meal-size salads, hearty pastas, and "creative island cuisine" (such as zesty wok-fired shrimp and scallops in a red coconut curry) continue to impress year after year. The playful children's menu ($8) also brims with healthful but enticing choices, including pasta and kalua turkey over rice.

Lower level of Kawaihae Shopping Center, 61-3665 Akoni Pule Hwy. (Hwy. 270, *makai* side), Kawaihae. www.cafepesto.com. ℭ **808/882-1071.** Main courses $11–$17 lunch, $15–$37 dinner. Pizza $10–$21. Sun–Thurs 11am–9pm; Fri–Sat 11am–10pm. To park in front of restaurant, take Kawaihae Harbor spur from Hwy. 270; Cafe Pesto is on the right.

**Pueo's Osteria ★★★** ITALIAN  Upcountry residents and night owls rejoiced when this inviting bistro opened in Waikoloa Village Highlands Center in 2013, but its appeal goes far beyond its location (an 8-minute drive uphill of the Waikoloa Beach Resort) and late hours. Executive chef-owner James Babian, who lined up more than 150 local food purveyors for Four Seasons Hualalai during his tenure there, continues to work his connections for the freshest seafood, meat, and produce, while importing only the finest of everything else (including olive oil and well-priced wines) to create a delicious Italian menu. Bargain hunters will love the "early owl" specials and bar menu, which includes a Tuscan burger made with local beef, provolone, and bruschetta tomatoes, served with house-made fries for just $12; build-your-own wood-fired pizzas start at $13. For dinner, the grilled octopus appetizer ($14) is a silky, smoky delight, while Babian has an equally tender touch with fresh pasta ($17–$25) and hearty meat dishes such as chicken Milanese ($18) or lamb osso buco ($33). Reserve early, and request a table on the covered patio.

In Waikoloa Village Highlands Center, 68-1845 Waikoloa Rd., Waikoloa. www.pueososteria.com. © **808/339-7566.** Main courses $16–$33; pizza $14–$18; bar menu $6–$13. Reservations recommended. Dinner 5–9pm daily; bar Sun–Thurs 5pm–1am, Fri–Sat 5pm–2am (bar menu 5pm–midnight daily).

## NORTH KOHALA

For a light meal or snack, stop at **Kohala Coffee Mill ★**, 55-3412 Akoni Pule Hwy. (*mauka* side, across from Bamboo, below; © **808/889-5577**). Known best for scoops of Tropical Dreams ice cream (p. 183) and well-crafted coffee drinks, it's open weekdays 6am to 6pm, weekends 7am to 6pm. In Kapaau, homey **Minnie's Ohana Lim Style ★**, 54-3854 Akoni Pule Hwy. (*mauka* side, at Kamehameha Rd.), serves heaping portions of fresh fish, roast pork, and plate-lunch staples (© **808/889-5288;** Mon–Thurs 11am–8pm, Fri 11am–3pm and 6–8:30pm).

### Moderate

**Bamboo ★★** PACIFIC RIM    Dining here is a trip, literally and figuratively. A half-hour away from the nearest resort, Bamboo adds an element of time travel, with vintage decor behind the screen doors of its pale-blue, plantation-era building; an art gallery and quirky gift shop provide great browsing if you have to wait for a table. And in these parts, the food is well worth the wait, from local lunch faves such as barbecued baby-back ribs to a veggie stir-fry of soba noodles or grilled chicken with a kicky Thai-style coconut sauce. Dinner adds more fresh-catch preparations, including a grilled filet with a tangy *lilikoi* mustard sauce balanced by crispy goat cheese polenta. If you're dining on Friday or Saturday night, you may luck into live music. **Note:** Bamboo's yummy *lilikoi* cocktails have inspired a line of drink mixes you can buy to re-create the hang-loose vibe at home.

55-3415 Akoni Pule Hwy. (Hwy. 270, just west of Hwy. 250/Hawi Rd.), Hawi. www.bamboorestaurant.info. © **808/889-5555.** Dinner reservations recommended. Main courses $10–$20 lunch, $15–$35 dinner (full- and half-size portions available at dinner). Tues–Sat 11:30am–2:30pm and 6–8pm; Sun brunch 11:30am–2:30pm.

## WAIMEA

Daunted by high-priced hotel breakfasts? Visit the inexpensive **Hawaiian Style Café** ★, 65-1290 Kawaihae

---

### Tropical Dreams: Ice Cream Reveries

Founded in North Kohala in 1983, ultra-rich **Tropical Dreams** ★★★ ice cream is sold all over the island now, but you'll find the most flavors at the retail store next to its Waimea factory, 66-1250 Lalamilo Farm Rd. (off Hwy. 19; www.tropicaldreamsicecream. com; © **888/888-8031**). For a truly tropical sensation, try ice creams such as Tahitian vanilla, lychee, or poha, or sorbets like dragonfruit, passion-guava, or white pineapple ($3.50 for an 8 oz. cup—the smallest size available). It's open weekdays 8am to 4:30pm.

Rd. (Hwy. 19, 1 block east of Opelo Rd.; ☏ **808/885-4925**), which serves pancakes bigger than your head (try them with warm *haupia*, a coconut pudding), kalua pork hash, Portuguese blood sausage, and other local favorites. It's cash only, and very crowded on weekends (Mon–Sat 7am–1:30pm; until noon Sun).

### Expensive

**Merriman's** ★★★ HAWAII REGIONAL   This is where it all began in 1988 for chef Peter Merriman, one of the founders of Hawaii Regional Cuisine and an early adopter of the farm-to-table trend. Now head of a statewide culinary empire that includes various Merriman's and Monkeypod Kitchen incarnations on the four major islands, the busy Merriman has entrusted chef Eric Purugganan with maintaining his high standards and inventive flair. Lunch offers terrific values, such as the grilled fresh fish ($15), while weekend brunch includes a luscious eggs Benedict with ham and jalapeño hollandaise, and a less guilt-inducing kale and beet salad with chèvre and smoke-marinated grape tomatoes. At dinner, you can order Merriman's

Wok charred ahi tuna from Merriman's.

famed wok-charred ahi, grass-fed steak, or molten chocolate purse with vanilla bean ice cream—but you'll also want to consider Purugganan's fresh-catch dish, often inspired by his herb garden, or his three-course "chef's choice" dinner ($69).

At the Opelo Plaza, 65-1227 Opelo Rd., off Hwy. 19, Waimea. www.merrimanshawaii.com. © **808/885-6822.** Reservations recommended. Main courses $11–$15 lunch, $29–$54 dinner (half-portions $23–$37). Mon–Fri 11:30am–1:30pm; daily 5:30–9pm; Sat–Sun brunch 10am–1pm.

### Moderate

**Village Burger** ★★ BURGERS Tucked into a cowboy-themed shopping center with a drafty food court (bring a jacket or sit by the fireplace), this burger stand run by former Four Seasons Lanai and Mauna Lani Bay chef Edwin Goto has a compact menu: plump burgers made with local grass-fed beef or "red veal," grilled ahi, or taro (when available); thick, sumptuous shakes made from Tropical Dreams ice cream (see above); and hand-cut, twice-cooked fries, with or without Parmesan "goop" (consider your salt intake first). Other than that, there's just an ahi Niçoise salad ($12) featuring island greens—but it's also delicious. Try the mamaki tea, if on offer; it's brewed from native plants grown by local school kids.

In the Parker Ranch Center, 67-1185 Mamalahoa Hwy., Waimea. www.villageburgerwaimea.com. © **808/885-7319.** Burgers $8–$12. Mon–Sat 10:30am–8pm; Sun 10:30am–6pm.

## The Hamakua Coast

This lovely but little-populated area holds few dinner options, and those tend to close early, so plan ahead. *Note:* You'll find these restaurants on "The Kohala Coast, Waimea & the Hamakua Coast" map on p. 151.

**Café Il Mondo** ★ PIZZA/ESPRESSO BAR   To order a medium or large version of the pleasantly crusty, stone-oven-baked pizzas, you'll have to get it to go. But if you can find a space in this very cozy bistro, pick your own pie ($12–$15), or consider one of the calzones with the cafe's signature pesto sauce, made with macadamia nuts in lieu of pine nuts. The best values may be the Mama Mia dinners ($13): roast chicken with twice-baked potatoes or beef lasagna with focaccia, both with a garden salad. Arrive before 5pm to try one of the sandwiches in freshly baked bread or focaccia buns. *Note:* Bring your own beer and wine (**Malama Market** is just around the corner); the pizzeria charges $2 to $5 for corkage, depending on how many are imbibing.

45-3626 Mamane St. (Hwy. 240, at Lehua St.), Honokaa. € **808/775-7711.** Main courses $7–$15 lunch, $11–$15 dinner. No credit cards. Mon–Sat 11am–8pm.

**Tex Drive-In & Restaurant** ★★ AMERICAN/LOCAL   The two stars here are only for the *malasadas,* Portuguese sweetbread doughnut holes fried to order, dusted in sugar, and available (for 65¢ more) with a filling, such as Bavarian cream, tropical jellies—guava, mango, pineapple—and chocolate. The Tex malasada is square, larger, and a little chewier than the traditional version, and sometimes Tex runs out of certain fillings, but the plain are quite satisfying. Often full of tour groups, Tex also serves burgers, hot dogs, sandwiches, and Hawaiian plate lunches that are modestly priced but adequate at best; you're better off checking out the whimsical gift shop and then continuing on to Waimea or central Honokaa for a full meal.

45-690 Pakalana St., off Hwy. 19, Honokaa. www.texdriveinhawaii.com. € **808/775-0598.** Malasadas $1.10 each, fillings 65¢. Main courses $5–$7 breakfast, $4–$9 lunch and dinner. Daily 6am–8pm.

# Hilo

Hawaii's second largest city hosts a raft of unpretentious eateries serving plate lunches and Japanese cuisine, reflecting East Hawaii's plantation heritage and largest ethnic group. A prime example of the former is **Ken's House of Pancakes ★**, 1730 Kamehameha Ave., at the corner of Hwys. 19 and 11 (www.kenshouseofpancakes.com; *©* **808/935-8711**), which serves large helpings of local dishes and American fare 24 hours a day. The ambience is even more basic (plastic trays and paper plates) at the venerable **Café 100** (www.cafe100.com; *©* **808/935-8683**), 969 Kilauea Ave., but the price is right, with hefty plate lunches for $7, burgers $2 and up, and more than 30 varieties of loco moco—meat, eggs, rice, and gravy—starting around $3; opt for brown rice to lessen the guilt. It's open daily at 6:45am, closing at 8:30pm Monday to Thursday, 9pm Friday, and 7:30pm Saturday.

**Miyo's ★**, 564 Hinano St. (www.miyosrestaurant.com; *©* **808/935-8825**), prides itself on "home-style" Japanese cooking, with locally sourced ingredients and a few welcome surprises, such as decadent pumpkin flan and a fluffy cheesecake. It's open daily except Sunday, 11am to 2pm for lunch (main courses $12–$16) and 5:30 to 8:30pm for dinner ($14–$18).

*Note:* You'll find the following restaurants and those listed above on the "Hilo" map on p. 56.

**Café Pesto ★★** PIZZA/PACIFIC RIM   The menu of wood-fired pizzas, pastas, risottos, fresh local seafood, and artfully prepared "creative island cuisine" such as mango-glazed chicken is much the same as at the original Kawaihae location (p. 181), and that's a good thing. Even better: the airy dining room in a restored 1912 building, with black-and-white tile floors and huge glass windows overlooking the vintage wooden buildings and palm trees of downtown Hilo. Service is attentive and swift, especially by island standards, but don't shy away from the two counters with high-backed chairs if the tables are full.

At the S. Hata Bldg., 308 Kamehameha Ave., Hilo. www.cafe pesto.com. © **808/969-6640.** Pizzas $10–$21; main courses $11–$17 lunch, $19–$30 dinner. Sun–Thurs 11am–9pm; Fri–Sat 11am–10pm.

**Hilo Bay Café ★★** PACIFIC RIM   Hidden in a strip mall for years, this ambitious restaurant moved in late 2013 to an elevated perch overlooking Hilo Bay, next to Suisan Fish Market and the lovely Liliuokalani Gardens. Fittingly, sushi and seafood dishes are the most reliable pleasers, including horseradish panko-crusted ono and grilled asparagus salad with pan-roasted salmon, but fresh produce from the Hilo Farmer's Market also inspires several dishes. Vegetarians will appreciate thoughtful options such as grilled herb eggplant with piquant chimichurri sauce or the Hamakua mushroom curry pot pie (one can add chicken or shrimp). The drink list is similarly creative, including locally sourced kombucha and craft beer. During daylight, ask for a seat on the covered lanai deck or at a table with a bay view.

123 Lihiwai St., just north of Banyan Dr., Hilo. www.hilobaycafe. com. © **808/935-4939.** Reservations recommended for dinner. Main courses $11–$17 lunch, $11–$20 dinner. Lunch 11am–5pm Mon–Sat (limited sushi 2–5pm). Dinner 5–9pm Sun–Thurs, 5–9:30pm Fri–Sat.

## Puna District

Options are limited and frankly often disappointing here, so plan mealtimes carefully and stock up on picnic supplies in Kailua-Kona or Hilo. *Note:* You'll find the following restaurants on the "Hotels & Restaurants in the Volcano Area" map (p. 163).

## VOLCANO VILLAGE

In addition to the listings below, look for the **Tuk-Tuk Thai Food** ★★ truck in front of the Volcano Inn, 19-3820 Old Volcano Rd. (www.tuk-tukthaifood.com; ✆ **808/747-3041**), from 11am to 6pm Tuesday to Saturday. You can even call ahead for its hearty curries and noodle dishes ($8–$10), about half the price of the Thai restaurant down the road.

### Expensive

**Kilauea Lodge Restaurant** ★★ CONTINENTAL Like his inn (for sale at press time), owner-chef Albert Jeyte's woodsy restaurant radiates *Gemütlichkeit,* that ineffable German sense of warmth and cheer, symbolized by the "International Fireplace of Friendship" studded with stones from around the world. Although starters can be ho-hum, the European-style main courses showcase unique proteins such as rabbit, antelope, buffalo, and duck, along with local grass-fed beef and lamb, plus the fresh catch (recommended). The wine list is well-priced, although *lilikoi* margaritas can quickly take the edge off a long day of exploring the nearby national park. Dinner prices are steep (perhaps due in part to the lack of competition), but lunch offers good values, including Kuahiwi Ranch grass-fed beef, buffalo and antelope burgers and a curried chicken bowl. Breakfast is another winner, especially the all-too-tempting French toast made with Punaluu Bake Shop's guava, taro, and white Portuguese sweetbread. 19-3948 Old Volcano Rd., Volcano. www.kilauealodge.com. ✆ **808/967-7366.** Reservations recommended. Main courses $8–$13 breakfast, $10–$13 lunch, $22–$49 dinner. Daily 7:30am–2pm and 5–9pm; Sun brunch 10am–2pm.

**Moderate**

**Café Ono** ★ VEGETARIAN  When burgers and plate lunches start to pall, this cafe and tearoom hidden in a quirky art studio/gallery provides a delectably light alternative. The all-vegetarian menu is concise: a soup or two, chili, lasagna, quiche (highly recommended), and sandwiches, most accompanied by a garden salad. Don't pass up the peanut butter and pumpkin soup if available, and ask if you can give Ernest the goat a bite to eat before you explore the lush gardens outside.

In Volcano Garden Arts, 19-3834 Old Volcano Rd., Volcano. www.volcanogardenarts.com. ✆ **808/985-8979.** Main courses $10–$15. Tues–Sun 11am–3pm.

## HAWAII VOLCANOES NATIONAL PARK

**The Rim** ★★ ISLAND FARM/SEAFOOD  By no means is this your typical national park concession, as some hot dog–seeking visitors are discouraged to find. Since the restored Volcano House hotel reopened in 2013, The Rim and the adjacent **Uncle George's Lounge** ★★ have tried to match their three-star views of Kilauea Caldera with a menu that's both artful and hyper-local. The bountiful breakfast buffet includes made-to-order eggs, tropical fruit smoothies, wild turkey hash, local bacon, and freshly baked pastries. Bento lunch boxes offer a choice of kalua pork, chicken braised with lemongrass and kaffir lime, an organic veggie/tofu stir-fry, or macadamia-nut fresh catch, plus four tasty sides and a *lilikoi* cream puff. Reserve well in advance for a window table at dinner, when lights are periodically dimmed to showcase the glow from Halemaumau Crater. Culinary highlights include *opakapaka* (pink snapper) wrapped in white pineapple, the rare-seared Kona *kampachi,* and the

## A TASTE of volcano wines

**Volcano Winery** (www.volcano winery.com; **☏ 877/967-7772**) has made a unique pit stop near Hawaii Volcanoes National Park since 1993, when it first started selling traditional grape wines, honey wines, and grape wines blended with tropical fruits. Del and Marie Bothof have owned the winery since 1999, planting Pinot Noir and Cayuga White grapes in 2000 and expanding into tea in 2006. Their latest wine is called Infusion, a macadamia-nut honey wine infused with estate-grown black tea. Wine tastings, for ages 21 and up, are $5 to $8; there's also a picnic area under cork and koa trees. The tasting room and store, 35 Pii Mauna Dr. in Volcano (just off Hwy. 11 near the 30-mile marker), are open 10am to 5:30pm daily.

Kuahiwi Ranch steak of the day, served with local wilted kale and mashed Okinawan sweet potatoes. The lounge serves excellent *pupus* ($12–$17) such as chicken satay and avocado dip. *Note:* Diners must pay park admission ($10 a vehicle, good for 7 days).

In Volcano House, 1 Crater Rim Dr., Volcano. www.hawaiivolcano house.com. **☏ 808/756-9625.** Reservations recommended. Breakfast buffet $18 adults, $9 children; lunch bentos $19 adults, $11 children; dinner main courses $19–$39. Daily breakfast buffet 7–10am, lunch 11am–2pm, dinner 5–9pm. Lounge daily 11am–9pm.

## PAHOA

**Kaleo's Bar & Grill ★★** ECLECTIC/LOCAL    The best restaurant for miles around has a wide-ranging menu, ideal for multiple visits, and a welcoming, homey atmosphere. Local staples such as chicken katsu and spicy Korean kalbi ribs won't disappoint, but look for dishes with slight twists, such as tempura ahi roll with spicy *lilikoi* sauce or the blackened-ahi BLT with avocado and mango mayo, served with organic greens or fries. The Mediterranean appetizer platter ($15) makes a great vegetarian meal with pesto tomatoes, hummus, grilled veggies, and other goodies. Kids can find pasta and burger choices to their liking. Save room for the *lilikoi* cheesecake or banana spring rolls with ice cream.

15-2969 Pahoa Village Rd., Pahoa. www.kaleoshawaii.com. *©* **808/965-5600.** Main courses $7–$16 lunch, $12–$27 dinner. Daily 11am–9pm.

## Kau District

When you're driving between Kailua-Kona and Hawaii Volcanoes National Park in Naalehu, it's good to know about two places on Highway 11 in Naalehu for a quick pick-me-up. The **Punaluu Bake Shop** ★ (www.bakeshophawaii.com; *©* **866/366-3501** or 808/929-7343) is the busier tourist attraction, famed for its varieties of Portuguese sweetbread (including taro, mango, and guava), now seen in stores across the islands; clean restrooms, a deli counter, and gift shop are also part of the appeal. It's open 9am to 5pm daily. Across the highway off a small lane lies **Hana Hou Restaurant** ★ (www.hanahourestaurant.com; *©* **808/929-9717**), which boasts a bakery counter with equally tempting sweets (try the macnut pie or *lilikoi* bar) and a small, retro dining room serving simple but fresh and filling plate lunches ($8–$17), burgers, sandwiches, and quesadillas; look for the large sign saying eat. It's open Sunday through Thursday 8am to 7pm (until 8pm Fri and Sat).

This island is fertile ground, not just for the coffee, tea, chocolate, macadamia nuts, and honey that make tasty souvenirs, but also for artists inspired by the volcanic cycle of destruction and creation, the boundless energy of the ocean, and the timeless beauty of native crafts. For those cooking meals or packing a picnic, see the "Edibles" listings.

**Note:** Stores are open daily unless otherwise stated.

## The Kona Coast
### KAILUA-KONA

For bargain shopping with an island flair, bypass the T-shirt and trinket shops and head 2 miles south from Kailua Pier to **Alii Gardens Marketplace,** 75-6129 Alii Dr., a friendly, low-key combination farmer's market, flea market, and crafts fair, with plenty of parking and tent-covered stalls. You'll find fun items handmade in Hawaii as well as China's factories. On Tuesday, Wednesday, and Saturday, visit the **Kona Natural Soap Company** stand (www.konanaturalsoapcompany.com) and let Greg Colden explain the all-natural ingredients he uses, many grown at his farm in Keauhou.

In Kailua-Kona's historic district, the funky, family-run **Pacific Vibrations** (© **808/329-4140**) has colorful surfwear; it's at 75-5702 Likana Lane, an alley

# SHOPPING

by Jeanne Cooper

off Alii Drive just north of Mokuaikaua Church. Across the street, the nonprofit **Hulihee Palace Gift Shop** stocks arts and crafts by local artists, including gorgeous feather lei, silk scarves, art cards, aprons, and woven lauhala hats (www.daughtersofhawaii.org; ✆ 808/329-6558; closed Sun).

**Keauhou Shopping Center**, above Alii Drive at King Kamehameha III Road (www.keauhouvillage shops.com), has more restaurants and services than shops, but check out **Kona Stories** (www.kona stories.com; ✆ 808/324-0350) for thousands of books, especially Hawaiiana and children's titles. Also in the mall, **Jams World** (www.jamsworld.com; ✆ 808/322-9361) has kicky, comfortable resort wear for men and women, from a Hawaii company founded in 1964. Local hula *halau* perform hour-long shows Fridays at 6pm on the Heritage Court Stage. (Be sure to peek inside the center's free Heritage Center Museum, too.)

## HOLUALOA

Charmingly rustic Holualoa, 1,400 feet and 10 minutes above Kailua-Kona at the top of Hualalai Road, is the perfect spot for visiting coffee farms (p. 32) and tasteful galleries, with a half-dozen or more within a short distance of each other on Mamalahoa Highway (Hwy. 180). Among them, **Studio 7 Fine Arts** (www.studio7hawaii.com; ✆ 808/324-1335), a virtual Zen garden with pottery, wall hangings, and paper collages by Setsuko Morinoue and paintings and prints by husband Hiroki. *Note:* Most galleries are closed Sunday and Monday; see www.holualoahawaii.com for more listings.

Lovers of lauhala, the Hawaiian art of weaving leaves (*lau*) from the pandanus tree (*hala*), revel in

**Kimura's Lauhala Shop,** farther south on the *makai* side of Mamalahoa Hwy. at Hualalai Rd. Founded in 1914, the store brims with locally woven mats, hats, handbags, and slippers, plus Kona coffee, koa wood bowls, and feather hatbands. It's closed Sunday.

## SOUTH KONA

Many stores along Highway 11, the main road, are roadside fruit and/or coffee stands, well worth pulling over for, if only to "talk story" and pick up a snack. One exception: the wonderfully eclectic **Antiques and Orchids,** 81-6224 Mamalahoa Hwy., Captain Cook, in a circa-1906 building (② 808/323-9851; closed Sun). Owner Beverly Napolitan's orchids grace Hawaiiana, Victorian, and other antiques and collectibles; an antiques mall sells fellow vendors' "mantiques": vintage tools, fishing gear, and sports memorabilia. Fabric aficionados must stop at **Kimura Store,** a quaint general store and textile emporium with more than 10,000 bolts of aloha prints and other colorful cloth, at 79-7408 Mamalahoa Hwy. (ocean side), Kainaliu (② 808/322-3771; closed Sun).

# The Kohala Coast
## SOUTH KOHALA

Three open-air shopping malls claim the bulk of stores here, with a few island-only boutiques amid state and national chains. The real plus is the malls' free entertainment (check their websites for current calendars) and prices somewhat lower than those of shops in resort hotels.

The Waikoloa Beach Resort has two malls, both off its main drag, Waikoloa Beach Road. **Kings' Shops** (www.kingsshops.com) has a *keiki* (children's) hula performance at 6pm Friday and music by Kahalanui, a

Hawaiian swing band, at 7pm Wednesday. Along with luxury stores (**Tiffany, Louis Vuitton, Coach**), find affordable swimwear at **Making Waves** (© 808/886-1814) and batik-print fashions at **Noa** (© 808/886-5449). **Queens' MarketPlace** (http://queensmarket place.net) includes two fun places for families: **Local Lizard & Friends** (© 808/886-8900), with gecko-themed clothes, toys and tchotchkes, and **Giggles** (© 808/886-0014). Its free shows include hula and Polynesian dance Monday, Wednesday, and Friday at 6pm.

The **Shops at Mauna Lani** (www.shopsat maunalani.com), on the main road of the Mauna Lani Resort, presents hula and Polynesian fire dancing Monday and Thursday at 7pm. As for its stores, **Hawaiian Island Creations** (www.hicsurf.com; © 808/881-1400) stands out for its diverse lineup of local, state, and national surfwear brands.

In **Kawaihae,** an unassuming shopping strip on Highway 270, just north of the Highway 19 intersection, hosts **Harbor Gallery** (www.harborgallery.biz; © 808/882-1510), displaying the works of more than 150 Big Island artists, and specializing in koa and other wood furniture, bowls, and sculpture. Stock up on savory souvenirs at **Hamakua Macadamia Nut Factory** (p. 38).

## NORTH KOHALA

When making the trek to the Pololu Valley Lookout, you'll pass a few stores of note along Hwy. 270. **As Hawi Turns,** 2 miles west of the Kohala Mountain Road (Hwy. 250), features eclectic women's clothing, locally made jewelry, home decor, and a consignment area cheekily called As Hawi Returns (© 808/889-5203).

Across from the King Kamehameha Statue in Kapaau, **Ackerman Gallery** features arts and crafts from the Big Island, including paintings by owner Gary Ackerman (www.ackermangalleries.com; © **808/889-5971;** closed Sun).

## WAIMEA

The barn-red buildings of **Parker Square,** on the south side of Highway 19 east of Opelo Road, hold several pleasant surprises. The **Gallery of Great Things** (www.galleryofgreatthingshawaii.com; © **808/885-7706**) has high-quality Hawaiian artwork, including quilts and Niihau shell leis, as well as pieces from throughout the Pacific. Sticking closer to home, literally, **Bentley's Home & Garden Collection** (www.bentleyshomecollection.com; © **808/885-5565**) is chock-full of Western and country-inspired clothes, accessories, and cottage decor.

# East Hawaii

## HAMUKUA COAST

Park on Mamane Street (Hwy. 240) in "downtown" **Honokaa** and stroll through a huge selection of antiques and collectibles at the warehouse-sized **Honokaa Trading Company** (© **808/775-0808;** closed Mon). If you'd like something newer, head to **Big Island Grown,** selling edibles such as coffee, tea, and honey, plus locally made gifts and clothing (© **808/775-9777;** closed Sun), or **Taro Patch Gifts** (www.taropatchgifts.com; © **808/775-7228**), which adds books to the mix. **Waipio Valley Artworks** (www.waipiovalleyartworks.com; © **808/775-0958**), on Kukuihaele Road near the overlook, has many handsome wood items, plus a cafe.

Hilo Farmers Market.

## HILO

Hawaii's second-largest city has both mom-and-pop shops and big-box stores. The **Hilo Farmer's Market** is the prime attraction (see "A Feast for the Senses," below), but you should also hit the following for *omiyage,* or edible souvenirs: **Big Island Candies,** 585 Hinano St. (www.bigislandcandies.com; ℂ **808/935-5510**) and **Two Ladies Kitchen,** 274 Kilauea Ave. (ℂ **808/961-4766,** closed Sun). Big Island Candies is a factory store and busy tourist attraction that cranks out addictive macadamia-nut shortbread cookies. A cash-only hole-in-the-wall, Two Ladies Kitchen makes delicious *mochi,* a pounded-rice treat (try the one with a giant strawberry inside, if available), and *manju,* a kind of mini-turnover.

Visit **Sig Zane Designs,** 122 Kamehameha Ave. (www.sigzane.com; ℂ **808/935-7077,** closed Sun), for apparel and home items with Zane's fabric designs, inspired by native Hawaiian plants and culture,

You can't beat the **Hilo Farmer's Market** (www.hilofarmersmarket.com), considered by many the best in the state, from its dazzling display of tropical fruits and flowers (especially orchids) to savory prepared foods such as pad Thai and bento boxes, plus locally made crafts and baked goods, all in stalls pleasantly crammed around the corner of Kamehameha Avenue and Mamo Street. The full version takes place 6am to 4pm Wednesday and Saturday; go early for the best selection and fewest crowds. (About 30 vendors set up at 7am–4pm the rest of the week, but it's not quite the same experience.)

including wife Nalani Kanakaole's hula lineage. **Basically Books,** 160 Kamehameha Ave. (www.basicallybooks.com; ✆ **808/961-0144**), is also happy to educate you with a wide assortment of maps and books emphasizing Hawaii and the Pacific.

## PUNA DISTRICT

One of the prettiest places to visit in **Volcano Village** is **Volcano Garden Arts,** 19-3834 Old Volcano Rd. (www.volcanogardenarts.com; ✆ **808/985-8979;** closed Mon), offering beautiful gardens with sculptures and open studios; delicious **Café Ono** (p. 190); and an airy gallery of artworks (some by owner Ira Ono), jewelry, and home decor by local artists. Look for Hawaiian quilts and fabrics, as well as island-made butters and jellies, at **Kilauea Kreations,** 19-3972 Old Volcano Rd. (www.kilaueakreations.com; ✆ **808/967-8090**).

In Hawaii Volcanoes National Park, the two **gift shops** at Volcano House (p. 165) have surprisingly tasteful gifts, many of them made on the Big Island, as well as attractive jackets for chilly nights. The original 1877 Volcano House, a short walk from the Kilauea Visitor Center, is home to the nonprofit **Volcano Art Center** (www.volcanoartcenter.org; © **808/967-7565**), which sells locally made artworks, including the intricate, iconic prints of Dietrich Varez, who worked at the modern Volcano House in his youth.

## Edibles

Since most visitors stay on the island's west side, the Hilo Farmer's Market isn't really an option to stock their larders. In in Kailua-Kona, visit the **Keauhou Farmer's Market** (www.keauhoufarmersmarket.com) from 8am to noon Saturday at the **Keauhou Shopping Center** (near Ace Hardware), for locally grown produce, fresh eggs, baked goods, coffee, and flowers. Pick up the rest of what you need at the center's **KTA Super Stores** (www.ktasuperstores.com; © **808/323-2311**), a Big Island grocery chain founded in 1916 at which you can find island-made specialties (poke, mochi) as well as national brands. Another **KTA** is in the Kona Coast Shopping Center, 74-5588 Palani Rd. (© **808/329-1677**), open daily until 11pm. Wine aficionados will be amazed at the large and well-priced selection in **Kona Wine Market,** in the Kona Commons Shopping Center, 74-5450 Makala Blvd. (www.konawinemarket.com; © **808/329-9400**). If you have a **Costco** membership, its only Big Island warehouse is at 73-4800 Maiau St., near Highway 19 and Hina Lani Street (© **808/331-4800**).

On the Kohala Coast, the best prices are in **Waimea,** home to a **KTA** in Waimea Center, Highway 19 at Pulalani Road (© **808/885-8866**). Buy smoked meat and fish, hot *malasadas* (doughnut holes), baked goods, and ethnic foods along with a cornucopia of produce at the **Waimea Homestead Farmer's Market,** Saturday 7am to noon at Kuhio Hale, 64-759 Kahilu Rd., near Hwy. 19's mile marker 55 (www.waimeafarmersmarket.com). The best deals for fresh fish are at **Da Fish House,** 61-3665 Akoni Pule Hwy. (Hwy. 270) in Kawaihae (✆ **808/882-1052;** closed Sun). Among resort options, **Foodland Farms** in the Shops at Mauna Lani (www.foodland. com; ✆ **808/887-6101**), has top-quality local produce and seafood, while the Kings' Shops hosts a decent **farmer's market** Wednesday 8:30am to 3pm. In the Queens' MarketPlace, **Island Gourmet Markets** (www.islandgourmethawaii.com; ✆ **808/886-3577**) has an almost overwhelming array of delicacies, including 200-plus kinds of cheese.

# NIGHTLIFE

by Jeanne Cooper

With few exceptions, the Big Island tucks in early, all the better to rise at daybreak, when the weather is cool and the roads (and waves) are open. But live Hawaiian music is everywhere, and it's easy to catch free, engaging hula shows, too, at several open-air resort malls (see "Big Island Shopping," p. 193).

## Kailua-Kona

When the sun goes down, the scene heats up around Alii Drive. Among the hot spots: **On the Rocks,** next to Huggo's restaurant, at 75-5824 Kahakai Rd. (www. huggosontherocks.com; ℃ **808/329-1493**), has Hawaiian music and hula nightly, going until midnight Friday and Saturday and 10pm Sunday. Across the way in the Coconut Grove Market Place, **Laverne's Sports Bar** (formerly Lulu's; www.laverneskona.com; ℃ **808/331-2633**) draws a 20-something crowd with happy-hour specials, theme nights, and late-night DJs on weekends; it's open until 2am nightly. Next door, an eclectic mix of musicians—including jazz, country, and rock bands—perform at **Bongo Ben's,** 75-5819 Alii Dr. (www.bongobens.com; ℃ **808/329-9203**), open until 10pm nightly. **Rays on the Bay,** at the **Sheraton Kona Resort & Spa** (p. 147), lures locals and visitors to Keauhou with firepits, a great happy hour, nightly live music, and perhaps best of all, free valet parking.

PREVIOUS PAGE: **Luau at the Hilton Waikoloa Village**

## Sharing Stories & Aloha Under the Stars

If your timing is right, your visit will include the best free entertainment on the island: **Twilight at Kalahuipua'a,** a monthly Hawaiian-style celebration on the lawn in front of the oceanside Eva Parker Woods Cottage on the Mauna Lani Resort (www. maunalani.com/about/big-island-hawaii-events; ✆ **808/ 881-7911**). On the Saturday closest to the full moon, revered entertainers and local *kupuna* (elders) gather to "talk story," play music, and dance hula. The 3-hour show starts at 5:30pm, but the audience starts arriving an hour earlier, with picnic fare and beach mats. Bring yours, and plan to share food as well as the fun. Parking is free, too.

## The Kohala Coast

All the resort hotels have at least one lounge with nightly live music, usually Hawaiian, often with hula. Members of the renowned **Lim Family** perform at varying times and venues in the **Mauna Lani Bay Hotel & Bungalows** (p. 155), while award-winning singer **Darlene Ahuna** sings from 7 to 10pm Tues–Thurs in the **Reef Lounge** of the Hapuna Beach Prince Hotel (p. 152). **Lava Lava Beach Club** (p. 180) has created a lively scene at the Waikoloa Beach Resort with nightly music and hula right on the sand of "A-Bay."

Just beyond the resorts, the **Blue Dragon,** 61-3616 Kawaihae Rd., Kawaihae (www.bluedragon restaurant.com; ✆ **808/882-7771**), is a great open-air music spot. Here you can enjoy music—jazz, rock, Hawaiian swing—often with dancing, Thursday through Sunday.

For a uniquely Big Island alternative to a luau, try **An Evening at Kahua Ranch** (www.kahuaranch.

com; © **808/882-7954**), a barbecue with open bar, line dancing, rope tricks, a campfire singalong, and stargazing, on a working North Kohala ranch. The 3-hour event costs $119 for adults and $60 for kids 6 to 11 (free for kids under 6) with hotel shuttle; drive yourself and it's $95 and $48, respectively. Festivities start at 6pm Wednesday in summer, 5:30pm in winter.

## Hilo & the Hamakua Coast

Opened in 1925, the neoclassical **Palace Theater,** 38 Haili St. (www.hilopalace.com; © **808/934-7010**), screens first-run independent movies and hosts concerts, festivals, hula, and theater to pay for its ongoing restoration. **Hilo Town Tavern,** 168 Keawe St. (© **808/935-2171**), is a Cajun restaurant and dive bar open until 2am daily, with a nice pool room and live music (hip-hop to Hawaiian). The tavern supports downtown Hilo's **First Friday Art Walk,** the first Friday of each month, when shops and galleries offer music and refreshments until 8pm. The **Honokaa First Friday** event has a similar format and monthly schedule, with stores open late, sidewalk vendors, and live music from 5 until 9pm.

## Puna District

Although the revered founder of **Uncle Robert's Awa Club** (© **808/443-6913**), Robert Keliihoomalu, passed away in 2015, the bustling Wednesday-night marketplace (5–10pm) continues at his family compound at the end of the road in Kalapana, with live music from 6 to 9pm. Sample the mildly intoxicating *awa* (the Hawaiian word for kava) at the tiki bar then, or come back Friday night for more live music,

# luaus' new taste **OF OLD HAWAII**

Let's face it: You may never have a truly great meal at a luau, due to the numbers served, but on the Big Island you can have a very good one, with a highly enjoyable—and educational—show to boot. Buffets now offer more intriguing, tasty items such as pohole ferns and Molokai sweet potatoes, while shows feature more local history, from the first voyagers to *paniolo* days, plus a spectacular fire knife dance and Polynesian revue. I recommend one of these oceanfront luaus:

○ **Haleo** (www.haleoluau. com) at the **Sheraton Kona Resort & Spa** (p. 147) is simply the best in Kailua-Kona (Mon 4:30pm; $95 adults, $45 children 6–12).

○ **Gathering of the Kings** (www.gatheringofthekings. com) at the **Fairmont Orchid Hawaii** (p. 150), has the best selection of island-style food, including the taro leaf stew that gave *lū'au* their name (Sat 4:30pm; $109 adults, $75 children 5–12).

○ **Legends of Hawaii** (www. hiltonwaikoloavillage.com/ resort-experiences) at **Hilton Waikoloa Village** (p. 153) is the most family-friendly, with pillow seating upfront for kids, plus a show-only option (Tues, Fri, and Sun 5:30pm; $112 adults, $102 seniors and teens 13–17, $57 children 5–12; free for children 4 and under); show only, $65 adults, $45 ages 5–12. Prices $2–$5 higher July to mid-Aug.)

starting at 6. In Pahoa, **Kaleo's Bar & Grill ★★** (p. 191) offers nightly live music, including jazz and slack key.

# HAWAII IN CONTEXT

by Shannon Wianecki

Since the Polynesians ventured across the Pacific to the Hawaiian Islands 1,000 years ago, these floating jewels have continued to call visitors from around the globe.

Located in one of the most remote and isolated places on the planet, the islands bask in the warm waters of the Pacific, where they are blessed by a tropical sun and cooled by gentle year-round trade winds—creating what might be the most ideal climate imaginable. Mother Nature has carved out verdant valleys, hung brilliant rainbows in the sky, and trimmed the islands with sandy beaches in a spectrum of colors. The indigenous Hawaiian culture embodies the "spirit of aloha," an easy-going generosity that takes the shape of flower leis freely given, monumental feasts shared with friends and family, and hypnotic Hawaiian melodies played late into the tropical night.

Visitors are drawn to Hawaii not only for its incredible beauty, but also for its opportunities for adventure. Go on, gaze into that fiery volcano, swim in a sea of rainbow-colored fish, tee off on a championship golf course, hike through a rainforest to hidden waterfalls, and kayak into the deep end of the ocean, where whales leap out of the water for reasons still mysterious. Looking for rest and relaxation? You'll discover that life moves at an unhurried pace here. Extra doses of sun and sea allow both body and mind to recharge.

FACING PAGE: **Fire dancers.**

Hawaii is a sensory experience that will remain with you, locked in your memory, long after your tan fades. Years later, a sweet fragrance, the sun's warmth on your face, or the sound of the ocean breeze will deliver you back to the time you spent in the Hawaiian Islands.

# THE FIRST HAWAIIANS

Throughout the Middle Ages, while Western sailors clung to the edges of continents for fear of falling off the earth's edge, Polynesian voyagers crisscrossed the planet's largest ocean. The first people to colonize Hawaii were unsurpassed navigators. Using the stars, birds, and currents as guides, they sailed double-hulled canoes across thousands of miles, zeroing in on tiny islands in the center of the Pacific. They packed their vessels with food, plants, medicine, tools, and animals: everything necessary for building a new life on a distant shore. Over a span of 800 years, the great Polynesian migration connected a vast triangle of islands stretching from New Zealand to Hawaii to Easter Island and encompassing the many diverse archipelagos in between. Archaeologists surmise that Hawaii's first wave of settlers came via the Marquesas Islands sometime after A.D. 1000, though oral histories suggest a much earlier date.

Over the ensuing centuries, a distinctly Hawaiian culture arose. Sailors became farmers and fishermen. These early Hawaiians were as skilled on land as they had been at sea; they built highly productive fish ponds, aqueducts to irrigate terraced *kalo loi* (taro patches), and 3-acre *heiau* (temples) with 50-foot-high rock walls. Farmers cultivated more than 400 varieties of *kalo,* their staple food; 300 types of sweet potato; and 40 different bananas. Each variety served a different need—some were drought resistant, others medicinal, and others good for babies. Hawaiian women fashioned intricately patterned *kapa* (barkcloth)—some of the finest in all of Polynesia. Each of the Hawaiian Islands was its own kingdom, governed by *alii* (high-ranking chiefs) who drew their authority from an established caste system and *kapu* (taboos). Those who broke the *kapu* could be sacrificed.

The ancient Hawaiian creation chant, the *Kumulipo,* depicts a universe that began when heat and light emerged out of darkness, followed by the first life form: a coral polyp. The 2,000-line epic poem is a grand genealogy, describing how all species are interrelated, from gently waving seaweeds to mighty human warriors. It is the basis for the Hawaiian concept of *kuleana,* a word that simultaneously refers to privilege and responsibility. To this day, Native Hawaiians view the care of their natural resources as a filial duty and honor.

# WESTERN CONTACT
## Cook's Ill-Fated Voyage

In the dawn hours of January 18, 1778, Captain James Cook of the HMS *Resolution* spotted an unfamiliar set of islands, which he later named for his benefactor, the Earl of Sandwich. The 50-year-old sea captain was already famous in Britain for "discovering" much of the South Pacific. Now on his third great voyage of exploration, Cook had set sail from Tahiti northward across uncharted waters. He was searching for the mythical Northwest Passage that was said to link the

Pacific and Atlantic oceans. On his way, he stumbled upon Hawaii (aka the Sandwich Isles) quite by chance.

With the arrival of the *Resolution,* Stone Age Hawaii entered the age of iron. Sailors swapped nails and munitions for fresh water, pigs, and the affections of Hawaiian women. Tragically, the foreigners brought with them a terrible cargo: syphilis, measles, and other diseases that decimated the Hawaiian people. Captain Cook estimated the native population at 400,000 in 1778. (Later historians claim it could have been as high as 900,000.) By the time Christian missionaries arrived 40 years later, the number of Native Hawaiians had plummeted to just 150,000.

In a skirmish over a stolen boat, Cook was killed by a blow to the head. His British countrymen sailed home, leaving Hawaii forever altered. The islands were now on the sea charts, and traders on the fur route between Canada and China stopped here to get fresh water. More trade—and more disastrous liaisons—ensued.

Two more sea captains left indelible marks on the Islands. The first was American John Kendrick, who in 1791 filled his ship with fragrant Hawaiian sandalwood and sailed to China. By 1825, Hawaii's sandalwood groves were gone. The second was Englishman George Vancouver, who in 1793 left behind cows and sheep, which ventured out to graze in the islands' native forest and hastened the spread of invasive species. King Kamehameha I sent for cowboys from Mexico and Spain to round up the wild livestock, thus beginning the islands' *paniolo* (cowboy) tradition.

King Kamehameha I was an ambitious *alii* who used western guns to unite the islands under single rule. After his death in 1819, the tightly woven Hawaiian society began to unravel. One of his successors,

King Kamehameha I.   King David Kalakaua.

Queen Kaahumanu, abolished the *kapu* system, opening the door for religion of another form.

## Staying to Do Well

In April 1820, missionaries bent on converting Hawaiians arrived from New England. The newcomers clothed the natives, banned them from dancing the hula, and nearly dismantled the ancient culture. The churchgoers tried to keep sailors and whalers out of the bawdy houses, where whiskey flowed and the virtue of native women was never safe. To their credit, the missionaries created a 12-letter alphabet for the Hawaiian language, taught reading and writing, started a printing press, and began recording the islands' history, which until that time had been preserved solely in memorized chants.

Children of the missionaries became business leaders and politicians. They married Hawaiians and

# IS EVERYONE hawaiian IN HAWAII?

Only *kanaka maoli* (Native Hawaiians) are truly Hawaiian. The sugar and pineapple plantations brought so many different people to Hawaii that the state is now a remarkable potpourri of ethnic groups: Native Hawaiians were joined by **Caucasians, Japanese, Chinese, Filipinos, Koreans, Portuguese, Puerto Ricans, Samoans, Tongans, Tahitians,** and other **Asian and Pacific Islanders.** Add to that a sprinkling of **Vietnamese,** **Canadians, African Americans, American Indians, South Americans,** and **Europeans** of every stripe. Many people retain an element of the traditions of their homeland. Some Japanese Americans in Hawaii, generations removed from the homeland, are more traditional than the Japanese of Tokyo. The same is true of many Chinese, Koreans, and Filipinos, making Hawaii a kind of living museum of Asian and Pacific cultures.

stayed on in the islands, causing one wag to remark that the missionaries "came to do good and stayed to do well." In 1848, King Kamehameha III enacted the Great Mahele (division). Intended to guarantee Native Hawaiians rights to their land, it ultimately enabled foreigners to take ownership of vast tracts of land. Within two generations, more than 80% of all private land was in *haole* (foreign) hands. Businessmen planted acre after acre in sugarcane and imported waves of immigrants to work the fields: Chinese starting in 1852, Japanese in 1885, and Portuguese in 1878.

King David Kalakaua was elected to the throne in 1874. This popular "Merrie Monarch" built Iolani Palace in 1882, threw extravagant parties, and lifted the prohibitions on the hula and other native arts. For this, he was much loved. He proclaimed that "hula is the language of the heart and, therefore, the heartbeat of the Hawaiian people." He also gave Pearl Harbor to the United States; it became the westernmost bastion of the U.S. Navy. While visiting chilly San Francisco in 1891, King Kalakaua caught a cold and died in the royal suite of the Sheraton Palace. His sister, Queen Liliuokalani, assumed the throne.

## The Overthrow

For years, a group of American sugar plantation owners and missionary descendants had been machinating against the monarchy. On January 17, 1893, with the support of the U.S. minister to Hawaii and the Marines, the conspirators imprisoned Queen Liliuokalani in her own palace. To avoid bloodshed, she abdicated the throne, trusting that the United States government would right the wrong. As the Queen waited in vain, she penned the sorrowful lyric "Aloha Oe," Hawaii's song of farewell.

U.S. President Grover Cleveland's attempt to restore the monarchy was thwarted by congress. Sanford Dole, a powerful sugar plantation owner, appointed himself president of the newly declared Republic of Hawaii. His fellow sugarcane planters, known as the Big Five, controlled banking, shipping, hardware, and every other facet of economic life on the islands. In 1898, through annexation, Hawaii became an American territory ruled by Dole.

Oahu's central Ewa Plain soon filled with row crops. The Dole family planted pineapple on its sprawling acreage. Planters imported more contract laborers from Puerto Rico (1900), Korea (1903), and the Philippines (1907–31). Many of the new immigrants stayed on to establish families and become a part of the islands. Meanwhile, Native Hawaiians became a landless minority. Their language was banned in schools and their cultural practices devalued, forced into hiding.

For nearly a century in Hawaii, sugar was king, generously subsidized by the U.S. government. Sugar is a thirsty crop, and plantation owners oversaw the construction of flumes and aqueducts that channeled mountain streams down to parched plains, where waving fields of cane soon grew. The waters that once fed taro patches dried up. The sugar planters dominated the territory's economy, shaped its social fabric, and kept the islands in a colonial plantation era with bosses and field hands. But the workers eventually went on strike for higher wages and improved working conditions, and the planters found themselves unable to compete with cheap third-world labor costs.

## Tourism Takes Hold

Tourism in Hawaii began in the 1860s. Kilauea volcano was one of the world's prime attractions for adventure travelers. In 1865, a grass Volcano House was built on the rim of Halemaumau Crater to shelter visitors; it was Hawaii's first hotel. The visitor industry blossomed as the plantation era peaked and waned.

The original Volcano House, Hawaii's first hotel.

In 1901, W. C. Peacock built the elegant

## SPEAKING hawaiian

Most everyone in Hawaii speaks English. But many folks now also speak *olelo Hawaii*, the native language of these Islands. You will regularly hear *aloha* and *mahalo* (thank you). If you've just arrived, you're a *malihini*. Someone who's been here a long time is a *kamaaina*. When you finish a job or your meal, you are *pau* (finished). On Friday, it's *pau hana*, work finished. You eat *pupu* (Hawaii's version of hors d'oeuvres) when you go *pau hana*.

The Hawaiian alphabet, created by the New England missionaries, has only 12 letters: the five regular vowels (*a, e, i, o,* and *u*) and seven consonants (*h, k, l, m, n, p,* and *w*). The vowels are pronounced in the Roman fashion: that is, *ah, ay, ee, oh,* and *oo* (as in "too")—not *ay, ee, eye, oh,* and *you,* as in English. For example, *huhu* is pronounced *who-who*. Most vowels are sounded separately, though some are pronounced together, as in Kalakaua: "kah-lah-cow-ah."

Beaux Arts Moana Hotel on Waikiki Beach, and W. C. Weedon convinced Honolulu businessmen to bankroll his plan to advertise Hawaii in San Francisco. Armed with a stereopticon and tinted photos of Waikiki, Weedon sailed off in 1902 for 6 months of lecture tours to introduce "those remarkable people and the beautiful lands of Hawaii." He drew packed houses. A tourism promotion bureau was formed in 1903, and about 2,000 visitors came to Hawaii that year.

The steamship was Hawaii's tourism lifeline. It took 4½ days to sail from San Francisco to Honolulu. Streamers, leis, and pomp welcomed each Matson liner at downtown's Aloha Tower. Well-heeled visitors brought trunks, servants, and Rolls-Royces and stayed for months. Hawaiians amused visitors with personal tours, floral parades, and hula shows.

Beginning in 1935 and running for the next 40 years, Webley Edwards's weekly live radio show, "Hawaii Calls," planted the sounds of Waikiki—surf, sliding steel guitar, sweet Hawaiian harmonies, drumbeats—in the hearts of millions of listeners in the United States, Australia, and Canada.

By 1936, visitors could fly to Honolulu from San Francisco on the *Hawaii Clipper,* a seven-passenger Pan American Martin M-130 flying boat, for $360 one-way. The flight took 21 hours, 33 minutes. Modern tourism was born, with five flying boats providing daily service. The 1941 visitor count was a brisk 31,846 through December 6.

## World War II & Statehood

On December 7, 1941, Japanese Zeros came out of the rising sun to bomb American warships based at Pearl Harbor. This was the "day of infamy" that plunged the United States into World War II.

The attack brought immediate changes to the Islands. Martial law was declared, stripping the Big Five cartel of its absolute power in a single day. German and Japanese Americans were interned. Hawaii was "blacked out" at night, Waikiki Beach was strung with barbed wire, and Aloha Tower was painted in camouflage. Only young men bound for the Pacific came to Hawaii during the war years. Many came back to graves in a cemetery called Punchbowl.

The postwar years saw the beginnings of Hawaii's faux culture. The authentic traditions had long been suppressed, and into the void flowed a consumable brand of aloha. Harry Yee invented the Blue Hawaii cocktail and dropped in a tiny Japanese parasol. Vic Bergeron created the mai tai, a drink made of rum and fresh lime juice, and opened Trader Vic's, America's first themed restaurant that featured the art, decor, and food of Polynesia. Arthur Godfrey picked up a ukulele and began singing *hapa-haole* tunes on early TV shows. In 1955, Henry J. Kaiser built the Hilton Hawaiian Village, and the 11-story high-rise Princess Kaiulani Hotel opened on a site where the real princess once played. Hawaii greeted 109,000 visitors that year.

In 1959, Hawaii became the 50th state of the United States. That year also saw the arrival of the first jet airliners, which brought 250,000 tourists to the state. By the 1980s, Hawaii's visitor count surpassed 6 million. Fantasy megaresorts bloomed on the neighbor islands like giant artificial flowers, swelling the luxury market with ever-swanker accommodations. Hawaii's tourist industry—the bastion of the state's economy—has survived worldwide recessions, airline industry hiccups, and increased competition from overseas. Year after year, the Hawaiian Islands continue to be ranked among the top visitor destinations in the world.

# HAWAII TODAY
## A Cultural Renaissance

Despite the ever-increasing influx of foreign people and customs, the Native Hawaiian culture is experiencing a rebirth. It began in earnest in 1976, when members of the Polynesian Voyaging Society launched *Hokulea,* a double-hulled canoe of the sort that hadn't been seen on these shores in centuries. The *Hokulea's* daring crew sailed her 2,500 miles to Tahiti without

**Hula girls.**

using modern instruments, relying instead on ancient navigational techniques. Most historians at that time discounted Polynesian wayfinding methods as rudimentary; the prevailing theory was that Pacific Islanders had discovered Hawaii by accident, not intention. The *Hokulea*'s successful voyage sparked a fire in the hearts of indigenous islanders across the Pacific, who reclaimed their identity as a sophisticated, powerful people with unique wisdom to offer the world.

The Hawaiian language found new life, too. In 1984, a group of educators and parents recognized that, with fewer than 50 children fluent in Hawaiian, the language was dangerously close to extinction. They started a preschool where *keiki* (children) learned lessons purely in Hawaiian. They overcame numerous bureaucratic obstacles (including a law still on the books forbidding instruction in Hawaiian) to establish Hawaiian-language-immersion programs across the state that run from preschool through post-graduate education.

Hula—which never fully disappeared despite the missionaries' best efforts—is thriving. At the annual Merrie Monarch festival commemorating King Kalakaua, hula *halau* (troupes) from Hawaii and beyond gather to demonstrate their skill and artistry. Fans of the ancient dance form are glued to the live broadcast of what is known as the Olympics of hula. *Kumu hula* (hula teachers) have safeguarded many Hawaiian cultural practices as part of their art: the making of *kapa,* the collection and cultivation of native herbs, and the observation of *kuleana,* an individual's responsibility to the community.

In that same spirit, in May 2014, the traditional voyaging canoe *Hokulea* embarked on her most ambitious adventure yet: an international peace delegation. During the canoe's 3-year circumnavigation of the globe, the crew's mission is "to weave a lei around the world" and chart a new course toward a healthier and more sustainable horizon for all of humankind. The sailors hope to collaborate with political leaders, scientists, educators, and schoolchildren in each of the ports they visit.

The history of Hawaii has come full circle: the ancient Polynesians traveled the seas to discover these Islands. Today, their descendants set sail to share Hawaii with the world.

# DINING IN HAWAII

In the early days of Hawaii's tourism industry, the food wasn't anything to write home about. Continental cuisine ruled fine-dining kitchens. Meats and produce arrived much the same way visitors did: jet-lagged

**Ahi poke.**

after a long journey from a far-off land. Island chefs struggled to revive limp iceberg lettuce and frozen cocktail shrimp—often letting outstanding ocean views make up for uninspired dishes. In 1991, 12 chefs staged a revolt. They partnered with local farmers, ditched the dictatorship of imported foods, and brought sun-ripened mango, crisp organic greens, and freshly caught *uku* (snapper) to the table. Coining the name "Hawaii Regional Cuisine," they gave the world a taste of what happens when passionate, classically trained cooks have their way with ripe Pacific flavors.

Two decades later, the movement to unite local farms and kitchens is still bearing fruit. The HRC heavyweights continue to keep things hot in island kitchens. But they aren't, by any means, the sole source of good eats in Hawaii.

Haute cuisine is alive and well in Hawaii, but equally important in the culinary pageant are good-value plate lunches, shave ice, and food trucks.

The **plate lunch,** which is ubiquitous throughout the islands, can be ordered from a lunch wagon or a restaurant and usually consists of some protein—fried mahimahi, say, or teriyaki beef, shoyu chicken, or chicken or pork cutlets served katsu style: breaded and fried and slathered in a rich gravy—"two scoops rice," macaroni salad, and a few leaves of green, typically julienned cabbage. Chili water and soy sauce are the condiments of choice. Like **saimin**—the local version of noodles in broth topped with scrambled eggs, green onions, and sometimes pork—the plate lunch is Hawaii's version of comfort food.

Shave ice.

Because this is Hawaii, at least a few fingerfuls of **poi**—steamed, pounded taro (the traditional Hawaiian staple crop)—are a must. Mix it with salty *kalua* pork (pork cooked in a Polynesian underground oven known as an *imu*) or *lomi* salmon (salted salmon with tomatoes and green onions). Other tasty Hawaiian foods include **poke** (pronounced *"po-kay,"* this popular appetizer is made of cubed raw fish seasoned with onions, seaweed, and roasted *kukui* nuts), **laulau** (pork, chicken, or fish steamed in *ti* leaves), **squid luau** (cooked in coconut milk and taro tops), **haupia** (creamy coconut pudding), and **kulolo** (a steamed pudding of coconut, brown sugar, and taro).

For a sweet snack, the prevailing choice is **shave ice.** Particularly on hot, humid days, long lines of shave-ice lovers gather for heaps of finely shaved ice topped with sweet tropical syrups. Sweet-sour *li hing mui* is a favorite, and new gourmet flavors include calamansi lime and red velvet cupcake. Aficionados order shave ice with ice cream and sweetened adzuki beans on the bottom or sweetened condensed milk on top.

# WHEN TO GO

Most visitors come to Hawaii when the weather is lousy most everywhere else. Thus, the **high season**—when prices are up and resorts are often booked to capacity—is generally from mid-December to March or mid-April. The last 2 weeks of December, in particular, are prime time for travel to Hawaii. Spring break is also jam-packed with families taking advantage of the school holiday. If you're planning a trip during peak season, make your hotel and rental car reservations as early as possible, expect crowds, and prepare to pay top dollar.

The **off season,** when the best rates are available and the islands are less crowded, is late spring (mid-Apr to early June) and fall (Sept to mid-Dec).

If you plan to travel in **summer** (June–Aug), don't expect to see the fantastic bargains of spring and fall—this is prime time for family travel. But you'll still find much better deals on packages, airfare, and accommodations in summer than in the winter months.

## Climate

Because Hawaii lies at the edge of the tropical zone, it technically has only two seasons, both of them warm. There's a dry season that corresponds to **summer** (Apr–Oct) and a rainy season in **winter** (Nov–Mar). It rains every day somewhere in the islands at any time of the year, but the rainy season can bring enough gray weather to spoil your tanning opportunities. Fortunately, it seldom rains in one spot for more than 3 days straight.

The **year-round temperature** doesn't vary much. At the beach, the average daytime high in summer is 85°F (29°C), while the average daytime high in winter is 78°F (26°C); nighttime lows are usually about 10° cooler. But how warm it is on any given day really depends on *where* you are on the island.

Each island has a **leeward** side (the side sheltered from the wind) and a **windward** side (the side that gets the wind's full force). The leeward sides (the west and south) are usually hot and dry, while the windward sides (east and north) are generally cooler and moist. When you want arid, sunbaked, desert-like weather, go leeward. When you want lush, wet, jungle-like weather, go windward.

Hawaii also has a wide range of **microclimates,** thanks to interior valleys, coastal plains, and mountain peaks. On the Big Island, Hilo ranks among the wettest cities in the nation, with 180 inches of rainfall a year. At Puako, only 60 miles away, it rains less than 6 inches a year. The summits of Mauna Kea on the Big Island and Haleakala on Maui often see snow in winter—even when the sun is blazing down at the beach. The locals say if you don't like the weather, just drive a few miles down the road—it's sure to be different!

## Holidays

When Hawaii observes holidays (especially those over a long weekend), travel between the islands increases, interisland airline seats are fully booked, rental cars are at a premium, and hotels and restaurants are busier.

Federal, state, and county government offices are closed on all federal holidays. Federal holidays in 2016 include New Year's Day (Jan 1); Martin Luther King,

### Hey, No Smoking in Hawaii

Well, not *totally* no smoking, but Hawaii has one of the toughest laws against smoking in the U.S. The Hawaii Smoke-Free Law prohibits smoking in public buildings, including airports, shopping malls, grocery stores, retail shops, buses, movie theaters, banks, convention facilities, and all government buildings and facilities. There is no smoking in restaurants, bars, and nightclubs. Most bed-and-breakfasts prohibit smoking indoors, and more and more hotels and resorts are becoming smoke-free even in public areas. Also, there is no smoking within 20 feet of a doorway, window, or ventilation intake (so no hanging around outside a bar to smoke—you must go 20 ft. away). Even some beaches have no-smoking policies.

Jr., Day (Jan 18); Washington's birthday (Feb 16); Memorial Day (May 30); Independence Day (July 4); Labor Day (Sept 5); Columbus Day (Oct 12); Veterans Day (Nov 11); Thanksgiving Day (Nov 24); and Christmas (Dec 25).

State and county offices are also closed on local holidays, including Prince Kuhio Day (Mar 25), honoring the birthday of Hawaii's first delegate to the U.S. Congress; King Kamehameha Day (June 11), a statewide holiday commemorating Kamehameha the Great, who united the islands and ruled from 1795 to 1819; and Admission Day (third Fri in Aug), which honors the admittance of Hawaii as the 50th state on August 21, 1959.

## Hawaii Calendar of Events

Please note that, as with any schedule of upcoming events, the following information is subject to change; always confirm the details before you plan your trip around an event.

### JANUARY

**Waimea Ocean Film Festival,** Waimea and the Kohala Coast, Big Island. Several days of films featuring the ocean, ranging from surfing and Hawaiian canoe paddling to ecological issues. Go to http://waimeaoceanfilm.org or call © **808/854-6095.** First weekend after New Year's Day.

### FEBRUARY

**Chinese New Year,** most islands. In 2015, lion dancers will be snaking their way around the state on February 19, the start of the Chinese Year of the Sheep. Visit www.chinesechamber.com or call © **808/533-3181.** On Maui, lion dancers perform at the historic Wo Hing Temple on Front Street (www.visitlahaina.com). Call © **888/310-1117** or 808/667-9175. Also in Wailuku; call © **808/244-3888** for location.

### MARCH

**Kona Brewers Festival,** King Kamehameha's Kona Beach Hotel Luau Grounds, Kailua-Kona, Big Island. This 5-day annual event features microbreweries from around the world, with beer tastings, food, and entertainment. Go to http://konabrewersfestival.com or call © **808/987-9196.** Mid-March.

**Prince Kuhio Day Celebrations,** all islands. On this state holiday, various festivals throughout Hawaii celebrate the birth of Jonah Kuhio Kalanianaole, who was born on March 26, 1871, and elected to Congress in 1902.

APRIL

**Merrie Monarch Hula Festival,** Hilo, Big Island. Hawaii's biggest, most prestigious hula festival features a week of modern *(auana)* and ancient *(kahiko)* dance competition in honor of King David Kalakaua, the "Merrie Monarch" who revived the dance. Tickets sell out by January, so reserve early. Go to www.merriemonarch.com or call © **808/935-9168.** March 27-April 2, 2016.

MAY

**Outrigger Canoe Season,** all islands. From May to September, canoe paddlers across the state participate in outrigger canoe races nearly every weekend. Go to www.ocpaddler.com for this year's schedule of events.

**Big Island Chocolate Festival,** Kona, Big Island. This celebration of chocolate (cacao) grown and produced in Hawaii features symposiums, candy-making workshops, and gala tasting events. It's held in the Fairmont Orchid hotel. Go to www.bigisland chocolatefestival.com or call © **808/854-6769.** First or second weekend in May.

JUNE

**Obon Season,** all islands. This colorful Buddhist ceremony honoring the souls of the dead kicks off in June. Synchronized dancers circle a tower where Taiko drummers play, and food booths sell Japanese treats late into the night. Each weekend, a different Buddhist temple hosts the Bon Dance. Go to www.gohawaii.com for a statewide schedule.

AUGUST

**Puukohola Heiau National Historic Site Anniversary Celebration,** Kawaihae, Big Island. This homage to authentic Hawaiian culture begins at 6am at Puukohola Heiau. It's a rugged, beautiful site where attendees make leis, weave lauhala mats, pound poi, and dance ancient hula. Bring refreshments and sunscreen. Go to http://www.nps.gov/puhe.htm or call ✆ **808/882-7218.** Mid-August.

**Admission Day,** all islands. Hawaii became the 50th state on August 21, 1959. On the third Friday in August, the state takes a holiday (all state-related facilities are closed).

**Queen Liliuokalani Canoe Race,** Kailua-Kona to Honaunau, Big Island. Thousands of paddlers compete in the world's largest long-distance canoe race. Go to www.kaiopua.org or call ✆ **808/938-8577.** Labor Day weekend.

**Parker Ranch Round-Up Rodeo,** Waimea, Big Island. This hot rodeo competition is in the heart of cowboy country. Go to http://parkerranch.com/labor-day-weekend-rodeo/ or call ✆ **808/885-7311.** Weekend before Labor Day.

**Aloha Festivals,** various locations on all islands. Parades and other events celebrate Hawaiian culture and friendliness throughout the state. Go to www.alohafestivals.com or call ✆ **808/923-2030.**

**Ironman Triathlon World Championship,** Kailua-Kona, Big Island. Some 1,500-plus world-class athletes run a full marathon, swim 2.5 miles, and bike 112 miles on the Kona-Kohala Coast of the Big Island. Spectators watch the action along the route for free. The best place to see the 7am start is along the Alii Drive seawall, facing Kailua Bay; arrive before 5:30am to get a seat. (Alii Dr. closes to traffic; park on a side street and walk down.) To watch finishers come in, line up along Alii Drive from Holualoa Street to Palani Road. The first finisher can arrive as early as 2:30pm. Go to www.ironmanworldchampionship.com or call ✆ **808/329-0063.** Saturday closest to the full moon in October.

**Kona Coffee Cultural Festival,** Kailua-Kona, Big Island. Celebrate the coffee harvest with a bean-picking contest, lei contests, song and dance, and the Miss Kona Coffee Pageant. Go to http://konacoffeefest.com or call ✆ **808/326-7820.** Events throughout November.

**Hawaii International Film Festival,** various locations throughout the state. This cinema festival with a cross-cultural spin features film-makers from Asia, the Pacific Islands, and the United States. Go to www.hiff.org or call ✆ **808/792-1577.** Mid-October to early November.

**Invitational Wreath Exhibit,** Volcano Art Center, Hawaii Volcanoes National Park, Big Island. Thirty-plus artists, including painters, sculptors, glass artists, fiber artists, and potters, produce both whimsical and traditional "wreaths" for this exhibit. Park entrance fees apply. Go to www.volcanoartcenter.org or call ✆ **808/967-7565.** Mid-November to early January.

**DECEMBER**

**Kona Surf Film Festival,** Courtyard Marriott King Kamehameha's Kona Beach Hotel, Big Island. An outdoor screening of independent films focusing on waves and wave riders. Go to www.konasurffilmfestival.org or call ✆ **808/936-0089.** Early December.

**9**

# PLANNING

H awaii is rich in natural and cultural wonders and that's especially true for the Big Island of Hawaii, home to the state's most important national park and intriguing ancient Hawaiian sites. Here we've compiled everything you need to know before escaping to the Islands.

Our biggest tip is to **fly directly to the island of your choice;** doing so can save you a 2-hour layover in Honolulu and another plane ride. Oahu, the Big Island, Maui, and Kauai now all receive direct flights from the Mainland; if you're heading to Molokai or Lanai, you'll have the easiest connections if you fly into Honolulu.

So let's get on with the process of planning your trip. For pertinent facts and on-the-ground resources in Hawaii, turn to "Fast Facts: Hawaii," at the end of this chapter on p. 240.

# GETTING THERE
## By Plane

Most major U.S. and many international carriers fly to **Honolulu International Airport** (HNL), on Oahu. Some also offer direct flights to **Kahului Airport** (OGG), on Maui; **Lihue Airport** (LIH), on Kauai; and **Kona International Airport** (KOA) and **Hilo Airport** (ITO), on the Big Island. If you can fly directly to the island of your choice, you'll be spared a 2-hour layover in Honolulu and another plane ride. If you're heading to Molokai (MKK) or Lanai (LNY), you'll have the easiest connections if you fly into Honolulu. See island chapters for detailed information on direct flights to each island.

**Hawaiian Airlines** offers flights from more mainland U.S. gateways than any other airline. Hawaiian's easy-to-navigate website makes finding the cheapest fares a cinch. Its closest competitor, price-wise, is **Alaska Airlines,** which offers daily nonstop flights from West Coast cities including Anchorage, Seattle, Portland, and Oakland. From points farther east, **United, American, Continental,** and **Delta** all fly to Hawaii with nonstop service to Honolulu and most neighbor islands. If you're having difficulty finding an affordable fare, try routing your flight through Las Vegas. It's a huge hub for traffic to and from the Islands.

For travel from beyond the U.S. mainland, check these airlines: Air Canada, Air New Zealand, Qantas Airways, Japan Air Lines, All Nippon Airways (ANA), the Taiwan-based China Airlines, Korean Air, and Philippine Airlines. Hawaiian Airlines also flies nonstop to Australia, American Samoa, Philippines, Tahiti, South Korea, and Japan.

## ARRIVING AT THE AIRPORT

**IMMIGRATION & CUSTOMS CLEARANCE** International visitors arriving by air should cultivate patience and resignation before setting foot on U.S. soil. U.S. airports have considerable security practices in place. Clearing Customs and Immigration can take as long as 2 hours.

**AGRICULTURAL SCREENING AT AIRPORTS** At Honolulu International and the neighbor-island airports, baggage and passengers bound for the Mainland must be screened by agriculture officials. Officials will confiscate local produce like fresh avocados, bananas, and mangoes, in the name of fruit-fly control. Pineapples, coconuts, and papayas inspected and certified for export; boxed flowers; leis without seeds; and processed foods (macadamia nuts, coffee, jams, dried fruit, and the like) will pass.

# GETTING AROUND HAWAII

Here are all the ways to see the sights once you hit the Big Island.

## Interisland Flights

The major interisland carriers have cut way back on the number of interisland flights. The airlines warn you to show up at least 90 minutes before your flight and, believe me, with all the security inspections, you will need all 90 minutes to catch your flight.

Hawaii has one major interisland carrier, **Hawaiian Airlines** (www.hawaiianair.com; ✆ **800/367-5320**), and two commuter airlines, **Island Air** (www.islandair.com; ✆ **800/323-3345**) and **Mokulele Airlines** (www.mokuleleairlines.com; ✆ **866/260-7070**).

---

### A Weeklong Cruise Through the Islands

If you're looking for a taste of several islands in 7 days, consider **Norwegian Cruise Line** (www.ncl.com; ✆ **866/234-7350**), the only cruise line that operates year-round in Hawaii. NCL's 2,240-passenger ship *Pride of America* circles Hawaii, stopping on four islands: the Big Island, Maui, Kauai, and Oahu.

The commuter flights service the neighbor islands' more remote airports and tend to be on small planes; you'll board from the tarmac and weight restrictions apply.

## By Car

Bottom line: You will likely need a car to get around the islands, especially if you plan to explore outside your resort—and you absolutely should. Public transit in the islands is spotty, but even so, it's set up for residents, not tourists carrying coolers and beach toys (all carry-ons must fit under the bus seat). So plan to rent a car.

That said, Hawaii has some of the priciest car-rental rates in the country. In fact, we recommend reserving your car as soon as you book your airfare.

To rent a car in Hawaii, you must be at least 25 years of age and have a valid driver's license and credit card. *Note:* If you're visiting from abroad and plan to rent a car in the United States, keep in mind that foreign driver's licenses are usually recognized in the U.S., but you should get an international one if your home license is not in English.

At Honolulu International Airport and most neighbor-island airports, you'll find many major car-rental agencies, including **Alamo, Avis, Budget, Dollar, Enterprise, Hertz, National,** and **Thrifty.** It's almost always cheaper to rent a car in Waikiki, or anywhere but at the airport, where you will pay a daily fee for the convenience of renting at the airport.

**GASOLINE** Gas prices in Hawaii, always much higher than on the U.S. mainland, vary from island to island. Expect to pay around $4 a gallon. Check www.gasbuddy.com to find the cheapest gas in your area.

**INSURANCE**   Hawaii is a no-fault state, which means that if you don't have collision-damage insurance, you are required to pay for all damages before you leave the state, whether or not the accident was your fault. Your personal car insurance may provide rental-car coverage; check before you leave home. Bring your insurance identification card if you decline the optional insurance, which usually costs from $9 to $45 a day. Obtain the name of your company's local claim representative before you go. Some credit card companies also provide collision-damage insurance for their customers; check with yours before you rent.

**DRIVING RULES**   Hawaii state law mandates that all car passengers must wear a **seat belt** and all infants must be strapped into a car seat. You'll pay a $92 fine if you don't buckle up. **Pedestrians** always have the right of way, even if they're not in the crosswalk. You can turn **right on red** after a full and complete stop, unless otherwise posted.

**ROAD MAPS**   The best and most detailed maps for activities are published by **Franko Maps** (www. frankosmaps.com); these feature a host of island maps, plus a terrific "Hawaiian Reef Creatures Guide" for snorkelers curious about those fish they spot

### Stay off the Cellphone

Talking on a cellphone while driving in Hawaii is a big no-no. Fines range from $100 to $200 and double in school or construction zones. An Oahu woman was even ticketed for talking on her cellphone while parked on the side of the road! Save yourself the money; don't use a cell while you are driving.

underwater. Free road maps are published by **"This Week Magazine,"** a visitor publication available on Oahu, the Big Island, Maui, and Kauai.

Another good source is the **University of Hawaii Press maps,** which include a detailed network of island roads, large-scale insets of towns, historical and contemporary points of interest, parks, beaches, and hiking trails. If you can't find them in a bookstore near you, contact **University of Hawaii Press,** 2840 Kolowalu St., Honolulu, HI 96822 (www.uhpress. hawaii.edu; ✆ **888/UH-PRESS [847-7377]**). For topographic maps of the islands, go to the **U.S. Geological Survey** site (www.pubs.usgs.gov).

# SPECIAL-INTEREST TRIPS & TOURS

This section presents an overview of special-interest trips and tours and outdoor excursions in Hawaii. We also list references for spotting birds, plants, and sea life. Always use the resources available to inquire about weather, trail, or surf conditions; water availability; and other conditions before you take off on your adventure.

## Air Tours

Nothing beats getting a bird's-eye view of Hawaii. Some of the islands' most stunning scenery can't be seen any other way. You'll have your choice of aircraft here: **helicopter or small fixed wing plane.**

Today's pilots are part Hawaiian historian, part DJ, part amusement-ride operator, and part tour guide, sharing anecdotes about Hawaii's flora, fauna, history, and culture. Top trips include: **Hawaii Volcanoes National Park** on the Big Island, where you stare into the molten core of a live volcano and watch lava spill into the sea.

## Farm Tours

Overalls and garden spades might not be the first images that come to mind when planning your Hawaii vacation, but a tour of a lush and bountiful island farm should be on your itinerary. Agritourism has become an important new income stream for Hawaii farmers, who often struggle with the rising costs of doing business in paradise. Farm tours benefit everyone: The farmer gets extra cash, visitors gain an intimate understanding of where and how their food is produced, and fertile farmlands stay in production—preserving Hawaii's rural heritage. There are so many diverse and inspiring farms to choose from: **100-year-old Kona coffee farms,** bean-to-bar **chocolate plantations, orchid nurseries.**

With its massive cattle ranches, tropical flower nurseries, and coffee-covered hillsides, the Big Island is the agricultural heart of Hawaii. Many agri-tours include sumptuous tasting sessions, fascinating historical accounts, and tips for growing your own food at home.

On the Big Island, the nonprofit **Hawaii Agri-Tourism Association** (www.hawaiiagtours.com; © **808/286-6559**) offers full-day immersions in Hilo's flower, fruit, and coffee industries, stopping at the Imiloa Astronomy Center for some cultural context. The educational tours cost $90 and take place Wednesday through Friday from 8:30am to 3:30pm.

# Volunteer Vacations & Ecotourism

If you're looking to swap sunbathing for something more memorable on your next trip to Hawaii, consider volunteering while on vacation. Rewards include new friends and access to spectacular wilderness areas that are otherwise off-limits.

To participate in beach and reef cleanups, or monitor nesting sea turtles, contact the **University of Hawaii Sea Grant College Program** (© 808/956-7031) or the **Hawaii Wildlife Fund** (www.wildhawaii.org; © 808/280-8124). For land-based adventures, **Malama Hawaii** (www.malamahawaii.org/get_involved/volunteer.php) is a statewide organization dedicated to malama (taking care) of the culture and environment of Hawaii. The website lists a range of opportunities, such as weeding and potting plants in botanical gardens, restoring taro patches, cleaning up mountain streams, and bird-watching.

Check out the **Hawaii Ecotourism Association** (www.hawaiiecotourism.org; © 808/235-5431), a comprehensive site that lists ecotourism volunteer opportunities, such as seabird habitat restoration.

A great alternative to hiring a private guide is taking a trip with the **Nature Conservancy** or the **Sierra Club.** Both organizations offer guided hikes in preserves and special areas during the year, as well as day- to week-long volunteer work trips to restore habitats and trails and root out invasive plants. It's a chance to see the "real" Hawaii—including wilderness areas that are ordinarily off-limits.

All Nature Conservancy hikes and work trips are free (donations appreciated). However, you must reserve a spot, and a deposit is required for guided hikes to ensure that you'll show up; your deposit is refunded when you do. For all islands, call the Oahu office for reservations. Contact the **Nature Conservancy of Hawaii** (www.nature.org/ourinitiatives/regions; ☎ **808/939-7171**)

The Sierra Club offers half- or all-day hikes on the Big Island. Hikes are led by certified Sierra Club volunteers and classified as easy, moderate, or strenuous. Donations of $1 for Sierra Club members and $5 for nonmembers (bring exact change) are recommended. Contact the **Hawaii Chapter of the Sierra Club** (www.sierraclubhawaii.com; ☎ **808/538-6616** on Oahu).

# [FastFACTS] HAWAII

**Area Codes**   Hawaii's area code is 808; it applies to all islands. There is a long-distance charge when calling from one island to another.

**Customs**   For details regarding U.S. Customs and Border Protection, consult your nearest U.S. embassy or consulate, or U.S. Customs (www.cbp.gov). You cannot take home fresh fruit, plants, or seeds (including some leis) unless they are sealed. You cannot seal and pack them yourself. For information on what you're allowed to bring home, contact one of the following agencies:

**U.S. Citizens:** U.S. Customs & Border Protection (CBP), 1300 Pennsylvania Ave., NW, Washington, DC 20229 (www.cbp.gov; ☎ 877/CBP-5511).

**Canadian Citizens:** Canada Border Services Agency (www.cbsa-asfc.gc.ca; ☎ 800/461-9999 in Canada, or 204/983-3500).

**U.K. Citizens:** HM Customs & Excise (www.hmce.gov.uk; ☎ 0845/010-9000 in the U.K., or 020/8929-0152).

**Australian Citizens:** Australian Customs Service (www.customs.gov.au; ☎ 1300/363-263).

**New Zealand Citizens:** New Zealand Customs, The Customhouse, 17–21 Whitmore St., Box 2218, Wellington (www.customs. govt.nz; ✆ 64/9-927-8036 outside of NZ, or 0800/428-786).

Electricity   Like Canada, the United States uses 110 to 120 volts AC (60 cycles), compared to 220 to 240 volts AC (50 cycles) in most of Europe, Australia, and New Zealand. Downward converters that change 220–240 volts to 110–120 volts are hard to find in the U.S., so bring one with you if you're traveling to Hawaii from abroad.

Embassies & Consulates   All embassies are in the nation's capital, Washington, D.C. Some consulates are in major U.S. cities, and most nations have a mission to the United Nations in New York City. If your country isn't listed below, check **www.embassy.org/ embassies** or call for directory information in Washington, D.C. (✆ **202/555-1212**).

The embassy of **Australia** is at 1601 Massachusetts Ave. NW, Washington, DC 20036 (www.usa.embassy.gov.au; ✆ **202/797-3000**). Consulates are in New York, Honolulu, Houston, Los Angeles, Denver, Atlanta, Chicago, and San Francisco.

The embassy of **Canada** is at 501 Pennsylvania Ave. NW, Washington, DC 20001 (www.canadainternational.gc.ca/washington; ✆ **202/682-1740**). Other Canadian consulates are in Chicago, Detroit, and San Diego.

The embassy of **Ireland** is at 2234 Massachusetts Ave. NW, Washington, DC 20008 (www.embassyofireland.org; ✆ **202/462-3939**). Irish consulates are in Boston, Chicago, New York, San Francisco, and other cities. See website for complete listing.

The embassy of **New Zealand** is at 37 Observatory Circle NW, Washington, DC 20008 (www.nzembassy.com; ✆ **202/328-4800**). New Zealand consulates are in Los Angeles, Salt Lake City, San Francisco, and Seattle.

The embassy of the **United Kingdom** is at 3100 Massachusetts Ave. NW, Washington, DC 20008 (http://ukinusa.fco.gov.uk; ✆ **202/588-6500**). Other British consulates are in Atlanta, Boston, Chicago, Cleveland, Houston, Los Angeles, New York, San Francisco, and Seattle.

Family Travel   With beaches to build castles on, water to splash in, and amazing sights to see, Hawaii is paradise for children.

The larger hotels and resorts offer supervised programs for children and can refer you to qualified babysitters. By state law, hotels can accept only children ages 5 to 12 in supervised activities programs, but can often accommodate younger kids by hiring babysitters to watch over them. Contact **People Attentive to Children (PATCH)** for referrals to babysitters who have taken a training course in childcare. On the Big Island, call ✆ **808/325-3864.** Tutoring services are also available.

**Baby's Away** (www.babysaway.com ✆ **800/996-9030**) rents cribs, strollers, highchairs, playpens, infant seats. The staff will deliver whatever you need to wherever you're staying and pick it up when you're done.

For a list of more family-friendly travel resources, turn to the experts at www.frommers.com.

Gay & Lesbian Travelers    Hawaii welcomes all people with aloha. The number of gay- or lesbian-specific accommodations on the islands is limited, but most properties welcome gays and lesbians as they would any traveler. Since 1990, the state's capital has hosted the **Honolulu Pride Parade and Celebration.** Register to participate at www.honolulupride.org.

**Gay Hawaii** (www.gayhawaii.com) and **Pride Guide Hawaii** (www.gogayhawaii.com) are websites with gay and lesbian news, blogs, business recommendations, and other information for the entire state. Also check out the website for **Out in Hawaii** (www.outinhawaii.com), which calls itself "Queer Resources and Information for the State of Hawaii," with vacation ideas, a calendar of events, information on Hawaii, and even a chat room.

For more gay and lesbian travel resources, visit www.frommers.com.

Health    **Mosquitoes, Centipedes & Scorpions**    While insects can get a little close for comfort in Hawaii (expect to see ants, cockroaches, and other critters indoors, even in posh hotels) few cause serious trouble. Mosquitoes do not carry disease here (barring an isolated outbreak of dengue fever in 2001). Giant centipedes—as long as 8 inches—are occasionally seen; scorpions are rare. Around Hilo on the Big Island, little red fire ants can rain down from trees and sting unsuspecting passersby. If you're stung or bitten by an insect and experience extreme pain, swelling, nausea, or any other severe reaction, seek medical help immediately.

**Hiking Safety**    Before you set out on a hike, let someone know where you're heading and when you plan to return; too many hikers spend cold nights in the wilderness because they don't take this simple precaution. It's always a good idea to hike with a pal. Select your route based on your own fitness level. Check weather conditions with the **National Weather Service** (www.prh.noaa.gov/hnl), even if it looks sunny: The weather here ranges from blistering hot to freezing cold and can change in a matter of hours or miles. Do *not* hike if rain or a storm is predicted; flash floods are common in Hawaii and have resulted in many preventable deaths. Plan to finish your hike at least an hour before sunset; because Hawaii is so close to the equator, it does not have a twilight period, and thus it gets dark quickly after the sun sets. Wear sturdy shoes, a hat, clothes to protect you from the sun and from getting scratches, and high-SPF sunscreen on all exposed areas. Take plenty of water, basic first aid, a snack, and a bag to pack out what you pack in. Watch your step. Loose lava rocks are famous for twisting ankles. Don't rely on cellphones; service isn't available in many remote places.

**Vog** When molten lava from Kilauea pours into the ocean, gases are released, resulting in a brownish, volcanic haze that hovers at the horizon. Some people claim that exposure to the smog-like air causes headaches and bronchial ailments. To date, there's no evidence that vog causes lingering damage to healthy individuals. Vog primarily affects the Big Island—Kona, in particular—but is often felt as far away as Maui and Oahu. You can minimize the effects of vog by closing your windows and using an air conditioner indoors. The University of Hawaii recommends draping a floor fan with a wet cloth saturated in a thin paste of baking soda and water, which captures and neutralizes the sulfur compounds. Cleansing your sinuses with a neti pot and saltwater also helps. ***Word of caution:*** If you're pregnant or have heart or breathing problems, avoid exposure to the sulfuric fumes in and around Hawaii Volcanoes National Park.

**Ocean Safety** The range of watersports available here is astounding—this is a prime water playground with conditions for every age and ability. But the ocean is also an untamed wilderness; don't expect a calm swimming pool. Many people who visit Hawaii underestimate the power of the ocean. With just a few precautions, your Pacific experience can be a safe and happy one. Before jumping in, familiarize yourself with your equipment. If you're snorkeling, make sure you feel at ease breathing and clearing water from the snorkel. Take a moment to watch where others are swimming. Observe weather conditions, swells, and possible riptides. If you get caught in big surf, dive underneath each wave until the swell subsides. Never turn your back to the ocean; rogue waves catch even experienced water folk unaware. Be realistic about your fitness—more than one visitor has ended his or her vacation with a heart attack in the water. Don't go out alone, or during a storm.

Note that sharks are not a big problem in Hawaii; in fact, local divers look forward to seeing them. Only 2 of the 40 shark species present in Hawaiian waters are known to bite humans, and then usually it's by accident. But here are the general rules for avoiding sharks: Don't swim at dusk or in murky water—sharks may mistake you for one of their usual meals. It should be obvious not to swim where there are bloody fish in the water, as sharks become aggressive around blood.

**Seasickness** The waters in Hawaii can range from calm as glass (off the Kona Coast on the Big Island) to downright turbulent (in storm conditions); they usually fall somewhere in between. In general, expect rougher conditions in winter than in summer and on windward coastlines versus calm, leeward coastlines. If you've never been out on a boat, or if you've been seasick in the past, you might want to heed the following suggestions:

- The day before you go out on the boat, avoid alcohol, caffeine, citrus and other acidic juices, and greasy, spicy, or hard-to-digest foods.

- Get a good night's sleep the night before.

- Take or use whatever seasickness prevention works best for you—medication, an acupressure wristband, ginger tea or capsules, or any combination. But do it **before you board;** once you set sail, it's generally too late.

- While you're on the boat, stay as low and as near the center of the boat as possible. Avoid the fumes (especially if it's a diesel boat); stay out in the fresh air and watch the horizon. Do not read.

- If you start to feel queasy, drink clear fluids like water, and eat something bland, such as a soda cracker.

**Stings** The most common stings in Hawaii come from jellyfish, particularly **Portuguese man-of-war** and box jellyfish. Since the poisons they inject are very different, you'll need to treat each type of sting differently.

A bluish-purple floating bubble with a long tail, the Portuguese man-of-war is responsible for some 6,500 stings a year on Oahu alone. These stings, although painful and a nuisance, are rarely harmful; fewer than 1 in 1,000 requires medical treatment. The best prevention is to watch for these floating bubbles as you snorkel (look for the hanging tentacles below the surface). Get out of the water if anyone near you spots these jellyfish. Reactions to stings range from mild burning and reddening to severe welts and blisters. Most jellyfish stings disappear by themselves within 15 to 20 minutes if you do nothing at all to treat them. "All Stings Considered: First Aid and Medical Treatment of Hawaii's Marine Injuries," by Craig Thomas and Susan Scott (University of Hawaii Press, 1997), recommends the following treatment: First, pick off any visible tentacles with a gloved hand or a stick; then, rinse the sting with salt- or fresh water, and apply ice to prevent swelling. Avoid applying vinegar, baking soda, or urine to the wound, which may actually cause further damage. See a doctor if pain persists or a rash or other symptoms develop.

Transparent, square-shaped **box jellyfish** are nearly impossible to see in the water. Fortunately, they seem to follow a monthly cycle: 8 to 10 days after the full moon, they appear in the waters on the leeward side of each island and hang around for about 3 days. Also, they seem to sting more in the morning, when they're on or near the surface. The stings from a box jellyfish can cause hive-like welts, blisters, and pain lasting from 10 minutes to 8 hours. "All Stings Considered" recommends the following treatment: First, pour regular household vinegar on the sting; this will stop additional burning. Do not rub the area. Pick off any vinegar-soaked tentacles with a stick and apply an ice pack. Seek medical treatment if you experience shortness of breath, weakness, palpitations, or any other severe symptoms.

**Punctures** Most sea-related punctures come from stepping on or brushing against the needle-like spines of sea urchins (known locally as *wana*). Be careful when you're in the water; don't put your foot down (even if you are wearing booties or fins) if you can't clearly see the bottom. Waves can push you into *wana* in a surge zone in shallow water. The spines can even puncture a wet suit. A sea urchin puncture can result in burning, aching, swelling, and discoloration (black or purple) around the area where the spines entered your skin. The best thing to do is to pull out any protruding spines. The body will absorb the spines within 24 hours to 3 weeks, or the remainder of the spines will work themselves out. Again, contrary to popular thought, urinating or pouring vinegar on the embedded spines will not help.

**Cuts**   Stay out of the ocean if you have an open cut, wound, or new tattoo. The high level of bacteria present in the water means that even small wounds can become infected. Staphylococcus, or "staph," infections start out as swollen, pinkish skin tissue around the wound that spreads and grows rather than dries and heals. Scrub any cuts well with fresh water and avoid the ocean until they heal. Consult a doctor if your wound shows signs of infection.

Internet & Wi-Fi   On every island, branches of the **Hawaii State Public Library System** have free computers with Internet access. To find your closest library, check **www.librarieshawaii. org/sitemap.htm**. There is no charge for use of the computers, but you must have a Hawaii library card, which is free to Hawaii residents and members of the military. Visitors can visit any branch to purchase a $10 visitor card that is good for 3 months.

If you have your own laptop, every **Starbucks** in Hawaii has Wi-Fi. For a list of locations, go to **www.starbucks.com/retail/ find/default.aspx**. Many, if not most, **hotel lobbies** have free Wi-Fi.

Most interisland airports have **Internet kiosks** that provide basic Web access for a per-minute fee that's usually higher than cybercafe prices. The **Honolulu International Airport** (http:// hawaii.gov/hnl) provides **Wi-Fi access** for a fee through Shaka Net. Check out copy shops like FedEx Office, which offers computer stations with fully loaded software (as well as Wi-Fi).

Mail   At press time, domestic postage rates were 35¢ for a postcard and 49¢ for a letter. For international mail, a first-class postcard or letter up to 1 ounce costs $1.15. For more information go to **www.usps.com**.

If you aren't sure what your address will be in the United States, mail can be sent to you, in your name, c/o General Delivery at the

main post office of the city or region where you expect to be. (Call
℃ **800/275-8777** for information on the nearest post office.) The
addressee must pick up mail in person and must produce proof of
identity (driver's license, passport, and the like). Most post offices
will hold mail for up to 1 month, and are open Monday to Friday
from 9am to 4pm, and Saturday from 9am to noon.

Always include zip codes when mailing items in the U.S. If you
don't know your zip code, visit www.usps.com/zip4.

**Medical Requirements**   Unless you're arriving from an area
known to be suffering from an epidemic (particularly cholera or
yellow fever), inoculations or vaccinations are not required for entry
into the United States.

**Mobile Phones**   Cellphone coverage is decent throughout
Hawaii, but tends to be inconsistent in the more remote and moun-
tainous regions of the Islands.

If you're not from the U.S., you'll be appalled at the poor reach
of our **GSM (Global System for Mobile Communications) wire-
less network,** which is used by much of the rest of the world. You
may or may not be able to send SMS (text messaging) home.

Do *not* use your cellphone while you are driving. Strict laws and
heavy fines ($97–$150) are diligently enforced.

**Money & Costs**   Frommer's lists exact prices in the local currency. The currency conversions quoted below were correct at press
time. However, rates fluctuate, so before departing consult a currency exchange website such as www.oanda.com or www.xe.com/
ucc/convert/classic to check up-to-the-minute rates.

THE VALUE OF US$ VS. OTHER POPULAR
CURRENCIES

| US$ | Can$ | UK£ | Euro (€) | Aus$ | NZ$ |
|-----|------|-----|----------|------|-----|
| 1 | C$1.25 | £.59 | €.90 | A$1.30 | NZ$1.45 |

ATMs (cashpoints) are everywhere in Hawaii—at banks, supermarkets, Longs Drugs, and Honolulu International Airport, and in

some resorts and shopping centers. The **Cirrus** (www.mastercard. com; © **800/424-7787**) and **PLUS** (www.visa.com; © **800/843-7587**) networks span the country; you can find them even in remote regions. Go to your bankcard's website to find ATM locations at your destination. Be sure you know your daily withdrawal limit before you depart.

**Note:** Many banks impose a fee every time you use a card at another bank's ATM, and that fee is often higher for international transactions (up to $5 or more) than for domestic ones (rarely more than $2.50). In addition, the bank from which you withdraw cash is likely to charge its own fee. Visitors from outside the U.S. should also find out whether their bank assesses a 1 to 3% fee on charges incurred abroad.

Credit cards are accepted everywhere except, most taxicabs (all islands), and some small restaurants and B&B accommodations.

Packing Tips   Hawaii is very informal. Shorts, T-shirts, and sandals will get you by at most restaurants and attractions; a casual dress or a polo shirt and long pants are fine even in the most expensive places. Aloha wear is acceptable everywhere, so you may want to plan on buying an aloha shirt or a Hawaiian-style dress while you're in the islands. If you plan on hiking, horseback riding, or ziplining, bring close-toed shoes; they're required.

The tropical sun poses the greatest threat to anyone who ventures into the great outdoors, so pack **sun protection:** a good pair of sunglasses, strong sunscreen, a light hat, and a water bottle. Dehydration is common in the tropics.

One last thing: **It can get really cold in Hawaii.** If you plan to see the sunrise from the top of Maui's Haleakala Crater, venture into the Big Island's Hawaii Volcanoes National Park, or spend time in Kokee State Park on Kauai, bring a warm jacket. Temperatures "upcountry" (higher up the mountain) can sink to 40°F (4°C), even in summer when it's 80°F (27°C) at the beach. Bring a windbreaker, sweater, or light jacket. And if you'll be in Hawaii between November and March, toss some **rain gear** into your suitcase, too.

Passports   Virtually every air traveler entering the U.S. is required to show a passport. All persons, including U.S. citizens, traveling by air between the United States and Canada, Mexico, Central and South America, the Caribbean, and Bermuda are

| Hamburger | 6.00–19.00 |
| --- | --- |
| Movie ticket (adult/child) | 11.00/7.50 |
| 20-ounce soft drink at convenience store | 2.50 |
| 16-ounce apple juice | 3.50 |
| Cup of coffee | 3.00 |
| Moderately priced three-course dinner without alcohol | 60.00 |

required to present a valid passport. **Note:** U.S. and Canadian citizens entering the U. S. at land and sea ports of entry from within the western hemisphere must now also present a passport or other documents compliant with the Western Hemisphere Travel Initiative (WHTI; check www.getyouhome.gov for details). Children 15 and under may continue entering with only a U.S. birth certificate, or other proof of U.S. citizenship.

**Australia**  Australian Passport Information Service (www.passports. gov.au; *©* **131-232** in Australia).

**Canada   Passport Office,** Department of Foreign Affairs and International Trade, Ottawa, ON K1A 0G3 (www.ppt.gc.ca; *©* **800/567-6868**).

**Ireland   Passport Office,** Setanta Centre, Molesworth Street, Dublin 2 (www.foreignaffairs.gov.ie; *©* **01/671-1633**).

**New Zealand   Passports Office,** Department of Internal Affairs, 47 Boulcott St., Wellington, 6011 (www.passports.govt.nz; *©* **0800/225-050** in New Zealand or 04/474-8100).

**United Kingdom**  Visit your nearest passport office, major post office, or travel agency, or contact the **Identity and Passport Service (IPS),** 89 Eccleston Sq., London, SW1V 1PN (www.ips.gov.uk; *©* **0300/222-0000**).

**United States**  To find your regional passport office, check the U.S. State Department website (http://travel.state.gov) or call the **National Passport Information Center** (*©* **877/487-2778**) for automated ivnformation.

**Safety**  Although tourist areas are generally safe, visitors should always stay alert, even in laidback Hawaii. It's wise to ask the island tourist office if you're in doubt about which neighborhoods are safe. Avoid deserted areas, especially at night. Don't go into any city park at night unless there's an event that attracts crowds. Generally speaking, you can feel safe in areas where there are many people and open establishments.

Avoid carrying valuables with you on the street, and don't display expensive cameras or electronic equipment. Hold on to your purse, and place your billfold in an inside pocket. In theaters, restaurants, and other public places, keep your possessions in sight. The Honolulu police department advises women to carry purses on the shoulder away from the street or, better yet, to wear the strap across the chest instead of on one shoulder. Women with clutch bags should hold them close to their chest.

Remember also that hotels are open to the public and that security may not be able to screen everyone entering, particularly in large properties. Always lock your room door—don't assume that once inside your hotel you're automatically safe.

Burglaries of tourists' rental cars in hotel parking structures and at beach parking lots have become more common. Park in well-lighted and well-traveled areas, if possible. Never leave any packages or valuables visible in the car. If someone attempts to rob you or steal your car, do not try to resist the thief or carjacker—report the incident to the police department immediately. Ask your rental agency about personal safety, and get written directions or a map with the route to your destination clearly marked.

Generally, Hawaii has the same laws as the mainland United States. Nudity is illegal in Hawaii. There are no legal nude beaches (we don't care what you have read). If you are nude on a beach (or anywhere) in Hawaii, you can be arrested.

Smoking marijuana also is illegal; if you attempt to buy it or light up, you can be arrested.

**Senior Travel**  Discounts for seniors are available at almost all of Hawaii's major attractions and occasionally at hotels and restaurants. The Outrigger hotel chain, for instance, offers travelers ages 50 and older a 20% discount on regular published rates—and an additional 5% off for members of AARP. Always ask when making hotel reservations or buying tickets. And always carry identification with proof of your age—it can really pay off.

Smoking    It's against the law to smoke in public buildings, including airports, shopping malls, grocery stores, retail shops, buses, movie theaters, banks, convention facilities, and all government buildings and facilities. There is no smoking in restaurants, bars, and nightclubs. Most B&Bs prohibit smoking indoors, and more and more hotels and resorts are becoming nonsmoking even in public areas. Also, there is no smoking within 20 feet of a doorway, window, or ventilation intake (so no hanging around outside a bar to smoke—you must go 20 ft. away).

Taxes    The United States has no value-added tax (VAT) or other indirect tax at the national level. Every state, county, and city may levy its own local tax on all purchases, including hotel and restaurant checks and airline tickets. These taxes will not appear on price tags.

Hawaii state general excise tax is 4.166%, which applies to all items purchased (including hotel rooms). On top of that, the state's transient Accommodation Tax (TAT) is 9.25%. These taxes, combined with various resort fees, can add up to 17% to 18% of your room rate. Budget accordingly.

Telephones    All calls on-island are local calls; calls from one island to another via a landline are long distance and you must dial 1, then the Hawaii area code (808), and then the phone number. Many convenience groceries and packaging services sell **prepaid calling cards** in denominations up to $50. Many public pay phones at airports now accept American Express, MasterCard, and Visa. **Local calls** made from most pay phones cost 50¢. Most long-distance and international calls can be dialed directly from any phone. **To make calls within the United States and to Canada,** dial 1, followed by the area code and the seven-digit number. **For other international calls,** dial 011, followed by the country code, city code, and the number you are calling.

Calls to area codes **800, 888, 877,** and **866** are toll-free. However, calls to area codes **700** and **900** (chat lines, bulletin boards, "dating" services, and so on) can be expensive—charges of 95¢ to $3 or more per minute. Some numbers have minimum charges that can run $15 or more.

For **reversed-charge or collect calls,** and for person-to-person calls, dial the number 0, then the area code and number; an operator will come on the line, and you should specify whether you are calling collect, person-to-person, or both. If your operator-assisted call is international, ask for the overseas operator.

For **directory assistance** ("Information"), dial 411 for local numbers and national numbers in the U.S. and Canada. For dedicated long-distance information, dial 1, then the appropriate area code plus 555-1212.

Time   The continental United States is divided into **four time zones:** Eastern Standard Time (EST), Central Standard Time (CST), Mountain Standard Time (MST), and Pacific Standard Time (PST). Alaska and Hawaii have their own zones. For example, when it's 7am in Honolulu (HST), it's 9am in Los Angeles (PST), 10am in Denver (MST), 11am in Chicago (CST), noon in New York City (EST), 5pm in London (GMT), and 2am the next day in Sydney.

**Daylight saving time,** in effect in most of the United States from 2am on the second Sunday in March to 2am on the first Sunday in November, is not observed in Hawaii, Arizona, the U.S. Virgin Islands, and Puerto Rico. Daylight saving time moves the clock 1 hour ahead of standard time.

Tipping   Tips are a major part of certain workers' income, and gratuities are the standard way of showing appreciation for services provided. (Tipping is certainly not compulsory if the service is poor!) In hotels, tip **bellhops** at least $2 per bag ($3–$5 if you have a lot of luggage) and tip the **housekeepers** $2 per person per day (more if you've left a disaster area for him or her to clean up). Tip the **doorman** or **concierge** only if he or she has provided you with some specific service (for example, calling a cab for you or obtaining difficult-to-get theater tickets). Tip the **valet-parking attendant** $2 to $5 every time you get your car.

In restaurants, bars, and nightclubs, tip **service staff** and **bartenders** 18 to 20% of the check, and tip **valet-parking attendants** $2 per vehicle.

As for other service personnel, tip **cab drivers** 15% of the fare; tip **skycaps** at airports at least $2 per bag ($3–$5 if you have a lot of luggage); and tip **hairdressers** and **barbers** 18 to 20%.

Toilets  You won't find public toilets or "restrooms" on the streets in Hawaii but they can be found in hotel lobbies, restaurants, museums, department stores, railway and bus stations, service stations, and at most beaches. Large hotels and fast-food restaurants are often the best bet for clean facilities. Restaurants and bars in heavily visited areas may reserve their restrooms for patrons.

Travelers with Disabilities  Travelers with disabilities are made to feel very welcome in Hawaii. Many hotels are equipped with wheelchair-accessible rooms and pools, and tour companies provide many special services.

For tips on accessible travel in Hawaii, go to the **Hawaii Tourism Authority** website (www.gohawaii.com/oahu/about/travel-tips/special-needs). The **Hawaii Centers for Independent Living,** 200 N. Vineyard Blvd., Bldg. A501, Honolulu, HI 96817 (www.cil-hawaii.org; © **808/522-5400**), can provide additional information about accessibility throughout the Islands.

**Access Aloha Travel** (www.accessalohatravel.com; © **800/480-1143**) specializes in accommodating travelers with disabilities. Agents book cruises, tours, accommodations, and airfare (as part of a package only).

For more on resources for travelers with disabilities, go to www.frommers.com.

Water  Generally the water in your hotel or at public drinking fountains is safe to drink (depending on the island, it may have more chlorine than you like).

Wi-Fi  See "Internet & Wi-Fi," earlier in this section.

# Index

## Accommodations

## Restaurants

# PHOTO CREDITS